SPORT GOVERNANCE

Sport governance has become an increasingly widespread subject for research and teaching in sports studies. This engaging and accessible textbook examines the governance of sport organisations in a changing political, legal, financial and socio-cultural context. It explains how sport organisations are governed, explores the issues and challenges faced by those governing sport today and looks ahead to how sport can be governed better in the future.

Covering sport at all levels, from community organisations and national governing bodies to international organisations such as the IOC and FIFA, this text examines key components of governance, such as legal and regulatory frameworks, stakeholding, performance, compliance and the reform of the non-profit sector in line with corporate governance. This text is also timely, given that recent corruption scandals in sport have served to highlight the central importance of good governance in sport. Its nine chapters draw upon more than 30 international case examples across a range of sports, including athletics, football, gymnastics, hockey, rowing, rugby, badminton and tennis.

With extensive lists of learning activities and resources, original empirical research and insights into the politics of policymaking and implementation, this textbook is essential reading for any course on sport governance, policy, management or development.

Neil King is Senior Lecturer in Sport at Edge Hill University, UK.

SPORT GOVERNANCE

An introduction

Neil King

LONDON AND NEW YORK

First published 2017
by Routledge
2 Park Square, Milton Park, Abingdon, Oxon OX14 4RN

and by Routledge

711 Third Avenue, New York, NY 10017

Routledge is an imprint of the Taylor & Francis Group, an informa business

© 2017 N. King

The right of Neil King to be identified as author of this work has been asserted by him in accordance with sections 77 and 78 of the Copyright, Designs and Patents Act 1988.

All rights reserved. No part of this book may be reprinted or reproduced or utilised in any form or by any electronic, mechanical, or other means, now known or hereafter invented, including photocopying and recording, or in any information storage or retrieval system, without permission in writing from the publishers.

Trademark notice: Product or corporate names may be trademarks or registered trademarks, and are used only for identification and explanation without intent to infringe.

British Library Cataloguing-in-Publication Data

A catalogue record for this book is available from the British Library

Library of Congress Cataloging in Publication Data
Names: King, Neil A., author.Title: Sport governance : an introduction / Neil King.
Description: New York : Routledge, 2016. | " 2017. | Includes bibliographical references and index.
Identifiers: LCCN 2016007308| ISBN 9781138654310 (Hardback) | ISBN 9781138654327 (Paperback) | ISBN 9781315623313 (eBook)
Subjects: LCSH: Sports administration.
Classification: LCC GV713 .K5 2016 | DDC 796.06/9--dc23
LC record available at http://lccn.loc.gov/2016007308

ISBN: 978-1-138-65431-0 (hbk)
ISBN: 978-1-138-65432-7 (pbk)
ISBN: 978-1-315-62331-3 (ebk)

Typeset in Bembo
by Saxon Graphics Ltd, Derby

CONTENTS

ABBREVIATIONS

ADB	Angling Development Board
AFL	Australian Football League
AGGIS	Action for Good Governance in International Sports Organisations
AGM	Annual General Meeting
ARA	Amateur Rowing Association
ASC	Australian Sports Commission
ATP	Association of Tennis Professionals
BAF	British Athletics Federation
CAS	Court of Arbitration for Sport
CASC	Community Amateur Sports Club
CEO	Chief Executive Officer
CIC	Community Investment Company
CICA	Canadian Institute of Chartered Accountants
COE	Council of Europe
CSP	County Sport Partnership
CSR	Corporate Social Responsibility
DCMS	Department for Culture, Media and Sport
EC	European Commission
ECJ	European Court of Justice
EGM	Extraordinary General Meeting
EHA	English Hockey Association
EMS	European model of sport
EU	European Union
FA	Football Association
FFA	Football Federation Australia
FGRC	Football Governance Research Centre
FIFA	International Federation of Association Football

FSA	Financial Services Authority
FSF	Football Supporters' Federation
IAAF	International Association of Athletics Federations
IAF	International Federation of American Football
ICAS	International Council of Arbitration for Sport
ICC	International Cricket Council
ICSA	Institute of Chartered Secretaries and Administrators
IFRS	International Financial Reporting Standards
INGSO	International Non-Government Sports Organisation
IOC	International Olympic Committee
IOR	Inter-Organisational Relations
ISCA	International Sport and Culture Association
LMA	League Managers' Association
LTA	Lawn Tennis Association
NAO	National Audit Office
NCVO	National Council for Voluntary Organisations
NGB	National Governing Body
NPM	New Public Management
NPSO	Non-Profit Sports Organisation
OCOG	Organising Committee for the Olympic Games
OECD	Organisation for Economic Co-operation and Development
PFA	Professional Footballers' Association
RFU	Rugby Football Union
SPARC	Sport and Recreation New Zealand
SRA	Sport and Recreation Alliance
SROI	Social Return On Investment
UEFA	Union of European Football Associations
UKAD	UK Anti-Doping
UKSI	UK Sports Institute
WADA	World Anti-Doping Agency

ILLUSTRATIONS

Figures

Tables

Chapter 5

Chapter 6

Chapter 7

Chapter 8

CASE EXAMPLES

Chapter 1

Chapter 2

Chapter 3

Chapter 4

INTRODUCTION TO THE STUDY TEXT

This study text is for undergraduate-level sport-related degree programmes and centres on the governance of, and by, Non-Profit Sports Organisations (NPSOs) at an international, national and local level. Governance can be defined as 'the process of granting power, verifying performance, managing, leading and/or administrating within an organization' (O'Boyle, 2013: 1). In this sense governance is both political and administrative, and both aspects are addressed in this text. It may be timely for the sports student to engage with sport governance as it has experienced significant change in the last decade, including increasing professionalisation, commercialisation, political intervention and administrative upheaval. This complex context presents graduates with significant challenges in the operation of NPSOs, pertaining to regulation, stakeholding, performance, ethical practice and compliance. These challenges can be located in a context of administrative reform or a 'modernisation' of the sport sector.

Rationale

ICSA (2014: 3) note that

> The increase in public funding for sport has provided the impetus for more professional sports administration and also highlighted areas of poor management and financial failure. These issues have been addressed by UK Sport and the Sports Councils as part of the need to protect public investment and improving NGB governance. There is however a growing demand for support and guidance for NGBs to assist them in meeting the standards expected and ultimately to help them improve their governance.

LIVERPOOL JOHN MOORES UNIVERSITY
LEARNING SERVICES

Specifically, it can be noted that a 'skills and knowledge gap' has emerged over the last decade, where the governance of sport has changed from volunteer-run organisations to 'businesses' managed by professionals utilising a model of corporate governance. Moreover, in some countries, such as England, NPSOs are expected to deliver services that the public sector previously provided to a larger extent. Therefore, with extended roles and responsibilities, it is timely to research, teach and study sports administration/governance.

In terms of studies of governance, non-profit sports governance is arguably under-theorised and the ongoing reform of the sector offers the opportunity to extend our understanding of sport governance. Also, sports governance is currently topical, given media and academic coverage of 'poor governance' in sport in recent years in the context of growing commercialisation and professionalisation. An emerging body of literature on 'good governance' and its application in practice also has currency. Further, the published literature on sport governance has not to date been collated, synthesised and summarised into one coherent and accessible study text for undergraduates. Given the vast literature extending across many aspects of governance, this text is intended to be an introduction or 'point of access', and is not intended to address sport governance in all countries or for all sports. Instead, case examples are utilised to highlight the key themes of sport governance that are organised into distinct, but overlapping, chapters.

For graduates entering the sport sector, this study text highlights the importance of effective and accountable governance for NPSOs in a context characterised by:

- changing public expectations and demand for greater accountability;
- a complex regulatory environment;
- an ongoing 'modernisation' and professionalisation of the non-profit sport sector;
- changing modes of local service delivery for sport; and
- public funding for sport becoming ever more conditional upon effective governance and management and compliance with national sport policy priorities.

Given this complex context, it can be argued that there are a series of benefits for NPSOs if graduates understand governance principles and practice relating to: improving business performance and managing risk for stakeholders; building the reputation of the organisation and attracting participants, members, volunteers, sponsors and other funders; enabling a longer view in strategising and forecasting; enhancing the capacity of the organisation; developing organisational resilience in a challenging financial environment; reducing dependence on public funding; and embedding sustainable practice.

Aim and objectives

The generic aim of this study text is to increase undergraduate understanding of sport governance. The specific objectives of the text are aligned to the key themes of sports governance. It is intended that undergraduates understand:

- definitions of governance (corporate and non-profit) and non-profit sport governance (legal forms, characteristics, key issues);
- the ongoing reform or 'modernisation' process in the UK;
- explanations of sport governance in the non-profit sector, where a number of theoretical approaches can be applied;
- the legislative context and regulatory aspects of sport governance;
- the administration of sports organisations, including the powers, roles and responsibilities of boards;
- stakeholding, partnership-working and collaboration in the sport sector;
- performance and leadership in sports organisations;
- the principles and practices pertaining to 'good governance', including ethical dimensions and issues of accountability and transparency;
- organisational compliance with legal, ethical and good practice codes and guidelines; and
- contemporary issues and challenges facing the sector.

It should be emphasised that the content of the text is largely generic rather than specific to certain sports, given that the sports sector is diverse across a vast array of sports with distinct histories, and which are governed across national, regional and local levels. Further, sports are led by NPSOs of different sizes and capacities, including differences in financial and human resources, membership numbers, active participants, stakeholders and funders.

Structure and scope

This study text consists of nine chapters. Chapter 1 outlines the organisational infrastructure for sport governance before analysing the ongoing reform or 'modernisation' of sport and citing the current issues and challenges facing the sector generally. Chapter 2 examines the differing explanations of sport governance, where a number of theoretical approaches can be applied to explain the governance of sport. Three broad theoretical approaches are included (hierarchies/steering, networks and the normative 'good governance') alongside specific models of governance. Chapter 3 details the administration of sports organisations, including the powers, roles and responsibilities of boards. Chapter 4 analyses the legislative context and regulatory aspects of sport governance in the UK, European Union (EU) and internationally. Chapter 5 addresses stakeholding and, more broadly, the challenges of partnership-working and collaboration in a sector. Chapter 6 examines performance in sports organisations and by sports organisations. Chapter

7 concerns the principles and practices pertaining to 'good governance', including ethical dimensions and issues of accountability and transparency. Chapter 8 addresses the issue of compliance to ensure legal, ethical and good practice guidelines are met. Finally, Chapter 9 assesses the key challenges facing NPSOs throughout the next decade. A short conclusion to the study text follows. The appendix is a list of learning resources that can be utilised by tutors and students alongside the chapter content (government and governing body documentation, sports organisation documentation and useful websites).

Case examples and learning activities

A series of case examples at the international, national and local level of sports governance permeate the text. These case studies are used to exemplify the core themes of sport governance. The case studies can be used in conjunction with the learning activities cited in each chapter. Each chapter commences with a number of learning objectives that precede specific learning activities, review questions and independent learning exercises that can be of value to students and tutors. Learning activities for students can be undertaken individually or in groups. How these activities are administered will depend on the tutor and the curriculum at different academic institutions. It is not the intention to prescribe specific learning exercises or to set a syllabus. Instead, each learning activity is intended to stimulate discussion and initiate further research on specific aspects of sport governance.

A brief introduction to governance in the non-profit sport sector

Definitions of 'governance' may be too many to be useful according to Rhodes (1997: 653). Nonetheless, it is clear from the vast literature on the subject that the term 'governance' can be defined in a *political* sense where the focus is on how power is exercised, who has influence, who decides and who benefits from decisions and actions. Alternatively, governance can be defined in an *administrative* sense, where governance is fundamentally concerned with: setting the rules and procedures for making organisational decisions; facilitating effective, entrepreneurial and prudent management; determining the means of optimising performance; ensuring statutory and fiduciary compliance; monitoring and assessing risk; and meeting ethical standards, for example.

Sport governance can be defined as

> the process by which the board sets strategic direction and priorities, sets policies and management performance expectations, characterizes and manages risks, and monitors and evaluates organizational achievements in order to exercise its accountability to the organization and owners.
>
> (SPARC, 2004: 16)

For the purposes of this study text, a generic definition of governance is utilised, namely: 'the process of granting power, verifying performance, managing, leading and/or administrating within an organization' (O'Boyle, 2013: 1).

This study text includes both meanings assigned to 'governance', although some chapters are clearly to do with *political* aspects of sport governance more so than *administrative* aspects. *Political* aspects of governance include:

- the reform or 'modernisation' of the sport sector by government (Chapter 1);
- the autonomy of sports organisations from government, and explanations of governance and power-relations (Chapter 2 and throughout the text);
- board representation, authority and influence (Chapter 3);
- compliance with UK legislation and regulation and EU directives (Chapter 4);
- stakeholder participation (Chapter 5);
- board–CEO relations in organisational performance (Chapter 6);
- understandings of accountability, transparency, fairness and democratic decision-making (Chapter 7); and
- the practice of ensuring compliance with regulations and policy (Chapter 8).

In this study text *administrative* aspects of governance include:

- organisational structures (Chapter 1);
- decision-making processes (Chapter 2);
- the role and responsibilities of boards (Chapter 3);
- legal structures (Chapter 4);
- methods to extend stakeholder engagement (Chapter 5);
- mechanisms for assessing performance (Chapter 6);
- codes of practice (Chapter 7); and
- compliance mechanisms (Chapter 8).

A distinction can be made between governance and management and also between governance and policy, where both management studies and policy studies are fields of research in their own right. 'Management' is usually associated with control within decision-making processes (e.g. managing staff or volunteers, managing budgets or planning) either individually as 'managers', or as an organisation. In this sense, there is clearly an overlap of management with governance in the administrative understanding of the term. In fact, management can be viewed as a component of 'governance'. 'Policy' can be conceived of as an agreed set of ideas underpinning a course of action and is usually framed within studies of power-relations or the political component of governance. Policy is also a term associated with government, whereas 'governance' is a broader construct that accounts for the decisions and actions of non-profit organisations as well as those performed by government departments or agencies responsible for sport.

For students studying sport governance, it is important to understand that the administration of sport takes place in a political context and, in many countries, a key driver underpinning the governance of sport is government or, more broadly, the state. This is in comparison to countries where the state plays an indirect or a marginal role in sport governance. The political and policy context to sport governance presents challenges for sports administrators, as is highlighted in this text.

The extent to which sports organisations operate within a framework of 'good governance' or governance through values, that may be expressed in a constitution or a code of conduct or practice, is a key focus of this study text. The growth in literature around 'good governance' in the last decade reflects a concern with the manner in which sport has been governed, its norms and values, given incidents of poor governance or corruption in sport as highlighted by the media in recent years, such as the behaviour of FIFA officials in the procurement of events, match-fixing in some sports and doping, for example. The call for 'good governance' (e.g. Council of Europe, 2012; IOC, 2008; Katwala, 2000; Pieth, 2011; Sugden and Tomlinson, 1998) and, in particular, the quality of the self-governance of international non-governmental sport organisations (INGSOs) has been subject to scrutiny due to the increasing commercialisation of sport in the context of global capitalism (Andreff, 2000; Sugden, 2002; Henry and Lee, 2004). Governance therefore has differing albeit overlapping definitions. Critically, understandings of governance have implications for practice, hence the rationale underpinning this introductory text for students of sport governance.

Bibliography

Andreff, W. (2000) Financing modern sport in the face of a sporting ethic. *European Journal for Sport Management*, 7: 5–30.

Council of Europe (COE) (2012) *Good Governance and Ethics in Sport*. Parliamentary assembly committee on Culture, Science Education and Media. Strasbourg: Council of Europe.

Henry, I.P. and Lee, P.C. (2004) Governance and ethics in sport. In: Chadwick, S. and Beech, J. eds, *The Business of Sport Management*. Harlow: Pearson Education, pp. 25–42.

Hoye, R. and Cuskelly, G. (2007) *Sport Governance*. Oxford: Elsevier Butterworth-Heinemann.

Institute of Chartered Secretaries and Administrators (ICSA) (2014) *Corporate Governance*, 5th edition. London: ICSA.

International Olympic Committee (IOC) (2008) *Basic Universal Principles of Good Governance of the Olympic and Sports Movement*. Lausanne: IOC. www.olympic.org/Documents/Conferences_Forums_and_Events/2008_seminar_autonomy/Basic_Universal_Principles_of_Good_Governance.pdf

Katwala, S. (2000) *Democratising Global Sport*, London: The Foreign Policy Centre.

O'Boyle, I. (2013) Managing organizational performance in sport. In: Hassan, D. and Lusted, J., eds *Managing Sport: Social and Cultural Perspectives*. Oxon: Routledge, pp. 1–16.

Pieth, M. (2011) *Governing FIFA*. Concept paper and report, Universität Basel.

Rhodes, R.A.W. (1997) *Understanding Governance: Policy Networks, Governance, Reflexivity and Accountability*. Milton Keynes: Open University Press.

Sport and Recreation New Zealand (SPARC) (2004) *Nine Steps to Effective Governance: Building High Performing Organisations*. Wellington: SPARC.

Sugden, J. (2002) Network football. In: Sugden, J. and Tomlinson, A., eds, *Power Games*. London: Routledge, pp. 61–80.

Sugden, J. and Tomlinson, A. (1998) *FIFA and the Contest for World Football: Who Rules the Peoples' Game?* Cambridge: Polity Press.

1

SPORT GOVERNANCE
Infrastructure and reform

LEARNING OBJECTIVES

At the completion of this chapter, students should be able to:

- outline the organisation and infrastructure for sport governance at the international and national levels;
- explain the reform of sport governance in the last two decades;
- assess the factors shaping sport governance; and
- critically evaluate the key governance issues and challenges facing sports organisations.

The infrastructure for sport governance

The sport sector consists of government bodies, Non-Profit Sports Organisations (NPSOs) including national governing bodies (NGBs) for specific sports, regional and county structures, leagues, associations and local-level sports clubs, and a raft of commercial organisations including sponsors. If the sector is viewed as a hierarchy, then international sports bodies sit above the national, regional and local levels of sport governance, with membership afforded to representatives of specific nations. Each country or nation state has a different infrastructure for sport, from almost wholly government (or state) run to almost wholly operated by non-profit (or voluntary) bodies. However, there are many commonalities across nation states, especially between Western nations. Hierarchies or networks are problematic to illustrate in diagrammatic form due to their complexity, but also due to the fact that the sport sector infrastructure changes, often on a regular basis. Nonetheless, a simple figure is included here (see Figure 1.1).

International Sporting Organisations

FIGURE 1.1 The infrastructure of international sport

International sports organisations can be separated into four types.

1. single sport, such as FIFA and the IAAF;
2. multi-sport, such as the IOC and Commonwealth Games Federation;
3. associations of clubs, such as the European Clubs Association, or athletes, such as the Association of Tennis Professionals (ATP);
4. regulators, such as the Court of Arbitration for Sport and the World Anti-Doping Agency (WADA).

All of these organisations are non-governmental, non-profit organisations. Nonetheless, these organisations have relationships with commercial bodies and with national and international government bodies (Foster, 2006). The location of major organisations such as the IOC and FIFA in Switzerland reflects their financial orientation, given the taxation advantages (Chappelet and Kuber-Mabbot, 2008, 2010). The expansion in the number and size of international sports bodies has in part been due to the rapid commercialisation of (professional) sport since the 1980s, resulting in resource-rich organisations such as the IOC and FIFA. It is important to understand relationships between such organisations and governments and regulatory bodies, and with transnational companies in order to understand the political and ethical issues that have arisen in recent years.

As a result of a series of 'scandals' and weak governance (Numerato et al., 2013), international sports organisations such as FIFA are undergoing reform, and sport governance across a range of countries has taken shape in recent years. For example, Parent and Patterson (2013) analyse the evolution of the Canadian sports system and governance changes related to hosting the 2010 Winter Olympic Games in Vancouver. Sport in Australia has experienced its own reform process (Stewart et *al.*, 2004) and there has been significant policy and governance developments in countries across Europe (Bergsgard *et al.*, 2007). The role of the EU and sports law in shaping governance is addressed in Chapter 4. Elsewhere, a body of literature has emerged on policy and governance change across different sports in different countries. For example, Smolianov (2013) analyses the Russian Modern Pentathlon Federation in the context of political change; Bester (2013) assesses the unique governance challenges facing Cycling South Africa; Hong and Fuhua (2013) trace the governance of sport in China from state-centred to semi-autonomous; and Dorsey (2016) examines sport governance in North Africa and the Middle East, where sport is shaped by the state intervention and the politics of the region. This text will explore the key themes in sport governance with reference to case examples, although not all countries or sports can be considered due to the limitations of space. Two major international sports organisations and one regulatory body that have had a significant level of influence on sport governance at the national and local levels are presented here as examples of powerful bodies shaping the sport sector.

International Olympic Committee

The IOC has the overall (legal) responsibility for the Olympic Games and other games using the Olympic name; its key role is to promote the Olympic 'Movement'. The organisation is overseen by a 15-member executive board and a president. It is an association of 205 National Olympic Committees, with European members making up the majority membership. There are also 35 Olympic Federations, and many NGBs are also members (39 alone in the USA, for example). There are also Organising Committees for the Olympic Games (OCOGs), of which LOCOG was one for the London 2012 Olympic Games. A president is elected every four years to oversee this vast hierarchy. The IOC has acquired significant influence over the development of sport in part due to the sale of broadcasting rights, marketing and a deepening relationship with multinational commercial partners. Key partners include WADA (see the case example to follow) and the Court of Arbitration for Sport (CAS) (see Chapter 3). The IOC has been subject to organisational change (Zakus and Skinner, 2008) following criticisms of its governance (Mallon, 2000).

FIFA

FIFA is a hierarchical organisation with a president at the top of the pyramid supported by eight vice-presidents and an executive committee. The president is elected every four years and the vice-presidents are appointed through 'mysterious … combination of election, patronage and historical precedent' (Sugden and Tomlinson, 1998). Various sub-committees (e.g. refereeing, tournaments) are responsible for specific components of FIFA's infrastructure. FIFA also has six regional (and independent) confederations that are: UEFA, CONMEBOL (South

America), CONCACAF (Central and North America), CAF (Africa), AFC (Asia) and OCF (Oceania). As a result, these regional power bases can support or challenge the centralised structure of governance. For example, UEFA generates significant income and proposed separating from FIFA in the 1990s. Given the wealth of FIFA and its power to decide who will host the football World Cup, senior members 'experience a lifestyle akin to that enjoyed by eminent world politicians, international celebrities and royalty' (Sugden and Tomlinson, 1997: 52). This, in turn, has led to investigations into the governance of FIFA (Jennings, 2006; Jennings and Sambrook, 2000) that will be addressed later in this text.

World Anti-Doping Agency (WADA)

WADA emerged from growing concerns regarding doping in sport dating back to the 1960s (Houlihan, 2002). By the 1980s, recognition emerged of a need for harmonisation of rules and out-of-competition testing, given significant differences in the method of tackling doping across sports and across different countries with differing resources. Accredited laboratories for testing and a list of banned substances emerged over time, but it was not until the 1998 Tour de France that a tipping point was reached when governments and police agencies became involved, opening criminal investigations. Thus doping was no longer an issue for governing bodies of sport alone to address. Subsequently, WADA was established in November 1999 prior to the 2000 Olympic Games.

Today, governments and the Olympic Movement share a commitment to fund anti-doping measures and share representation on WADA's council and executive bodies. Moreover, a *World Anti-Doping Code* has been established to address: definitions of doping, prohibited substances, procedures for testing, sanctions and appeals and education and research (David, 2008). However, challenges remain for WADA that include: difficulties of harmonisation and compliance across sports and countries; legal challenges from athletes; enforcing the monitoring of athletes (the 'whereabouts' rule); and addressing the networks involved in doping (Reid and Kitchin, 2013). Additionally, a report (WADA, 2015, 2016) cited significant doping issues in athletics and questioned the role of the IAAF as the international governing body in addressing the issue effectively. Doping and the role of WADA are addressed further in later sections of this text (Houlihan, 1999, 2000; UNESCO, 2012).

In terms of the national infrastructure for sport, this differs per country, but for most there exists a raft of NPSOs, from NGBs to regional or county bodies to local sports clubs and associations. These organisations work in partnership with the government department dedicated or partly dedicated to sport (e.g. the DCMS in England), alongside other departments that oversee school sport and local authority provision for sport, and 'arms-length' government agencies (e.g. Sport England and other UK sports councils) that have oversight for grass-roots sport; in elite sport it is UK Sport that oversees performance-related objectives. The non-profit sector has representation from an 'umbrella' organisation, namely the Sport and Recreation Alliance (SRA). In the UK it is local authorities that are the major provider of community sport (see King, 2009). Further, a raft of commercial sports organisations and non-sport organisations are in partnership with NPSOs.

National governance of sport: the policy context

Political priorities as manifested in public policy have had a significant impact on sport governance. A central tension in the UK and European context and in Australia and Canada, for example, has been between investment in elite sport and investment in the goal of mass participation (Bergsgard *et al.*, 2007; Collins, 2008; Green, 2006, 2007, 2009; Green and Houlihan, 2005; Houlihan, 1997; Houlihan and White, 2002; Oakley and Green, 2001; O'Boyle and Bradbury, 2013; Stewart *et al.*, 2004). A number of these authors have noted a shift towards an emphasis on elite sport, particularly in the last decade, with consequences for the governance of sport by NPSOs, as is discussed in the following section. It can also be observed that, despite differences in the relationship between the state (or national or regional government more specifically) and NPSOs, a policy convergence towards elite sport has been demonstrated in Western countries in part based on the pursuit of success in the Olympic Games and other mega-events. However, as Bergsgard *et al.* (2007) note in comparing policy in England, Canada, Germany and Norway, national policy and sport governance differ because of historical, cultural and socio-economic trajectories, where the role and relative influence of NPSOs differs (also see Henry, 2009). As an example of sport policy shaping governance reform, the following case example highlights the significance of policy for NPSOs.

CASE EXAMPLE: POLICY STATEMENTS AND THE UK SPORTS GOVERNANCE CODE

Policy statements set the tone for governance change. *Creating a Sporting Habit for Life* (DCMS, 2012) continued a trajectory of non-profit sector reform that requires organisations to manage change and comply with government policy. A resource dependency on public funding enables funding conditions to be imposed in all but those sports that are financially independent. This statement proposes a decentralised and locally determined approach to delivery of school and community sport where NPSOs play an enhanced role in the delivery of sport. This is in contrast to the central government-led approach to delivering school and community sport primarily via local authority funding. Specifically, the statement states that:

- up to 2017, over £50m will be spent to 'open well-run sports clubs' (whether or not they are connected to an NGB), voluntary groups and others to enhance the 'sporting experience';

- NGBs are expected to utilise their sports club structure to deliver more coaching opportunities and to improve the quality of experience and drive up participation;
- sports clubs are expected to 'modernise' and become more 'business-like'.

Following on from this statement is a government proposal that by September 2016 NGBs will adopt a *UK Sports Governance Code*. This forms one part of the latest strategy for sport (DCMS, 2015). Essentially, sports bodies must align practices to a corporate sector model of governance. This includes a minimum of 25 per cent female representation on sports boards by 2017. Critically, public funding can only be accessed if the code is adopted. Further, this model is intended to be encouraged across countries and at the level of International Non-Government Sports Organisations (INGSOs), although it cannot be enforced outside of the UK.

The reform of sport governance

Houlihan and White (2002: 168) observed that 'For many years governments had displayed a surprising level of deference towards governing bodies of sport, often being prepared to distribute public money with little control over how it was spent.' However, since the mid-1990s this began to change, in the UK at least, with a restructuring of the Sports Councils and the introduction of the National Lottery, where sport was awarded beneficiary status. Green (2006, 2009) analysed the shift towards professionalisation of the sector and reform in line with goals to meet Olympic Games success on the one hand, and social policy goals on the other (also see King, 2009). Further, in the UK, a number of NGBs have met with financial difficulties, such as the former British Athletics Federation (BAF), which in turn led to reform of the sport and the founding of UK Athletics, which in turn sought to 'modernise' the governance of athletics (Grix, 2009). This is one example of a wider reform or 'modernisation' of the sport sector as a whole (Houlihan and Green, 2009). It can be noted that in the last decade in particular, UK sports bodies have to some extent adopted the principles and practices of the corporate sector to the point that there are more similarities than differences, especially where sports organisations have adopted a 'business model'. For example, NGBs have introduced *Whole Sport Plans* that aim not only to establish a business model for specific sports, but performance-related targets, and good governance principles and codes into the practices of NGBs. While some international-level governing bodies have struggled to adapt or have resisted change – such as FIFA, where 'the specific structure of FIFA makes it difficult to adapt what is considered best business practice to the governance challenges it is facing' (Transparency International, 2011: 2) – many NPSOs in the UK have more readily embraced aspects of reform.

The reform or 'modernisation' of sport has been defined as 'the process of continuing development of a Governing Body towards greater effectiveness, efficiency and independence' (UK Sport, 2003: 1). The UK government stated that NGBs would receive increased control over the allocation of public funding on the condition that NGBs become more accountable on the one hand, and more efficient and effective on the other. Features of this reform were revising administrative structures and practices, implementing robust management and planning and monitoring all activities. NGB modernisation was further advocated in *Game Plan* (DCMS/Stategy Unit, 2002), where clear performance indicators were introduced as the basis on which to determine the distribution of funding.

In order to support this extensive programme of reform, UK Sport invested government funding into NGB projects across the UK as part of the Modernisation Programme between 2001 and 2005 (Houlihan and Green, 2009: 18). Further, in 2003, a high-level review of the Modernisation Programme, entitled *Investing in Change*, was undertaken in order to identify the optimum models for NGB performance and to develop action plans to guide performance (UK Sport, 2003: 5). Performance is understood here as increasing participation, developing talent and delivering elite-level success (UK Sport, 2004a, 2004b). In regard to elite-level success as a performance indicator, UK Sport launched 'Mission 2012' in 2007 in preparation for the 2012 London Olympic Games.

The reform programme fundamentally sought to address poor corporate governance defined in terms such as a lack of transparency, financial control and monitoring and reporting (UK Sport, 2003: 34–39). Sport England and UK Sport now require that all funded NGBs have to meet certain standards found in corporate governance that can be applied to NPSOs. It is intended that NPSOs, and in particular NGBs of sport, increase their level of responsibility for driving sport, so that autonomy can be 'earned' rather than viewed as a right. Further aspects of the modernisation programme are highlighted in the chapters of this text, where more recent developments continue to build on the momentum for reform set between 2000 and 2007.

CASE EXAMPLE: COMPONENTS OF SPORT GOVERNANCE REFORM IN THE UK

Aspects of reform or 'modernisation' that have had consequences for the governance of sport in the UK mirror those in other countries and include the following:

- Government agencies now require that all funded NGBs have to meet certain standards relating to corporate governance in the areas of strategic planning, financial management, human resources and organisational policy in order to receive funding.

- The introduction of targets, measurable outcomes, Key Performance Indicators and the need to demonstrate compliance with certain standards.
- Increased scrutiny of NGBs via the introduction of *Whole Sport Plans*.
- The introduction of conditional funding arrangements linked to performance-related targets in elite sport and raising and widening participation in grass-roots sport.
- NGBs must take part in an annual self-assurance process which provides the basis on which government funding is determined.
- The introduction of a Competencies Framework (a tool for NGBs to use to benchmark their modernisation process) that includes: risk management; transparent financial disclosure; effective financial controls; compliance with laws and regulations; revisions to management structures; a long-term strategic plan; strategic review procedures; and the role and responsibility of the Chief Executive Officer (UK Sport, 2003: 48).
- Improvements in monitoring and reporting (UK Sport, 2003: 34–39), including continually monitoring NGB performance against targets and the evaluation of standards.
- A self-assurance process has encouraged NGBs to work towards increasing autonomy and responsibility as part of the modernisation process. This may be deemed 'earned autonomy' (Houlihan and Green, 2009).
- NGBs receive increased control over the allocation of public funding on the proviso that NGBs become more accountable by modernising administration structures and practices, and implementing robust management and planning activities.
- The *UK Sports Governance Code* requires NPSOs to comply or lose funding.

In respect of the reform of specific sports, two short case examples are included here: the role of the Football Association (FA) in grass-roots football (soccer) in England and the reform of Football Federation Australia. These cases foreground how NGBs are adapting to external pressures from stakeholders and revising internal practices.

CASE EXAMPLE: THE MODERNISATION OF GRASS-ROOTS FOOTBALL IN ENGLAND

As detailed by O'Gorman (2013), since the 1990s grass-roots football (soccer) in England has been subject to a modernisation process originating both from pressure within the sport by clubs, volunteers and administrators, and externally from government. A series of reports outlined the issues facing the sport, such as safety in facilities, coaching quality and child welfare. The FA subsequently produced *Blueprint for the Future of Football*, which was a catalyst for change. County-level football associations became limited companies to be operated along business lines and a *Charter for Quality* was developed. Following this the FA produced a *Football Development Strategy* in 2001 that foregrounded club development. Also, the *FA Charter Standard Club Programme* focused on raising the standards of behaviour in the sport by using a three-level accreditation process.

CASE EXAMPLE: GOVERNANCE REFORM OF FOOTBALL FEDERATION AUSTRALIA

Hoye and Cuskelly (2007) examined the governance review of the Football Federation Australia (FFA) in 2002/2003 (then known as Soccer Australia). A combination of political infighting, debt, the absence of strategic direction, factionalism and wider concerns regarding mixed results in international football (soccer) competition led to the review. The outcome of the review process included separating governance from management of the FFA; altering membership, electoral processes and voting structures; establishing a new constitution; and changing relationships between the key stakeholders, which had been affected by mistrust. These administrative aspects of sport governance are addressed more fully in Chapter 3.

As an example of sport governance in a specific country, or in this case, a collective of three countries – Denmark, Norway and Sweden – an overview is included here to highlight differences between the 'Scandinavian model' and governance elsewhere, such as the UK. A growing body of literature has emerged that is specific to sport governance in social democratic countries within Europe (Carlsson *et al.*, 2011; Enjolras and Waldahl, 2010; Persson, 2011; Thing and Ottesen, 2010) in addition to studies of policy (Bergsgard *et al.*, 2007; Fahlén *et al.*, 2015; Skille, 2011).

CASE EXAMPLE: SPORT GOVERNANCE IN SCANDINAVIA

It is important to note that the political orientation of countries shapes sport governance, alongside socio-cultural characteristics. Within the social democratic 'welfare' model, sport receives substantial state support but the governance of sport has been semi-autonomous of the state historically and therefore self-regulation, rather than regulation by the state, was the norm. However, more recently, sport governance in Scandinavia has been subject to the effects of professionalisation, commercialisation and globalisation, as has been the case elsewhere. A key characteristic of policy has been an ideological focus on sport for all or mass participation in sports alongside public health and voluntarism. In countries with a stronger market orientation, operating within an ideology of neo-pluralism, sport for all as a concept and practice has diminished – an example is the UK. However, to what extent sport for all is central to the practices of NPSOs in Scandinavia is disputed, given an increasing focus of NGBs on elite sport as in the UK case. Sport governance in Scandinavia may therefore be going through a period of transformation, especially given the emergence of 'good governance' (see Chapter 7) as a focus in sport across national boundaries.

Compliance with reform

In terms of enforcing reform, Walters *et al.* (2010) found that adherence to aspects of the reform programme was evidenced by the majority of NGBs. For example,

- almost all NGBs had a strategy in place that covered at least three years;
- the majority of these NGBs stated that the strategy was well-defined;
- a very high proportion of NGBs engage with stakeholders through their websites and annual reports;
- the majority seek stakeholder feedback;
- the majority of NGBs have stakeholder representation at board/committee level;
- the majority of NGBs are involved with corporate responsibility initiatives; and
- issues of transparency, accountability, participation and communication are important issues for NGBs.

However, in other respects, compliance with aspects of the reform agenda in the period 2003–2010 had proven to be more problematic. For example:

- Only one-third of NGBs had formalised the management of human resources despite increasing professionalisation, increases in the number of paid staff, changes in government policy and funding criteria and an increasingly strict compliance climate.
- Training was identified as a key action to be undertaken by NGBs in 2003, yet only one-third provided training opportunities for both paid and volunteer staff in 2010.
- Although the value of NGBs managing human resources effectively can improve business outcomes and competitive advantage in the context of scarce resources, many NGBs had not, as of 2010, adjusted practices accordingly.

Despite these 'shortfalls' in expected outcomes, it should be noted that UK NGBs are a diverse and heterogeneous group and not all aspects of the reform agenda can be applied easily, even if these aspects are appropriate for the particular sport at a particular level or organisation, especially in a challenging economic context. Walters *et al.* (2010) also found that many NGBs suffer from resource constraints, as do NPSOs generally, excluding the small minority of relatively wealthy sports organisations where private-sector funding supports sport at the elite performance level. Therefore, implementing change can be difficult. Nonetheless, a raft of support and guidance exists from umbrella organisations such as the SRA and the government funding agencies driving reform.

Managing the reform process and governance change is usually conducted within the framework of a series of recommendations following a review. This might be organised by a sports council recommending change to NGB governance or the NGB recommending change in county associations or local clubs, for example. Drivers of change nationally may originate in international sports bodies or non-sport bodies connected to the EU, taking the form of codes of practice or, in the case of the EU and national government, legislation and regulated practices. Self-assessment exercises as opposed to external pressures may also initiate change that may result from pressure from members, participants, funders or other stakeholders.

The process of change for a sports board will usually include undertaking an audit or review; a re-orientation of objectives; a re-organisation of structures and processes; drawing up a strategy or action plan; implementing the planned changes; and an evaluation of outcomes and impact. Although there is scope for negotiation in responding to external pressures, the scope may be limited in practice, particularly for NPSOs with few resources. The *UK Sport Modernisation Programme* (Hoye and Cuskelly, 2007; UK Sport, 2003) was prescriptive and included specific actions to be undertaken, such as drawing up templates for implementation and timeframes for delivery. Meeting targets is, however, not always feasible in the short term and a challenge for a NPSO in building the capacity for meaningful reform.

CASE EXAMPLE: THE GOVERNANCE OF ENGLISH PROFESSIONAL FOOTBALL CLUBS

Hamil *et al.* (2004) researched corporate governance performance in English professional football clubs and noted that the turnover in income had increased rapidly since the creation of a Premier League of clubs in 1994/1995, mainly due to revenues from television broadcasting. However, overall club profitability had declined. Hamil *et al.* offered three explanations: the non-profit status of clubs as 'community assets'; the 'consumers' (spectators/fans) are stakeholders in clubs (see Chapter 5); and football leagues operate on a cooperative basis by sharing revenue between member clubs. A distinction can therefore be made between NPSOs and corporate bodies with shareholders and consumers who are not stakeholders. Of note is that the standard of corporate governance in football clubs found in research by the Football Governance Research Centre (FGRC) was poor, and in many cases it can be argued that this observation remains true today. In particular, the level of compliance with company law and codes of corporate governance was weak. As a result, the management of risk was poor and many clubs, as of 2015/2016, remain in a perilous financial position, with others in administration, and others now run as community clubs by representatives of the fans. This, however, is in stark contrast to the few wealthy clubs in England, many of whom are under foreign ownership. Compliance issues are addressed more fully in Chapter 8.

The extent of compliance with the reform across the diverse non-profit sport sector has varied depending on a number of factors. In respect of sports clubs, Nichols *et al*. (2012) observe that there are three types – formal, semi-formal and informal clubs – where club type (and legal status) is a factor in the extent of compliance with government agenda. The average club is very small and is run almost entirely by volunteers with very limited resources. 'These characteristics of clubs have implications for their capacity to contribute to sport development objectives' (Nichols, 2013: 215). For example, the introduction of the *Clubmark* accreditation scheme was embraced by more formal clubs within a broader acceptance of professionalism (Taylor *et al*., 2003: 149–150), while more informal clubs found it to be a constraint on their planning. By contrast, informal clubs can perceive professionalisation to be a fundamental threat. Sports councils, via NGBs, have to find a balance in supporting clubs and creating conditions which may further burden volunteers, recognising that without volunteers the club structure would not exist. In a context where informal personal relations, rather than formal roles, is a characteristic of sports governance, and where a club may not have a clear set of aims and objectives, introducing demands on volunteers may be counterproductive for the sport. In 'Promoting more "professional" management practices to clubs, one has to be careful to retain, at the same time, the ethos of volunteering on which the club relies' (Nichols, 2013: 224–225).

Harris *et al*. (2009) found that there are four main views from clubs on delivering government-steered NGB objectives: (1) resistant – club volunteers do not perceive their role as being to support government policy; (2) indifferent – volunteers are not particularly interested in, or motivated by, achieving policy agenda, but they will recognise a level of synergy between club aspirations and those of NGBs; (3) reactive – the club board may respond in order to secure funding, for example; and (4) supportive – wholly embracing 'modernisation' and in some cases lobbying for it. The research found that few clubs were delivering or interested in delivering national policy objectives, although in 2015 the impact of reform may have gathered more momentum in some sports, e.g. athletics (see case example to follow).

In sum, the key compliance-related challenges faced by clubs of all sizes and relative adjustment to the ongoing reform process can be identified as:

- attracting, managing and retaining volunteers;
- developing new volunteers for fundamental club management roles;
- coaches need to be recruited and trained to the standard required by accreditation schemes;
- attracting and maintaining members;
- responding to pressures to 'professionalise';
- reacting to policy priorities of national and local government;
- reacting to changes in legislation (e.g. health and safety, child protection, charitable status, licensing); and
- applications for funding where conditions apply.

(Nichols, 2013: 213)

CASE EXAMPLE: GOVERNANCE REFORM IN UK ATHLETICS

With the collapse of the British Athletics Federation (BAF), a new governing body, UK Athletics, was formed in 1999. The new body brought together a diverse group of disciplines under one umbrella organisation. In the context of a declining level of performance in international competition, UK Sport (the government agency for elite sport) identified a need for athletics to undergo a modernising process. The long-standing amateur focus with reliance on volunteers was gradually replaced with a 'professional approach', e.g. full-time athletes supported by National Lottery monies distributed in this case by UK Sport. A *Whole Sport Plan* was introduced that included: developing a 'sustainable strategic business plan focusing on the needs of athletes'; an 'integrated delivery, management and governance'; the establishment of targets and measurable outcomes in consultation with clubs/athletes; and setting-up delivery partnerships with UK Athletics as the lead facilitator.

Subsequently, in compliance with this agenda, a UK Athletics Action Plan was drawn up and included:

- developing pathways through the Sports Development Continuum;
- developing athletics in schools;
- resourcing club development;
- improving coaching standards;
- improving links with athletes and clubs.

In 2003 the Action Plan linked to key funding of £41m from the National Lottery.

Grix (2009) argues that UK Athletics is unique among NGBs in how it has been modernised, where the outcome is an Olympic Games-driven governance 'model' to meet government 'medals targets', and with little focus and investment in the grass-roots of the sport. Whereas the former BAF was accountable to grass-roots clubs and 'downwards' to volunteers, UK Athletics is accountable 'upwards' to UK Sport. Nonetheless, there are now coherent pathways for elite development emerging using the UK Sports Institute network (UKSI) facilities, whereas previously there was limited access to world-class facilities for elite athletes and no national stadium capable of hosting mega-events until the UKSI network was established. Moreover, the 2012 London Olympics were an athletics 'success story' alongside success in the Paralympic Games for disabled athletes. National Lottery funding has also supported the *Community Refurbishment Programme* with a grass-roots focus. Nonetheless, this approach to reform in other sports may not be feasible or desirable and volunteers at the local level do not necessarily benefit from compliance with central government/NGB reform agenda if club objectives are recreational (non-competitive) or prioritise public benefit where the club has charitable status, for example (also see Green and Houlihan, 2006).

Governance change

A number of NGBs in the UK have experienced significant change in governance. The following case examples trace the early stages of transformation for four NGBs specific to England. Each sport, NGB and club has a different history, organisational culture and approach to governance. Nonetheless, these NGBs have clearly experienced 'modernisation' since the late 1990s. The issues raised by these case studies are explored and analysed further in the forthcoming chapters of this study text.

CASE EXAMPLES: GOVERNANCE MODELS IN THREE NGBS: HOCKEY, ROWING AND TENNIS

When assessing the challenges facing NGBs specifically, Houlihan and White (2002) analysed the work of NGBs. One aspect of this research was a focus on governance. For rowing, the Amateur Rowing Association (ARA) devised a strategy or 'Forward Plan' (2001–2005) that cited corporate governance as underpinning the development of the sport. A relatively high level of investment via the National Lottery and good relations with government agencies has in part been based on success in the Olympic Games. Support for the ARA was also forthcoming because of the approach to governance taken by the governing body.

Houlihan and White (2002) also investigate governance of the English Hockey Association (EHA), formed in 1997 with a merger of three governing bodies. The key unit of organisation for hockey is the club, who affiliate directly to the EHA, the county and the regional association. With the introduction of national league competition, the role of the club became more significant in the governance of the sport. The merger of many clubs at the time rationalised the governance of the sport although a redefinition of the role of the remaining clubs was an issue: whether clubs had a role in talent identification and development for elite competition or whether the role was participation and non-elite competition. Another concern was the financial viability of many smaller clubs that did not choose to merge (and some that did).

In contrast to the EHA, the Lawn Tennis Association (LTA) has a long history dating back to the nineteenth century. The LTA is one of the larger NGBs, with a relatively high annual turnover and over 200 paid staff. It was not until the year 2000 that a Club Strategy was produced, however, signalling a shift towards a form of governance that could be described as 'corporate'. Unlike many sports and their NGBs, tennis has not been resource-dependent on government and therefore has maintained a high level of autonomy. Clubs, too, have not fit into a structure for developing competition from a foundation level to national and international success. Whereas many clubs in other sports work with local authority sport/recreation services and local schools, it is only relatively recently that tennis clubs have formed these types of partnerships.

CASE EXAMPLE: CORPORATE GOVERNANCE OF THE RUGBY FOOTBALL UNION

One key aspect of the corporate model as applied to sport is business generation, and this is a core function of the Rugby Football Union (RFU), alongside the development of elite and community rugby. The mission statement of the RFU emphasises commercial and financial strength and the specific 'business generation' objective has its own strategic plan (Houlihan and White, 2002). A resource-rich sports organisation, with a relatively high number of paid staff, the RFU in effect is governed along the lines of a private sector operation. For example, the business plan includes sponsorship and commercial enterprises; a marketing plan; the negotiation of television rights, the development of e-commerce and consideration of licensing. Since this study took place, corporate governance has expanded in Rugby Union.

In terms of administrative governance, the RFU is set up as an industrial and provident society with responsibility for the administration and regulation of the sport. In terms of structure, it has a board of directors to manage the RFU; a council which can initiate and veto decisions; and shareholders who vote at general meetings. Following the termination of the former CEO's contract in 2011, the RFU commissioned an independent review. The *UK Corporate Governance Code* was used to benchmark best practice and recommendations were put forward in a report. A number of recommendations were approved to do with auditing and risk, codes of conduct, confidentiality in policy formulation, conflicts of interests and relationships with the media. Other recommendations were rejected. Advisory groups were subsequently established to assess the remaining recommendations, including reducing the number of board members and council members; introducing independent non-executive members; and, more fundamentally, reviewing the powers of the board, term limits and the role of key personnel. These issues, which are common to NPSOs, are explored in later chapters.

Sport governance today: issues and challenges

NPSOs face a series of inter-related challenges (Kitchin and Howe, 2012; Nichols, 2013; Shulz *et al.*, 2011; Walters and Tacon, 2013; Weed *et al.*, 2005) relating not only to the modernisation programme, but issues in sport, such as doping, betting and gambling, safeguarding children and vulnerable adults, ensuring inclusion and diversity in provision and a declining volunteer base; ethical leadership, operating as a business and negotiating a complex legal and sometimes litigious environment; and wider non-sport issues impacting on NPSOs such as an economic recession and political change. This short list is by no means comprehensive and all issues cited pose challenges that are not mutually exclusive. It is clear that there are significant exogenous pressures on NPSOs (see Figure 1.2) that become internalised by sports organisations and shape behaviour.

Steering a course through this complex and sometimes hostile environment has on occasion led to unintended outcomes due to manifold complications involved in the decision-making process. The media have been quick to highlight how sports organisations can struggle to cope with this environment, as was the case with the proposals for the redevelopment of Wembley Stadium, the lack of infrastructure investment for Picketts Lock (athletics facilities) and the failed bid for the 2006 FIFA World Cup Finals. Commentators have referred to the need for significant shift from volunteer-run 'kitchen table operations' to organisations with professional managers attempting to function in a rational and bureaucratic manner. Specifically, both the sports media and academics, and many within the governance of sport, have called for greater organisational effectiveness and for more controls on potential abuse of executive power (particularly at the international level), and by demands for more effective stakeholder representation and far greater accountability of board members.

What is clear is that pressures on NPSOs at the local level (e.g. sports clubs) have increased in the last two decades for a number of reasons, including:

* pressures to meet NGB standards, guidance and specific requirements;
* declining volunteer numbers related to the pressures on available time for volunteering (although not in all sports or at all levels);

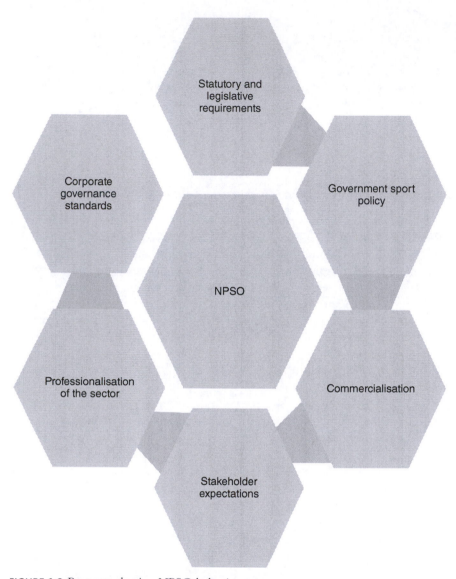

FIGURE 1.2 Pressures shaping NPSO behaviour

- increasing time allocated to paid employment and child care, especially in higher socio-economic groups where sports participation is highest;
- raised expectations among the general public of higher-quality services provided by NPSOs; and
- increased choice and competition for people's leisure time and expenditure.

More specifically, for NPSO boards, a series of administrative and operational challenges have emerged over the last decade. SPARC (2004) cite many challenges, including:

- boards focusing too much on operational rather than strategic issues;
- failing to define appropriate accountability measures for the board and staff;
- failing to define the results an organisation is striving to achieve;
- poor delineation of the roles of the board and staff;
- focusing on compliance issues at the expense of enhancing organisational performance;
- poorly skilled and inexperienced board members;
- failing to provide a clear framework for board members to carry out their duties;
- having low performance expectations of board members; and
- complex and confusing governance structures which fail to ensure accountability.

These governance challenges clearly focus on weaknesses in the core components of 'good governance' or best practice, namely: accountability, performance and compliance. Governance challenges matter for all sports bodies because failures such as those listed here tend to result in:

- a decline in membership numbers;
- a decline in participation;
- withdrawal of sponsorship;
- increased intervention from government-funded agencies (in some cases); and
- negative publicity and reputation.

Of particular significance for NPSOs is the volunteer base (Adams, 2011; Adams and Deane, 2009). Volunteers are critical to sporting organisations, whether large or small, and even where there is paid staff. Taylor (2004) identifies a number of trends related to volunteers as a key resource for NPSOs, including:

- an ageing volunteer workforce;
- fewer volunteers entering sport governance and administration;
- difficulties in recruiting volunteers;
- volunteers spending more time implementing new legislation and complying with NGB or government agency directives; and
- the expansion of a 'pay and play' culture replacing member contribution to clubs. This puts additional pressure on the active volunteers.

As a result of these trends, opportunities for developing a sports organisation, in building its capacity, for example, are diminished. Core operational tasks may therefore become the focus, rather than developing 'forward planning' or strategy.

Clearly, challenges facing NPSOs will vary depending on the size and resource base of any organisation. Taylor (2004) highlights differences between voluntary sports organisations across a spectrum from traditional, informal bodies that operate as cooperatives and perceive government intervention in sport as a 'threat', to

NPSOs that are professionalised, operate as a business and are receptive to government involvement or 'intervention' in sport. Moreover, as most NPSOs have relatively small bureaucracies, and in some cases an unbalanced political-administrative arrangement between volunteer board members and paid professionals working within a model resembling corporate governance, many sports organisations are susceptible to deviation from 'good governance' (Forster and Pope, 2004).

Further, the governance challenges facing sports clubs and associations and smaller NGBs with fewer resources can be treated differently in any analysis than those challenges faced by relatively resource-rich NGBs such as the majority of those sports cited by Houlihan and White (2002). For the majority of clubs and associations and smaller NGBs, the issues affecting governance include:

- the financial capacity of voluntary providers;
- government investment in grass-root sports (via Sport England) between 2013 and 2017 is across 46 sports (where the NGB has submitted a *Whole Sport Plan*) of approximately 126 recognised sports (in 2015), meaning many are not receiving government monies or have limited access to finance;
- government investment in elite sport (via UK Sport) is in specific sports related to success in major competitions, and others have had their funding reduced or curtailed;
- service standards and quality and the conditions attached to acquiring accreditation;
- the sustainability of provision in an economic recession where local authority support via grants has diminished;
- balancing equity with diversity and addressing the needs of disability sport;
- an increasingly litigious culture;
- volunteer numbers are declining in some sports;
- over two-thirds of volunteers are currently employed full-time in addition to their contribution to sport, resulting in time constraints on participation;
- volunteers are more likely than average to be 'wealthy achievers' – characterised as affluent, likely to live in rural or commuter areas, from large families living in large houses, older affluent professionals and farming communities (DCMS, 2011);
- professional (paid) staff and unpaid volunteers working towards common objectives; and
- increased competition between delivery agencies locally has in some cases led to a situation where there is 'no coordination of the offer'.

Given that there are approximately 1.5 million sports volunteers in the UK (one-quarter of *all* volunteering activity) and 150,000 clubs (approximately 50,000 have been operational for 50 years or more and have a long history of autonomy), across many sports and recreational activities, represented by NGBs of different sizes, resources, legal form, governance structures and relationships with government and a range of stakeholders, it is perhaps unsurprising that the non-profit sport sector faces many governance-related challenges.

Hoye and Cuskelly (2007: 19) summarise the influences on governance affecting NPSOs as:

- changes in the relationship between government and the non-profit sector;
- the regulatory environment in which non-profit sport organisations operate;
- the emergence of elite sport development as a priority in government sport policy;
- governance guidelines developed by government for sport organisations as part of the reform or 'modernisation' process;
- the impact of globalisation processes on sport; and
- the raised expectations of stakeholder groups.

Specific governance challenges for NPSOs are explored further at the end of this study text (see Chapter 9). It should also be noted that sport governance issues and challenges will vary by geographical region, where, for example, differences in sports administration and the wider political context between the European experience and that of North America (Hums and MacLean, 2004; Thoma and Chalip, 2006) will shape practice. Nonetheless, the influences cited by Hoye and Cuskelly (2007) apply across geographical and political boundaries, at least for sport governance in Western democracies. Moreover, at an international level of sport governance, NPSOs face global issues that transcend geographical boundaries where many sports are subject to increasing commercialisation and professionalisation.

Summary

This chapter sought to highlight the challenging environment in which NPSOs operate and specific issues and governance challenges faced since the reform or 'modernisation' of the sector began to take effect. The following chapters will explore the governance challenges facing NPSOs from a number of perspectives. The key themes that permeate each chapter relate to the core components of governance: board roles and responsibilities, performance, accountability and transparency including ethical frameworks and codes of practice, legislation regulation, stakeholding and partnerships, risk and compliance. The text will locate administrative challenges in a political context when assessing 'best practice' and 'good governance' by boards of NPSOs.

LEARNING ACTIVITIES

- Describe the infrastructure for sport governance at the international or at a national level.
- Identify the key characteristics of NPSOs and state how these characteristics influence governance.
- Why has reform of sport governance been necessary?
- Explain how reform measures introduced to modernise sports organisations have reshaped sport governance in the UK.
- As an independent task, with reference to a specific NPSO in the UK, assess the current challenges facing the board.
- To what extent are the challenges NPSOs face similar or different when comparing a resource-rich NGB operating within a corporate governance model and a small sports club run by volunteers?

Bibliography

Adams, A. (2011) Between modernisation and mutual aid: the changing perceptions of voluntary sports clubs in England. *International Journal of Sport Policy and Politics*, 3, 1: 23–43.

Adams, A. and Deane, J. (2009) Exploring formal and informal dimensions of sports volunteering in England. *European Sport Management Quarterly*, 9, 2: 119–140.

Bergsgard, N.A., Houlihan, B., Mangset, P., Nodland, S.I. and Rommetvedt, H. (2007) *Sport Policy: A Comparative Analysis of Stability and Change*. Oxford: Butterworth-Heineman.

Bester, P. (2013) South Africa. In: O'Boyle, I. and Bradbury, T., eds, *Sport Governance: International Case Studies*. London: Routledge, pp. 90–106

Carlsson, B. Norberg, J.R. and Persson, H.T.R. (2011) The governance of sport from a Scandinavian perspective. *International Journal of Sport Policy and Politics*, 3, 3: 305–309.

Chappelet, J.L. and Kuber-Mabbot, B. (2008) *The International Olympic Committee and the Olympic System: The Governance of World Sport*. Abingdon: Routledge.

Chappelet, J.L. and Kubler-Mabbott, B. (2010) A brief overview of the Olympic system. In Girginov, V., ed., *The Olympics*. Abingdon: Routledge.

Collins, M. (2008) Public policies on sports development: can mass and elite sports hold together? In: Girginov, V., ed., *Management of Sports Development*. Oxford: Butterworth-Heinemann, pp. 59–87.

Cuskelly, G., Hoye, R. and Auld, C. (2006) *Working With Volunteers In Sport: Theory And Practice*. London: Routledge.

David, P. (2008) *A Guide to the World Anti-Doping Code: A Fight for the Spirit of Sport*. Cambridge: Cambridge University Press.

DCMS (2011) *Taking Part: The National Survey of Culture, Leisure and Sport*. London: DCMS.

DCMS (2012) *Creating a Sporting Habit for Life: A New Youth Sport Strategy*. London: DCMS.

DCMS (2015) *Sporting Future: A New Strategy for an Active Nation*. London: DCMS.

DCMS/Strategy Unit (2002) *Game Plan: A Strategy for Delivering Government's Sport and Physical Activity Objectives*. London: DCMS/SU.

Deloitte and Touche (2003) *Investing in Change: High Level Review of the Modernisation Programme for Governing Bodies of Sport*. London: UK Sport.

Dingemans, J. (2011) Review of allegations of misconduct in relation to the Football Associations 2018 World Cup Bid. www.fifa.com/mm/document/affederation/administration/01/44/40/85/jdcreview-summary.pdf

Dorsey, J.M. (2016) *The Turbulent World of Middle East Soccer*. London: Hurst.

Enjolras, B. and Waldahl, R.H. (2010) Democratic governance and oligarchy in voluntary sport organizations: the case of the Norwegian Olympic Committee and Confederation of Sports. *European Sport Management Quarterly*, 10, 2: 215–239.

Fahlén, J., Eliasson, I. and Wickman, K. (2015) Resisting self-regulation: an analysis of sport policy programme making and implementation in Sweden. *International Journal of Sport Policy and Politics*, 7, 3: 391–406.

FIFA (2009) *FIFA Code of Ethics*. Zurich: FIFA.

FIFA/Independent Governance Committee (2014) FIFA Governance Reform Project: final report by the Independent Governance Committee to the Executive Committee of FIFA. Basel.

Forster, J. and Pope, N. (2004) *The Political Economy of Global Sporting Organisations*. Routledge: London.

Foster, J. (2006) Global sports organisations and their governance. *Corporate Governance*, 6, 1: 72–83.

Ganesh, S. and McCallum, K. (2011) Volunteering and professionalization: trends in tension? *Management Communication Quarterly*, 26, 1: 152–158.

Green, M. (2006) From 'sport for all' to not about 'sport' at all? Interrogating sport policy interventions in the United Kingdom. *European Sport Management Quarterly*, 6, 3: 217–238.

Green, M. (2007) Olympic glory or grassroots development? Sport policy priorities in Australia, Canada and the United Kingdom 1960–2006. *The International Journal of the History of Sport*, 24, 7: 921–953.

Green, M. (2008) Non-governmental organisations in sports development. In: Girginov, V., ed., *Management of Sports Development*. London: Elsevier, pp. 89–109.

Green, M. (2009) Podium or participation? Analysing policy priorities under changing modes of sport governance in the United Kingdom. *International Journal of Sport Policy and Politics*, 1, 2: 121–144.

Green, M. and Houlihan, B. (2005) *Elite Sport Development: Policy Learning and Political Priorities*. London: Routledge.

Green, M. and Houlihan, B. (2006) Governmentality, modernisation and the 'disciplining' of national sporting organisations: athletics in Australia and the United Kingdom. *Sociology of Sport Journal*, 23, 1: 47–71.

Grix, J. (2009) The impact of UK sport policy on the governance of athletics. *International Journal of Sport Policy and Politics*, 1, 1: 31–49.

Hamil, S., Holt, M., Michie, J., Oughton, C. and Shailer, L. (2004) The corporate governance of professional football clubs. *Corporate Governance: The International Journal of Business in Society*, 4, 2: 44–51.

Harris, S., Mori, K. and Collins, M. (2009) Great expectations: voluntary sports clubs and their role in delivering national policy for English sport. *Voluntas*, 20, 4: 405–423.

Henry, I.P. (2009) European models of sport: governance, organisational change and sports policy in the EU. *Journal of Policy for Physical Education and Sport*, 18: 1–22.

Hong, F. and Fuhua, F. (2013) China. In: O'Boyle, I. and Bradbury, T., eds, *Sport Governance: International Case Studies*. London: Routledge, pp. 124–136.

Houlihan, B. (1997) *Sport, Policy and Politics: A Comparative Analysis*. London: Routledge.

Houlihan, B. (1999) Anti-doping policy in sport: the politics of international policy co-ordination. *Public Administration*, 77: 311–334.

Houlihan, B. (2000) The World Anti-Doping Agency: prospects for success. In: O'Leary, J., ed., *Drugs and Doping in Sport*. London: Cavendish, p. 125.

Houlihan, B. (2002) *Dying to Win*, 2nd edition. Strasbourg: Council of Europe.

Houlihan, B. and Green, M. (2009) Modernization and sport: the reform of Sport England and UK Sport. *Public Administration*, 87, 3: 678–698.

Houlihan, B. and White, A. (2002) Sports development and four national governing bodies of sport. In: Houlihan, B. and White, A., *The Politics of Sports Development*. London: Routledge, pp. 164–205.

Hoye, R. and Cuskelly, G. (2007) *Sport Governance*. Oxford: Elsevier Butterworth-Heinemann.

Hums, M.A. and MacLean, J.C. (2004). *Governance and Policy in Sport Organizations*. Scottsdale, AZ: Halcomb Hathaway Publishers.

Jennings, A. (2006) *Foul! The Secret World of FIFA: Bribes, Vote Rigging and Ticket Scandals*. London: HarperSport.

Jennings, A. and Sambrook, C. (2000) *The Great Olympic Swindle: When the World Wanted its Games Back*. London: Simon & Schuster.

King, N. (2009) Sports development. In: *Sport Policy and Governance: Local Perspectives*. Oxford: Butterworth-Heinemann.

Kitchin, P. and Howe, D. (2012) The ramifications of modernization on community sport organizations: a critically informed case study. In: *ISSA World Congress of Sociology of Sport, Glasgow. International Sociology of Sport Association*: 55.

Mallon, B. (2000) The Olympic bribery scandal. *Journal of Olympic History*, May: 11–27.

May, T., Harris, S. and Collins, M. (2013) Implementing community sport policy: understanding the variety of voluntary club types and their attitudes to policy. *International Journal of Sport Politics and Policy*, 5, 3: 397–419.

Nichols, G. (2013) Voluntary sport clubs and sports development. In: Hylton, K., ed., *Sports Development: Policy, Process and Practice*, 3rd edition. London: Routledge.

Nichols, G. and James, M. (2008) One size does not fit all: implications of sports club diversity for their effectiveness as a policy tool and for government support. *Managing Leisure*, 13, 2: 104–114.

Nichols, G., Taylor, P., James, M., Holmes, K., King, L. and Garrett, R. (2005) Pressures on the UK Voluntary Sport Sector. *Voluntas*, 16, 1: 33–50.

Nichols, G., Padmore, J., Taylor, P. and Barrett, D. (2012) The relationship between types of sports clubs and English government policy to grow participation. *International Journal of Sport Policy and Politics*, 4, 2: 187–200.

Numerato, D., Baglioni, S. and Persson, H.T.R. (2013) The dark sides of sport governance. In: Hassan, D. and Lusted, J., eds, *Managing Sport: Social and Cultural Perspectives*. London: Routledge, pp. 284–300.

Oakley, B. and Green, M. (2001) Still playing the game at arm's length? The selective re-investment in British sport 1995–2000. *Managing Leisure*, 6: 74–94.

O'Boyle, I. (2013) Managing organizational performance in sport. In: Hassan, D. and Lusted, J., eds, *Managing Sport: Social and Cultural Perspectives*. Abingdon: Routledge, pp. 1–16.

O'Boyle, I. and Bradbury, T., eds. (2013) *Sport Governance: International Case Studies*. London: Routledge.

O'Gorman, J. (2013) The changing nature of sports volunteering: modernization, policy and practice. In: Hassan, D. and Lusted, J., eds, *Managing Sport: Social and Cultural Perspectives*. Abingdon: Routledge, pp. 218–238.

Palmer, C. (2013) *Global Sports Policy*. London: Sage.

Parent, M.M. and Patterson, D. (2013) Canada. In: O'Boyle, I. and Bradbury, T., eds, *Sport Governance: International Case Studies*. London: Routledge, pp. 54–73.

Persson, H.T.R. (2011) Good governance and the Danish Football Association: between international and domestic sport governance. *International Journal of Sport Policy and Politics*, 3, 3: 373–384.

Pieth, M. (2011) Governing FIFA. Concept paper and report, Universität Basel.

Reid, D. and Kitchin, P. (2013) The management of anti-doping: an ongoing challenge for sport. In: Hassan, D. and Lusted, J., eds, *Managing Sport: Social and Cultural Perspectives*. Abingdon: Routledge, pp. 34–50.

Schulz, J., Nichols, G. and Auld, C. (2011) Issues in the management of voluntary sports organisations and volunteers. In: Houlihan, B. and Green, M., eds, *Routledge Handbook of Sports Development*. London: Routledge.

Skille, E.A. (2011) Sport for all in Scandinavia: sport policy and participation in Norway, Sweden and Denmark. *International Journal of Sport Policy and Politics*, 3, 3: 327–339.

Smolianov, P. (2013) Russia. In: O'Boyle, I. and Bradbury, T., eds, *Sport Governance: International Case Studies*. London: Routledge, pp. 74–89.

SPARC (Sport and Recreation New Zealand) (2004) *Nine Steps to Effective Governance: Building High Performing Organisations*. Wellington, NZ: SPARC.

Stewart, B., Nicholson, M., Smith, A. and Westerbeek, H. (2004) *Australian Sport: Better by Design? The Evolution of Australian Sport Policy*. London: Routledge.

Sugden, J. and Tomlinson, A. (1998) *FIFA and the Contest for World Football: Who Rules the Peoples' Game?* Cambridge: Polity Press.

Taylor, P. (2004) Driving up participation: sport and volunteering. In: Sport England, *Driving Up Participation: The Challenge for Sport*. London: Sport England.

Taylor, P., Nichols, G., Holmes, K., James, M., Gratton, C., Garrett, R., Kokolakakis T., Mulder, C. and King, L. (2003) *Sports Volunteering in England, 2002, Summary Report*. London: Sport England.

Thing, L.F. and Ottesen, L. (2010) The autonomy of sports: negotiating boundaries between sports governance and government policy in the Danish welfare state. *International Journal of Sport Policy and Politics*, 2,2: 223–235.

Thoma, J.E. and Chalip, L. (2006) *Sport Governance in the Global Community*. Morgantown, WV: Fitness Information Technology, Inc.

Transparency International (2011) *Safe Hands: Building Integrity and Transparency at FIFA*. Berlin: Transparency International.

UK Sport (2003) '*Investing in Change': High Level Review of the Modernisation Programme for Governing Bodies of Sport*. London: Deloitte and Touche

UNESCO (2012) *International Convention against Doping in Sport*. www.unesco.org/eri/la/convention.asp?KO=31037&language=E&order=alpha

World Anti-Doping Agency (2015) *Independent Commission Report 1. Final Report*. Montreal: WADA.

World Anti-Doping Agency (2016) *Independent Commission Report 2. Final Report*. Montreal: WADA.

Walters, G. and Tacon, R. (2013) United Kingdom. In: O'Boyle, I. and Bradbury, T., eds, *Sport Governance: International Case Studies*. London: Routledge.

Walters, G., Trenberth, L. and Tacon, R. (2010) *Good Governance in Sport: A Survey of UK National Governing Bodies of Sport*. London: Birbeck University.

Weed, M., Robinson, L., Downward, P., Green, M., Henry, I., Houlihan, B. and Argent, E. (2005) *Academic Review of the Role of Sports Clubs*. Loughborough: Loughborough University.

Zakus, D.H. and Skinner, J. (2008) Modelling organizational change in the International Olympic Committee. *European Sport Management Quarterly* 8, 4: 421–442.

2

UNDERSTANDING SPORT GOVERNANCE

LEARNING OUTCOMES

At the completion of this chapter, students should be able to:

- identify the similarities and differences between corporate and non-profit governance;
- account for the characteristics of non-profit sport organisations;
- describe and explain different theoretical approaches and models for understanding sport governance;
- explain different understandings of 'autonomy' and how each relates to sport governance;
- decide which theoretical approaches or models possess utility for understanding sport governance for specific sports and in specific countries or geographical regions;
- critically assess the value of theory for practice by NPSOs.

Introduction

This chapter provides an overview of the theories of governance that apply to the administration of sport set within wider debates on governance (Rhodes, 1997, 2007; Stoker, 1998; Weiss, 2000). In comparison to corporate governance, the governance of non-profit organisations is relatively under-theorised (Cornforth, 2003). Nonetheless, administrators of sports bodies can acquire valuable insights for the management of their organisations from comparing and reflecting upon a range of governance theories. In order to understand 'governance', both the role of institutions and structures shaping decisions and actions, and the role of beliefs and ideas held by individuals and groups within networks or organisational cultures, need to be analysed. Further, power-relations between the various 'actors' (individuals, groups, organisations) need to be explained in order to make sense of 'governance' and how sports bodies are governed.

Research on governance

The body of literature on governance is written from three perspectives. First, 'governance' is understood as a system in which an organisation is steered (similar to understandings of 'governing'). From this perspective, SPARC (2004) define governance as a process by which the board of a sports organisation establishes a strategic direction based on its values, beliefs and priorities; sets policy and management performance expectations; identifies and manages risks; monitors and evaluates organisational achievements; and reports to the key stakeholders in order to be accountable. Second, governance can be understood as managing and delivering sport through networks, where cooperation and collaboration replace hierarchical authority. From this perspective, policy emerges as a result of bargaining and negotiation between organisations. Third, governance can be understood as 'good governance', where the focus of sports organisations is on management that is underpinned by ethical standards and adherence to a legal framework. Each of these perspectives is explored in more detail in this chapter. First, however, it is necessary to make a distinction between governance in the corporate and non-profit sectors.

Corporate and non-profit governance

A distinction can be made between corporate governance and governance related to non-profit organisations in the voluntary sector (Alexander and Weiner, 1998). Corporate governance is concerned with the governance of profit-seeking organisations that focus on maximising shareholder value, whereas non-profit governance is concerned with the governance of voluntary organisations that focus on services for their members and wider stakeholder value. In the UK, the sport sector is primarily made up of non-profit organisations such as national governing bodies (NGBs) of sport, sports clubs and associations. However, differences in the legal status, size, resources and objectives of the Non-Profit Sports Organisation (NPSO), whether NGB or club, impacts on the mode of governance adopted and governance in practice.

Fishel (2003) identified the internal characteristics of non-profit organisations that are shared with NPSOs. These characteristics have important implications for governance in sport, including the following:

- Organisations depend on the contribution of volunteers for both governance and service delivery.

- Organisations embody values and beliefs around a core purpose and specific priorities that can be interpreted differently.
- Organisations tend to have imprecise objectives that are difficult to monitor and quantify.
- Organisations are accountable to many stakeholders.
- Organisational structures are often complex to accommodate many stakeholders.
- Organisations tend to embody tensions between the board and paid staff in respect of decision-making and strategy.
- Organisations are not driven by financial (profit-seeking) motives.

Following on from these generic characteristics of non-profit organisations, the characteristics of Non-Profit Sports Organisations (NPSOs) can be identified (based on Watt, 2004):

- Dependence on volunteers to deliver the objectives of the organisation.
- One vote per member underpins governance but in practice organisations tend to be dominated by specific influential individuals or groups.
- Most operate on an individual-member basis but some have organisations as members too.
- Many are grant-aided via central government, although sources of income have been diversified in recent years. A resource dependency on public sector organisations exists for many organisations such as elite sport institutes and local government sport and recreation services to provide facilities, grants, advice and other forms of support.
- Despite being resource dependent, non-profit organisations are considered autonomous (or semi-autonomous) bodies operating at 'arms-length' from government.
- Clubs rely on member contributions in large part for their financial survival.
- Clubs depend on volunteer support, without which many organisations would fold.
- Volunteers in governance enact their duties and responsibilities in their spare time.
- Individual members in governance roles are critical to the implementation of decisions.
- NGBs provide advocacy for their sport or sports and therefore take on lobbying roles.

NPSO characteristics therefore typically resemble other types of non-profit bodies, albeit there are differences depending on the legal form adopted and 'business model'. In sum, sports organisations tend to act in self-organising, inter-organisational networks characterised by interdependence, resource-exchange, rules of the game and significant autonomy from the state (Rhodes, 1997). However, this level of autonomy has been questioned in recent years, as noted in

Chapter 1, as calls for 'good governance' have gathered momentum. Arguably, there is no substantive difference between the corporate and non-profit sector in terms of 'good governance' (see Chapter 7).

In terms of similarities between corporate and non-profit organisations, many non-profits are entrepreneurially similar to corporate bodies and this is increasingly the case as government grant support is reduced in the sport sector. In fact, many Non-Profit Sports Organisations, such as NGBs and international governing bodies in resource-rich sports, operate a 'business model' that employs professionals utilising business techniques such as marketing, human resource management and a focus on 'customer' service.

Historically, almost all NPSOs were structured akin to hierarchical corporate bodies, where a 'command and control' model supersedes consultation and consensus-seeking across a range of stakeholders. Nonetheless, many corporate organisations have adopted horizontal structures in the last two decades, where governance is managed through networks; this is also the case in some aspects of the non-profit sport sector, albeit that hierarchical models remain embedded in the governance of sport at the international level. Further similarities between corporate and non-profit governance can be related to the reform of the sport sector, e.g. the measurement of performance found in the corporate sector has also become central to the operations of NPSOs. Moreover, social responsibility (as one component of good governance) has become a powerful narrative in both the corporate and non-profit sectors. The accounting rules for non-profits are, for the most part, similar to those in the corporate sector too. One key difference remains, however. Whereas

TABLE 2.1 Similarities and differences between corporate governance and non-profit sport governance

Similarities	Operation via a business model (although not in many smaller sports clubs)
	A shift from vertical to horizontal modes of governance (hierarchies to networks)
	Pressures to achieve 'good governance' (e.g. social responsibility, accountability, transparency)
	Compliance strategies and tactics
	Measurement of performance (financial and social)
	Accounting rules
Differences	Legal status (some sports bodies are limited companies)
	Organisational mission and objectives
	Board leadership: volunteers in the sport sector or paid professionals in the corporate sector (some sports bodies employ a CEO to 'steer' or independent directors sit on boards)
	Management: the balance of paid and voluntary staff
	Financial indicators of performance

corporate and non-profits use financial and non-financial measurements apart from shareholder value, it is only in the corporate sector that earnings per share, return on investment, dividend yield and share price are critical elements of measurement.

Despite the many similarities cited, NPSOs retain a strong tradition of voluntarism and therefore adopting the corporate model in its entirety is not viewed as desirable even if it was feasible. It should also be noted that many NPSOs have not adopted a 'business model', especially smaller organisations with limited financial resources and a workforce that is entirely made up of volunteers. Nonetheless, as detailed in Chapter 1, the sport sector has been subject to reforms or 'modernisation' that has inculcated a 'business-orientation' in NGBs and some clubs (see Table 2.1).

The governance narrative

The narrative of governance can be viewed from three broad perspectives: steering, networks and good governance. Each of these approaches is explored below.

Governance as 'steering'

Organisations that employ 'steering' strategies believe this approach will result both in improved performance (efficiencies, effectiveness) and improved levels of accountability (Pierre, 2000). In this approach, compliance with key goals or objectives is sought via setting parameters and targets that can subsequently be measured. Non-compliance can result in a reduction of organisational autonomy, a reduction or loss of funding, curtailment of local discretion or even a threat of replacing horizontal network governance with top-down governance from central government (see Chapter 8 on compliance). As Wolf (2008) noted, the effectiveness of steering is ensured when governance networks operate 'in the shadow of hierarchy'. Although 'steering' (as opposed to 'rowing') implies a dispersal, rather than a concentration, of power, and therefore increased autonomy and responsibilities for NPSOs, this approach to governance is underpinned by a strategy of adherence to the parameters of central government policy. A notable example here is the introduction of *Whole Sport Plans* (Sport England, 2005) that set parameters and policy priorities for NGBs to govern their sports. In turn, NGBs seek the compliance of clubs and their management boards.

Governance as 'networks'

Although the governance of sport involves 'steering', it also involves governing through networks of individuals, groups or organisations. Steering mechanisms may rely on contracts that can be legally binding, whereas network governance is founded on socially binding 'contracts' and compromises. These arrangements, either formal or informal, create both resource dependency and interdependency in the sport sector, and tend to result from external pressures (political and financial, for example) faced by sport organisations (Hoye and Cuskelly, 2007).

Interdependency and resource dependency have become core characteristics of the non-profit sport sector, which in turn has an impact on both performance and compliance. The study of network governance is therefore about the strategies, structures and processes organisations put in place to cope with these pressures.

Clearly, a shift from governance by hierarchies to governance by networks poses difficulties in steering decisions and actions. Further, questions are raised regarding accountability (Considine, 2002). John and Cole (2000: 82) argue that 'systems must adapt to form more horizontal, cooperative and trusting relationships with the many actors who need to be involved in the policy process. Command and control does not work; networking, bargaining and cooperation are part of the answer.' A key point is that although there are a multitude of sports organisations, not all stakeholder groups influence decisions and actions. In the UK, given the multitude of NPSOs, many with overlapping and unspecified roles in the delivery of sport, combined with the many government agencies or non-departmental public bodies (for example, Sport England and UK Sport), a Sports Minister, an Olympics Minister, a UK Sports Institute, the Department for Culture, Media and Sport (DCMS) and, not least, local authority services, the fact that a 'shared understanding of who did what and which organisation was the lead' in delivering sport (DCMS/Strategy Unit, 2002: 129) is difficult to reach. This highlights the need for bargaining, collaboration, trust and cooperation to address interoperability issues (see Chapter 5).

In summary, network-based governance suggests partnership, cooperation and collaboration as an alternative to governance by hierarchical authority. The network approach focuses on relations between organisations, thereby implying that sports bodies arrive at decisions and actions as a result of bargaining between organisations, although not necessarily on a 'level playing field'. Henry and Lee (2004) coin the term 'systematic governance' to capture these processes, being a study of competition, cooperation and mutual adjustment between sports organisations. Clearly, in a sector as diverse and fragmented as the sport sector, the networks approach foregrounds the need for boards of NPSOs to build partnerships and stakeholder consultation into the design and delivery of services. Further, the network governance approach implies that boards replace 'rowing' (intervening at the operational level of policy delivery) with 'steering' (guiding, shaping and leading).

CASE EXAMPLE: AUTHORITY AND POWER-RELATIONS – THE CASE OF THE FOOTBALL ASSOCIATION (FA)

An understanding of governance can be gained through an analysis of the decisions and actions of an NGB for sport. The FA has a hierarchical organisational infrastructure in which the national FA has oversight for county associations that set rules for their members, including competitions, clubs and individuals. Their remit includes overseeing the development of football, enforcing the rules and ensuring the integrity of football. However, the governance of football has undergone a transformation since the inception of the FA Premier League in 1992 and the growing commercial influence of its elite clubs. The authority and capacity of the FA to 'steer' the sport has been challenged in a commercial environment characterised by the following:

- Broadcasting contracts previously organised centrally and at a national level are organised today via clubs across Europe in partnerships with media groups. Clubs can break away from binding contractual relationships with NGBs.
- Media companies are challenging the rules governing club ownership through strategically obtaining stakes in many elite-level clubs.
- Clubs are cultivating relationships with other clubs both within domestic and across international boundaries, bypassing NGB protocols.
- The increasing levels of migration of overseas players raises questions around the jurisdiction of NGBs.
- An expansion of the foreign ownership of Premier League clubs.

Although power and governance are now dispersed through networks rather than centralised within the FA, it can also be argued that the Premier League (representing elite clubs), its media partners and corporate sponsors, are now at the hub of (professional) football and this is a 'concentration' of power. The diminishing authority of the FA by contrast has to be located in the context of the power of FIFA and UEFA at the international level; the growth of elite 'player power' since the Bosman case (see Chapter 3); and to a lesser extent, the influence of the Professional Footballers' Association (PFA), the League Managers' Association (LMA) and perhaps the influence of supporter groups and trusts at the local level via their national representatives, the Football Supporters' Federation (FSF). These organisations put pressure on the FA as key stakeholders in the sport (see Chapter 5). In this context, the decisions and actions of the FA centre on facilitating and coordinating rather than direction and control (Geeraert *et al.*, 2013; Hindley, 2004, 2008; Michie, 2000).

Governance as 'good governance'

Newman (2001) observes that governance has been used both as a descriptive and a normative term. In other words, governance can centre on how organisations operate in practice, or how organisations *should* be governed, or *could* be governed, in an ideal situation. The 'good governance' literature is therefore concerned with organisational change towards 'best practice' where organisations currently fall short of what might be defined as 'best practice'. Given the extensive literature on 'good governance' that has emerged in recent years, and its critical importance in the next decade for UK sports bodies, this component of the governance literature is addressed separately in this study text (see Chapter 7). Nonetheless, a theoretical overview of good governance is included here.

In brief, good governance concerns ethical standards underpinning the relationships, methods and instruments used by organisations. While there may be no best way of achieving good governance, it is founded on a number of common elements. These are accountability, transparency, combating corruption, stakeholder participation and a clear legal framework (Agere, 2000: 7–9). For NPSOs, good governance relates to 'best practice' within an organisation, e.g. in the arrangement of relationships between the NPSO and its primary and secondary stakeholders. Primary stakeholders include those without whose continuing participation the organisation would cease to exist and in sports terms may include members/volunteers, participants/athletes and funders/sponsors (including government/public funding). Secondary stakeholders refer to those groups who influence or affect, or are influenced or affected by, the organisation but are not essential for its survival. This group might therefore include supporters, broadcasters/ media, local government services, local community groups and others, although many NPSOs rely on local authority facilities to deliver their activities. The overlapping concepts of good governance and stakeholding have emerged as part of the language in discourses around reform and 'modernisation' (see Chapter 1).

Hierarchies, networks and good governance

On the one hand Rhodes (1997: 53) defines governance as a network structure with a large number of stakeholders 'that interact continuously because they need to exchange resources and negotiate shared purposes'. As noted, power and authority are diffused across the network, rather than under the control of a single organisation. However, on the other hand, Rhodes refers to governance as 'good governance', which involves the principles of effective, transparent and democratic management (Rhodes, 1997: 49–50). This has important implications for stakeholders in a network, but it is of special significance for governing bodies who are responsible for good governance in a sport. It is important to note that the notions of good governance and network governance are complementary, where NPSOs observe good governance principles.

Nonetheless, good governance should in theory be achievable in hierarchical forms of sport governance. Proponents of the networks approach emphasise a distribution of power as desirable in order to increase accountability, whereas proponents of hierarchies emphasise a concentration of power as desirable in order to increase performance. The relationship between hierarchies, networks and good governance principles is complex and NPSO boards are located at the heart of these debates. The introduction of corporate governance models into the sport sector, given the commercialisation of sports, has added to this complexity. What is clear is the need for NPSOs to understand the governance context in which each operates prior to setting goals, including the identification of the most powerful organisations and how organisations utilise their power.

Governance theories

This section examines the established theories of governance that may further illuminate power-relations shaping sport governance.

Agency theory

Agency theory is the dominant theory of corporate governance. This approach assumes that owners of organisations have different interests to those that manage organisations, where managers seek to maximise their own interests over shareholders. Nonetheless, in this relationship, shareholder interests are presented as paramount. This theory therefore focuses on management *compliance* with shareholder interests and expectations. Authors have argued that this theory has limited applicability for sport governance in the non-profit sector where a diverse range of stakeholders, rather than shareholders, shape governance. As Hoye *et al.* (2014) observe, for the majority of non-profit sport organisations, stakeholders do not have a financial share in the organisation and therefore it is claimed that agency theory is too narrowly focused on the financial component of governance for it to offer an explanation of sport governance.

Nonetheless, although not widely used by researchers, this approach is potentially useful for understanding sport governance for at least four reasons:

1. Directors at board level may have different interests to other members and stakeholders and may seek to maximise their interests ahead of the wider interests of the club.
2. Financial compliance has become important in the governance of NGBs and NPSOs, which are increasingly subject to accountability and transparency in regard to financial management, both from government and local stakeholders.
3. Where sports organisations operate a limited company, theory grounded in corporate governance applies to some extent.
4. Corporate governance models form a basis for non-profit governance today in many larger and wealthier sports.

New Public Management

New Public Management (NPM) (Newman, 2001, 2002, 2005), as a set of practices, originates in corporate governance and has been applied to the public sector (e.g. local government) and has latterly begun to impact on the non-profit sector. NPM reforms centre on:

- a definition of explicit standards and performance indicators;
- a strong emphasis on controlling and measuring performance;
- a separation of policymaking and service delivery;

- an effort to increase competition between public, private and non-profit sector providers;
- 'value for money' where service users are 'customers'.

In the UK further modifications of modes of governance are emerging and tend to include a more significant role for non-profit organisations as providers in the sport sector alongside public- and private-sector providers and trusts, with direct provision by the public sector downgraded (APSE, 2012; King, 2014a, 2014b). Grix (2010) highlights a trend towards 'agencification' in the sport sector, including arm's-length agencies, new forms of 'partnership', networks, charities, advisory bodies, boards, commissions, councils and trusts. In the non-profit sport sector, modes of governance are under review in many cases, given this rapidly changing context, with a general trend from autonomous self-governance to mixed modes of governance. *Performance*, as the central concern of NPM, remains a key concern of organisations managing sport, irrespective of the type of delivery agency; this theme is explored further in Chapter 6.

Stakeholder and stewardship theories

Related to the networks approach to governance is *stakeholder theory*, which is built on an analysis of relationships between organisations and their 'stakeholders' (however defined). This theoretical approach focuses on the responsibilities of organisations in governance. These responsibilities belong not only to the volunteer members and staff of an NPSO and its 'in-house' stakeholders (e.g. members/participants) but also for societal groups and the wider community. Organisations therefore seek to assimilate the viewpoints and interests of differing stakeholder groups at board level (see Chapter 5). In reference to the UK sport sector, it can be argued that the professionalisation of the non-profit sector for sport has impacted on volunteer stakeholding as a 'business model' based on performance has emerged.

A less positive view of the concept of the 'stakeholder' is that it represents a poor substitute for the more robust concept of 'citizen'. This raises questions regarding the rights of participants, athletes or other groups within an NPSO. Nonetheless, the study of stakeholding has become the dominant lens through which to view the relationship between an organisation and the various internal and external groups with which it directly or indirectly interacts (Houlihan, 2013).

In contrast to agency theory, *stewardship theory* assumes that managers are motivated less by control and more by a need for achievement, responsibility and recognition and therefore, rather than compliance, the focus of an organisation is on performance. From this perspective, board directors and club members, for example, share common interests and extended stakeholding can be realised in practice. These governance issues are discussed further in Chapter 5.

Inter-Organisational Relations theory

Inter-Organisational Relations (IOR) theory is based on an analysis of how organisations relate to one another. Although the governance of sport has traditionally been achieved via pyramidal structures, this is no longer the whole picture. Three 'ideal types' of Inter-Organisational Relations (IORs) can be identified, namely: coordination, cooperation and competition. These modes are generally associated with, respectively, the state, the voluntary sector and the market. According to Robinson *et al.* (2000) competition refers to both the competition for scarce resources as well as competition over ideas, constituencies, values and definitions of needs. Coordination is 'the description of relationships which are ordered by the exercise of authority through hierarchy and rules, rather than by the hidden hand of competition or by solidarity based on trust and reciprocity' (Robinson *et al.*, 2000: 7–8). Market relations tends to be a focus on research on corporate governance. IOR theory (Hoye and Cuskelly, 2007: 51–53) therefore focuses on these types of relationships through an analysis of structural efficiencies, inefficiencies and performance; resource exchange between sports bodies; decision-making and strategic planning; and the area of autonomy and compliance. Clearly, each of these research areas can be related to sport governance.

Areas for research that can shed light on the governance of sport include the study of relationships between:

- clubs and NGBs, regional or county bodies;
- NGBs and government bodies (and differences across the UK for comparative studies);
- NGBs and international governing bodies or EU bodies;
- clubs and government agencies or local government;
- NGBs and local government.

(King, 2009)

This theory can be related to relationships between non-profit sector bodies and government where a balance is attempted between coordination, cooperation and competition. Notions of co-production, co-management and co-governance have emerged in recent years, where sports clubs, for example, can co-produce services previously provided directly by local government sport or recreation services (see APSE, 2012). However, in practice these practices are not extensive in the UK sport sector to date. Co-production can be defined as the delivery of a public service by citizens, community groups and non-profit organisations at arm's length from government. Co-management could take the form of managerial co-ordination between an NGB and government body in the implementation of services. The related concept of co-governance is related to policy development by public-sector bodies in partnership with NPSOs, rather than NPSOs being delivery agencies for government policy priorities.

Resource dependency theory

Resource dependency theory highlights the fact that the majority of organisations are dependent on other organisations for their survival and therefore need to manage relationships effectively to sustain resources. The governing board of an NPSO therefore plays a critical role in relationship-building and may play a boundary-spanning role across a number of partnerships, including with organisations in the public and private sectors and others outside the sport sector. Due to resource dependencies impacting on the governance structure of a sports body, in addition to its level of flexibility and autonomy, NPSOs need to develop a specific skill-set to manage resource dependencies and Inter-Organisational Relations across a diverse sector. The non-profit sport sector is clearly dependent on government/public resources from the investment made by local authorities in facilities and spaces to play (parks, playing fields) to government and EU grants and National Lottery monies. This allows government to insist that NGBs and clubs operate within governance parameters set by policy guidance, funding conditions and legislation. However, some NPSOs are semi-autonomous of government due to another form of resource dependency, namely commercial sector sponsorship.

Resource dependence, IOR, stakeholder and stewardship theories are within a 'family' of theoretical perspectives linked to the research on network governance. In common is the analysis of how pressures in the external environment, in which organisations compete for resources, shape organisational behaviour. Other theories complement this approach to understanding governance, such as *institutional theory* (Hoye and Cuskelly, 2007: 13), which foregrounds how governance is shaped by pressures to conform with business practices and legal requirements.

Organisational theory

Organisational theory analyses governance issues through five inter-related processes, namely: formalisation, centralisation, specialisation, departmentalisation and structural isomorphism. Most research to date has centred on the process and impact of professionalisation on NPSOs. Clearly, the impact of professionalisation will differ across organisations of a different size, resources, objectives and governance structures. Another facet of this theoretical approach that can be related to the non-profit sport sector is the study of organisational change. More specifically, research has explored change as a result of conflict between organisations; organisational capacity for change; and resistance, adaptation or compliance with pressures to change, e.g. modify governance practices (Kikulis *et al.*, 1995). As a result of the ongoing reform of the sport sector, formalisation and specialisation have tended to increase. Other aspects of organisational theory are under-utilised in the study of NPSOs, apart from one recent study that analysed the impact of commercialisation in professional football (soccer) clubs (Gammelsæter, 2010).

Governance models

From the *governance models* perspective, governance issues are analysed through idealised policies, systems and processes. The components of governance 'models' are a set of structures, policies and processes that set out the remit, role and responsibilities of the board (and CEO where applicable) within an organisation. The literature on governance models consists of three core themes that can be applied to NPSOs:

1. The relative merits of NPSOs adopting the corporate model of governance.
2. The relative merits of three governance types: the traditional model; the executive-led model; and the policy governance model, for sport governance.
3. The application of governance models, including the appropriateness of smaller NPSOs managed by volunteers adapting to a model more suited to larger NPSOs with paid staff.

In respect of NPSOs adapting to or adopting corporate models of governance, Hodgkin (1993) defines corporate governance in terms of:

- the CEO has leadership responsibilities;
- the CEO determines the policy direction of the organisation;
- the CEO has administrative authority;
- the CEO is a voting member of the board; and
- the board focuses on employing and evaluating CEO performance.

However, Hodgkin (1993: 416) states that adopting a 'corporate model would be a dangerous error for non-profit organizations'. Instead, the model adopted needs to fit the purpose of an organisation. Critical differences between corporate and non-profit organisations that need to be considered include:

- the absence of a profit motive in NPSOs meaning that a sports club, for example, must focus on its mission and balancing stakeholder interests rather than shareholder value;
- NPSOs develop policy and strategy based on value judgements;
- NPSOs make detailed policy decisions at board level;
- volunteers on the board exercise control over decisions made by paid staff;
- high levels of accountability to stakeholders is expected; and
- NPSOs have wider social responsibilities beyond the organisation and its members.

Key issue: autonomy

The quest for 'autonomy' by NPSOs has proven to be a key issue in the sport sector and poses a significant challenge in the context of sector reform or 'modernisation'. The term is often assimilated with broader concepts such as 'independence' or narrower concepts such as 'self-determination' or 'self-regulation'. In order to add clarity to an understanding of autonomy in the sport sector, a distinction can be made between:

- political autonomy
- legal autonomy
- financial autonomy
- pyramidal autonomy.

Each of these definitions and understandings of autonomy can be related to and have consequences for sports governance.

Political autonomy concerns the relationship between government agencies and NPSOs that historically resist any form of state (or more narrowly, 'government') intervention, especially those operating at the level of international sport. This contrasts with other European nations where voluntary sports associations and the state were not treated as distinct spheres of political life, and the level of state intervention varies (Henry, 2009). In the UK, from the 1960s onwards, the state has increasingly shaped the governance of sport, and particularly from the 1970s with the introduction of the national sports councils and local government services for sport and recreation (King, 2009). More recently, as noted, the 'modernisation' agenda has served to highlight the emergence of a new 'social contract' where government (and, more broadly, the state) has a significant stake in sport and how it is governed. In this context, the changing relationship between the state and sport is of critical significance for the governance of sport. Moreover, in recognising the economic and social function of sport, the EU has acquired a certain degree of legitimacy in the political steering of sports governance (Garcia, 2009).

The *legal autonomy* of a sports organisation (Chapter 3) relates to the capacity of that organisation to adopt its own rules and norms within a national or regional legal framework. At national level, the legal autonomy of sports organisations is located in:

- civil law for organisational construct;
- fiscal law for tax exemptions;
- corporation law for contractual issues.

At international level, in Europe, the Council of Europe (COE) recognises a legal conceptualisation of autonomy through the *European Sports Charter* (1992), which states that voluntary sports organisations have the right to establish autonomous decision-making processes within the law. Further, the European Council's *Nice Declaration* on sport emphasised that it is the task of sporting organisations to organise and promote their particular sports (EC, 2000). In many cases, however, the legal autonomy of sport has been challenged by the decisions of the EU Court of Justice (see Chapter 4). Further change in EU law and sport-specific law (Parrish, 2003) may impact on the autonomy of NPSOs in the UK.

The third understanding of 'autonomy' as it relates to sport is *financial autonomy*. As noted in the section on resource dependency theory, NPSOs have to some extent become resource dependent on public financial support. As also noted, with the commercialisation of sport, some NPSOs are dependent more on corporate sponsors than state funding, resulting in a huge disparity across the sport sector between those that depend on government support and those that do not. A key factor here, of course, is sports broadcasting, from which some sports have benefited significantly. What is important for board members (and CEOs) of NPSOs is an understanding of the extent to which a sports organisation is financially autonomous and to what extent it is resource dependent, in order to establish a strategy to maximise autonomy, if this is an objective of the organisation.

A fourth understanding of autonomy is *pyramidal autonomy*. Historically, sport is governed via a vertical chain of command with the major international governing bodies at the apex. The IOC, for example, was created as a 'top-down' organisation with oversight for Olympic sports. The *Olympic Charter* is in effect a 'constitution' that represents fundamental principles and rules governing the Olympic Movement. Membership requires compliance with the Olympic Charter. However, most other international sports organisations were created 'bottom-up' by NGBs that in effect gave up a degree of autonomy and sovereignty over the governance of their sport as sports grew beyond national boundaries. In practice, many NPSO boards operating locally or regionally have a level of autonomy from NGBs but are nonetheless resource dependent and subject to scrutiny and compliance measures in many if not most cases. As noted, networked forms of governance have emerged alongside hierarchical forms of governance, which has raised issues around authority, control and leadership. How pyramidal autonomy functions in networks requires an investigation of power-relations in the sport sector.

Another conceptualisation of 'autonomy' can be related to sport governance, namely *supervised autonomy*. Where government does not have the power to 'intervene strongly' in the governance of a sport sector, it can take a supervisory role and limit activities to the promotion of codes of practice and dissemination of good practice or targeted support to specific initiatives. Compliance is therefore achieved through persuasion rather than coercion. In the day-to-day governance of NPSOs, supervised autonomy, in this case from government agencies such as UK Sport and Sport England, may be considered sufficient. However, within the 'modernisation' of sport in the UK, it can be argued that NGBs and clubs 'earn' a level of autonomy through modifying how their organisations are governed. Hence the concept of *earned autonomy* (Green and Houlihan, 2006). However, sports organisations may view this approach to understanding the meaning of autonomy as a subtle form of coercion and a case of 'moving the goalposts'. This concept overlaps with the notion of *negotiated autonomy* (Chappelet, 2010). This is achieved via 'arenas of deliberation' (sports forums, social dialogue, expert groups).

Although the 'balance of power' is never fully equitable, social dialogue fosters cooperation and enables the practice of sports governance to be enacted.

The *White Paper on Sport* (EC, 2007: 18) states that 'European sport is characterised by a multitude of complex and diverse structures which enjoy different types of legal status and levels of autonomy in Member States'. At the national and local level, NGBs and clubs similarly operate via complex and diverse structures, with NPSOs characterised by differences in legal status, and levels of autonomy, however conceptualised, defined and understood, vary to a wide degree. NPSOs must therefore assess their level of autonomy as one aspect of designing and employing a strategy to achieve their objectives. NPSO boards could raise questions such as:

- Is the organisation financially, politically and legally autonomous enough to implement 'good governance'?
- To what extent is the level of EU supervision binding?
- Can reforms in governance be made without the loss of autonomy?
- Does a negotiated form of autonomy compromise the authority of the board and its competence to implement decisions?

Finally, the concept and meaning of 'autonomy' as it is traditionally understood by many International Non-Government Sports Organisations (INGSOs) (i.e. independence from government intervention or limited regulation) has been challenged in recent years in the context of the misuse of power and allegations of corruption by some INGSOs. For example, in respect of INGSOs' relationship with EU law, Geeraert (n.d.), as part of the AGGIS project, reconceives 'autonomy' as a negotiated 'settlement' between sports organisations and government (or the state more broadly, to include legislative bodies), where the role of the state in sport governance is legitimate, as opposed to a context where sport governance operates 'outside' of the state.

INDEPENDENT LEARNING EXERCISES

- Read Geeraert's report 'Limits to the autonomy of sport: EU law' and discuss to what extent sport governance should be regulated by the state.
- Read the article linked below. Click on the links and explore the issue of autonomy in the sport sector. State your five key findings. www.playthe game.org/news/news-articles/2013/scientists-discuss-limits-to-the-autonomy-of-sport

---

Summary

In summary, although no single theory of governance in isolation from others adequately explains sport governance, as is the case for sport policy (Houlihan,

2005), a number of theories do offer valuable insights for those governing sport in the UK. Specifically, the study of governance offers the NPSO director and practitioner insights into problems of coordination and cooperation; resource dependency; autonomy; effective performance and greater accountability, for example. As Cornforth (2003: 11) concludes, adopting a theoretical approach that combines theories would allow for the reality of paradox and ambiguity involved in sport governance. To fully understand sport governance, both how sports bodies *should be* governed and how they *are* governed needs to be accounted for.

LEARNING ACTIVITIES

- Identify the key similarities and differences between governance in the corporate and non-profit sectors, with reference to NPSOs.
- Why have many NPSOs adopted or adapted to practices in the corporate sector?
- Compare the strengths and weaknesses of two theories of governance with reference to a single sport.
- How do resource dependencies impact on sport governance?
- Identify three ways in which theory informs practice in the sport sector.
- Analyse the level of autonomy of NPSOs in a country of your choice.

Bibliography

Agere, S. (2000) *Promoting Good Governance: Principles, Practices and Perspectives.* London: Commonwealth Secretariat.

Alexander, J.A. and Weiner, B.J. (1998) The adoption of the corporate governance model by nonprofit organisations. *Nonprofit Management and Leadership*, 8, 3: 224–242.

Association of Public Service Excellence (APSE) (2012) *Local Authority Sport and Recreation Services in England: Where Next?* Manchester: APSE.

Barnes, M., Cousens, L. and MacLean, J. (2007) From silos to synergies: a network perspective of the Canadian sport system. *International Journal of Sport Management and Marketing*, 2, 5/6: 555–571.

Bergsgard, N.A., Houlihan, B., Mangset, P., Nodland, S.I. and Rommetvedt, H. (2007) *Sport Policy: A Comparative Analysis of Stability and Change.* Oxford: Butterworth/Heinemann.

Bevir, M. and Rhodes, R. (2003) *Interpreting British Governance.* London: Routledge.

Bruyninckx, H. (2012) Sports governance: between the obsession with rules and regulation and the aversion to being ruled and regulated. In: Segaert, B., Theeboom, M., Timmerman, C. and Vanreusel, B., eds, *Sports Governance, Development and Corporate Responsibility.* Oxford: Routledge, pp. 107–121.

Chappelet, J.L. (2010) *Autonomy of Sport in Europe.* Strasbourg: Council of Europe.

Chappelet, J.L (2012) From daily management to high politics: the governance of the International Olympic Committee. In: Robinson, L., Chelladurai, P., Bodet, G. and Downward, P., eds, *Routledge Handbook of Sport Management.* New York: Routledge, pp. 7–25.

Considine, M. (2002) The end of the line? Accountable governance in the age of networks, partnerships and joined up services, *Governance*, 15, 1: 21–40.

Cornforth, C. (2003) Introduction: the changing context of governance – emerging issues and paradoxes. In: Cornforth, C., ed., *The Governance of Public and Non-profit Organisations: What Do Boards Do?* London: Routledge, pp.1–19.

DCMS/Strategy Unit (2002) *Game Plan: A Strategy for Delivering Government's Sport and Physical Activity Objectives*. London: DCMS/SU.

European Commission (2000) *Nice Declaration on the Specific Characteristics of Sport and its Social Function in Europe*. http://ec.europa.eu/sport/documents/doc244_en.pdf

European Commission (2007). *The EU and Sport: Background and Context, Accompanying Document to the White Paper on Sport*. SEC(2007) 935 final.

Fishel, D. (2003) *The Book of the Board: Effective Governance for Non-Profit Organisations*. Sydney: Federation Press.

Gammelsæter, H. (2010) Institutional pluralism and governance in 'commercialized' sport clubs. *European Sport Management Quarterly*, 10, 5: 569–594.

Garcia, B. (2009b) The new governance of sport: what role for the EU? In: Parrish, R., Gardiner, S. and Siekmann, R., eds, *EU, Sport, Law and Policy: Regulation, Re-regulation and Representation*. The Hague: TMC Asser Press, pp. 115–136.

Geeraert, A. (n/d) *Limits to the Autonomy of Sport: EU Law*. Action for Good Governance in International Sports Organisations (AGGIS). HIVA, Research Institute for Work and Society, KU Leuven.

Geeraert, A., Scheerder, J. and Bruyninckx, H. (2013) The governance network of European football: introducing new governance approaches to steer football at the EU level. *International Journal of Sport Policy and Politics*, 5, 1: 113–132.

Green, M. and Houlihan, B. (2006) Governmentality, modernisation and the 'disciplining' of national sporting organisations: athletics in Australia and the United Kingdom. *Sociology of Sport Journal*, 23, 1: 47–71.

Grix, J. (2010) The 'governance debate' and the study of sport policy. *International Journal of Sport Policy and Politics*, 2, 2: 159–171.

Henry, I.P. (2009) European models of sport: governance, organisational change and sports policy in the EU. *Journal of Policy for Physical Education and Sport*, 18: 1–22.

Henry, I.P. and Lee, P.C. (2004) Governance and ethics in sport. In: Chadwick, S. and Beech, J., eds, *The Business of Sport Management*. Harlow: Pearson Education.

Henry, I.P. and Theodoraki, E. (2000) Management, organisations and theory in the governance of sport. In: Coakley, J. and Dunning, E., eds, *Handbook of Sports Studies*. London: Sage, pp. 490–503.

Hindley, D. (2004) Stakeholding and trusts: a framework for good governance within the football industry. In: Papapanikos, G.T., ed., *4th International Conference on Sports*, Athens Institute of Education and Research, Athens, Greece, 31 May–2 June.

Hindley, D. (2008) Playing the game: the challenge of corporate social responsibility in English professional football. *The Social Impact of Sport Governance & Management*, University of Bocconi, Milan, 20–22 November.

Hodgkin, C. (1993) Policy and paper clips: rejecting the lure of the corporate model. *Nonprofit Management and Leadership*, 3: 415–428.

Houlihan, B. (2005) Public sector sport policy: developing a framework for analysis. *International Review for the Sociology of Sport*, 40, 2: 163–185.

Houlihan, B. (2010) Managing complexity and fluidity. In: Houlihan, B. and Green, M., ed., *Routledge Handbook of Sports Development*. Abingdon: Routledge, pp.4–28.

Houlihan, B. (2013) Stakeholders, stakeholding and good governance in international sport federations. In: Play the Game, *Action for Good Governance in International Sports Organisations*. Copenhagen: Play the Game/Danish Institute for Sports Studies, pp. 185–189.

Houlihan, B. and Green, M. (2006) Governmentality, modernization and the 'disciplining' of national sporting organizations: athletics in Australia and the United Kingdom. *Sociology of Sport Journal*, 23, 1: 47–71.

Hoye, R. and Cuskelly, G. (2007). *Sport Governance*. Oxford: Elsevier Butterworth-Heinemann.

Hoye, R., Smith, A.C.T., Nicholson, M. and Stewart, B. (2014) *Sport Management: Principles and Applications*, 4th edition. London: Routledge.

John, P. and Cole, A. (2000) When do institutions, policy sectors, and cities matter? Comparing networks of local policy makers in Britain and France. *Comparative Political Studies*, 33: 248–268.

Kikulis, L.M., Slack, T. and Hinings, B. (1995) A structural taxonomy of amateur sport organisations. *Journal of Sport Management*, 3: 129–150.

King, N. (2009) Sports development. In *Sport Policy and Governance: Local Perspectives*. Oxford: Butterworth-Heinemann.

King, N. (2014a) Questionable ethics: good governance or terminal decline for FIFA. In: *Governance and Compliance*. London: ICSA.

King, N. (2014b) Local authority sport services under the UK coalition government: retention, revision or curtailment? *International Journal of Sport Policy and Politics*, 6, 3: 349–369.

McDonald, I. (2005) Theorising partnerships: governance, communicative action and sport policy. *Journal of Social Policy*, 34, 4: 579–600.

McLaughlin, K., Osborne, S.P. and Ferlie, E., eds (2002) *New Public Management: Current Trends and Future Prospects*. London: Routledge.

Mason, D., Thibault, L. and Misener, L. (2006) An agency theory perspective on corruption in sport: the case of the International Olympic Committee. *Journal of Sport Management*, 20, 1: 52–73.

Michie, J. (2000) The governance and regulation of professional football. *The Political Quarterly*, 71, 2: 184–191.

Newman, J. (2001) *Modernising Governance: New Labour, Policy and Society*. London: Sage.

Newman, J. (2002) The new public management, modernisation and institutional change: disruptions, disjunctures and dilemmas. In: McLaughlin, K., Osborne, S.P. and Ferlie, E., eds, *New Public Management: Current Trends and Future Prospects*. London: Routledge, pp. 77–91.

Newman, J. (2005). Participative governance and the remaking of the public sphere. In: J. Newman, ed., *Remaking Governance: Peoples, Politics and the Public Sphere*. Cambridge: Polity Press, pp. 119–138.

Parrish, R., (2003) The politics of sports regulation in the EU. *Journal of European Public Policy*, 10, 2: 246–262.

Pierre, J. (2000) *Debating Governance: Authority, Steering and Democracy*. Oxford: Oxford University Press.

Rhodes, R.A.W. (1997) *Understanding Governance: Policy Networks, Governance, Reflexivity and Accountability*. Milton Keynes: Open University Press.

Rhodes, R.A.W. (2007) Understanding governance: ten years on. *Organization Studies*, 28, 8: 1243–1264.

SPARC (Sport and Recreation New Zealand) (2004) *Nine Steps to Effective Governance: Building High Performing Organisations.* Wellington, NZ: SPARC.

Sport England (2005) *Whole Sport Plans: Key Performance Indicator Manual.* London: Sport England.

Stoker, G. (1998) Governance as theory: five propositions. *International Social Science Journal,* 50, 1: 17–28.

Watt, D.C. (2004) *Sports Management and Administration,* 2nd edition. London: Routledge.

Weiss, T. (2000) Governance, good governance and global governance: conceptual and actual challenges. *Third World Quarterly,* 21, 5: 795–814.

Wolf, K.D. (2008) Emerging patterns of global governance: the new interplay between the state, business and civil society. In: Sherer, A.J. and Palazzo, G., eds, *Handbook of Research on Global Corporate Citizenship.* Cheltenham: Edward Elgar, pp. 225–248.

3

ADMINISTRATION AND SPORT GOVERNANCE

LEARNING OBJECTIVES

At the completion of this chapter, students should be able to:

- describe typical organisational structures for sport governance;
- analyse the role and responsibilities of the board in sport governance;
- assess the processes and procedures defining the administration of sports organisations;
- highlight the pressures on sports administrators and how these pressures are mediated;
- understand best practice in the administration of sports organisations.

Introduction

As a core component of sport governance, this chapter centres on the administration of Non-Profit Sports Organisations (NPSOs). Given that there are differing types of NPSO with different legal structures, financial liability, funding procurement and management board roles and responsibilities, in addition to variance in organisational size and available resources, this chapter will focus on what is generic rather than specific across a wide range of sports organisations.

Governance structures in sport

Components of the governance structure of NPSOs usually include a board or management committee (the decision-making body) and sub-committees (responsible for operational aspects). It is the board (that includes individuals with titles such as Chair, President, Secretary, Treasurer) which has the authority for setting the tone for the organisation and its strategic oversight. Most NPSOs employ sub-committees to implement the decisions of the board. Sub-committees have a remit to address specific issues pertaining to rules and regulations, financial management, human resource management, event management, marketing, sport development or coach development, for example. Volunteers take on many of these roles, working alongside paid members of staff, which is a unique feature of governance for NPSOs. Alongside this structural arrangement are the salaried staff that may include a Chief Executive Officer (CEO) and other paid staff, depending on the size of the organisation and its business orientation. Precise structural arrangements vary across sports and levels of organisation and across countries and regions.

The typical governance structure for an NPSO 'has been criticized for being unwieldy and cumbersome, slow to react to changes in market conditions, subject to potentially damaging politics or power plays … and imposing significant constraints on organizations wishing to change' (Hoye *et al.*, 2014: 169). On the other hand, traditional governance structures do enable contributions from members and also tend to ensure a degree of operational autonomy from government intervention. Governance structures for NPSOs create challenges such as: negotiating the relationship between paid staff and volunteer members; acquiring a level of compliance among the members with key decisions made by the board; and brokering the interests and sometimes competing agendas across complex partnerships with multiple stakeholders. These themes are explored further in later chapters of this study text.

For examples of organisational structures of NPSOs, see Figures 1.1, 3.1 and 3.2. Figure 1.1 provides an overview of the organisation of international sport. Figure 3.1 is typical of the governance structure of international non-government sports organisation (INGSOs), in this case UEFA, which tend to be hierarchical organisations of authority and power. Many national-level sports bodies are similar to this standard model. Figure 3.2, by contrast, represents the governance of a non-traditional sport in which members steer the National Governing Body (NGB). In effect, the governance structure for Parkour UK is an 'inverted pyramid'. Critically, term limits are capped at two terms of four years for Elected and Independent Directors and board appointments are also limited to one member for each home country (England, Northern Ireland, Scotland and Wales). Term limits are addressed later in this chapter.

The board

The strategic and governance role of the board is separated from the operational and management roles of the various committees and sub-committees (Taylor and O'Sullivan, 2009). Given the ongoing reform of the non-profit sport sector (see Chapter 1), the role of the board becomes critical in sport governance. The board typically has responsibility for functions including leadership, decision-making,

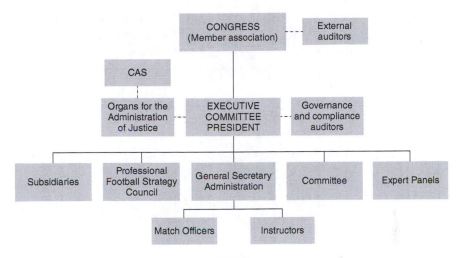

FIGURE 3.1 The governance structure of UEFA

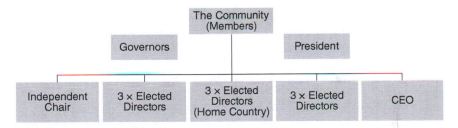

FIGURE 3.2 The governance structure of Parkour UK

representation and accountability (Ingram, 2003; UK Sport, 2004: 4) and oversight for strategic planning, policy formulation, legal compliance, the management of financial resources, stakeholder management, recruiting senior management, reviewing performance, monitoring the overall performance of the organisation and managing risk. Given the breadth of these functions, the executive body (management board or highest committee) is pivotal to the governance of the NPSO and to the sector.

The role of the board can be defined as to:

- focus on policy and strategy, and not on operational issues;
- ensure that financial and corporate governance targets are met;
- ensure that the organisation operates effectively;
- explain decisions to members;
- set financial policy;
- allocate budgets;
- raise funds; and
- plan for the longer term.

To a lesser extent, boards also tend to focus on hiring senior staff, and this may involve developing a human resource strategy including recruiting people with the competencies to manage change. Larger-sized NPSOs (with more than 25 full-time employees) tend to place more emphasis on establishing and developing a human resource strategy.

Fishel (2003: 10) identifies a similar and overlapping set of activities where non-profit boards should be involved. These are:

- attending board meetings and organisational activities;
- approval of the mission, participating in the planning process;
- selection and evaluation of the CEO;
- ensuring legal and financial obligations are met;
- support and oversight of programmes;
- assistance with fundraising;
- assurance of board effectiveness; and
- community relations and advocacy.

NPSO boards tend to allocate specific titles, roles and responsibilities to individual members. These roles are briefly discussed here. Specific roles will differ depending on the legal status of the NPSO.

Role of the president

Where an NPSO has a president, the key question is whether the role is executive or not. 'President' can be an honorary or symbolic role in some organisations. The role can in effect combine aspects of the chairman/woman role and that of the CEO. Typically, the role can: ensure that a common interest emerges from the many different interests within the board, where members are defending their own interest; help broker solutions across a range of potential conflicts within an organisation or across formal partnerships or informal collaborations; and represent an organisation in a lobbying or reputational capacity at events.

Role of the chair

A chair can be elected or appointed as set out in the constitution. The chair leads the organisation's strategy and vision for the future (in some sports bodies, the CEO will assume a strategic role, as the person responsible for implementation of the vision or mission). In smaller NPSOs, the chair may have many roles in practice, when there is the authority to do so. These roles can include: supervising and supporting the CEO or senior staff; acting as a channel of communication or broker between the board and staff; acting as a figurehead (where an NPSO does not have a president); and ensuring board decisions are implemented.

Role of the secretary

The role and responsibilities of the secretary vary depending on the size and resources of the NPSO. In smaller organisations, the role of honorary secretary is largely administrative, e.g. scheduling board meetings, taking minutes and distributing the minutes of meetings. In larger organisations, the role of company secretary (where the NPSO has the legal status of a company limited by guarantee, for example) is partly a legal role where the secretary must ensure compliance with company law. A company secretary also schedules meetings, takes minutes and distributes them, and also has responsibilities for updating public records at Companies House, and may have responsibilities to stakeholders, scheduling Annual General Meetings (AGMs), Extraordinary General Meetings (EGMs) or other meetings, for example.

Role of the treasurer

The treasurer assumes financial responsibilities and oversight for the board and organisation. Specifically, the treasurer: presents financial reports to the board and explains the data in the report; advises the board on financial matters; and oversees the preparation and scrutiny of annual accounts. In smaller NPSOs, the treasurer may also have responsibilities for budgeting or other financial duties; liaising with external funders, sponsors, financial authorities or other stakeholders.

Independent board members

In corporate governance theory an 'independent' board member refers to independence from management and the corporation. In other words, where 'The Board should be able to exercise objective independent judgement on corporate affairs', independent board members can contribute significantly to the decision-making of the board and 'can bring an objective view to the evaluation of the performance of the board and management' (OECD, 2004: 64). In the non-profit sport sector, there has also been a shift towards 'independent' board members (SRA, 2011). The issue is whether independent non-executive directors can exert any meaningful control over management decisions or actions. On the other hand, some NGBs in the UK have reported a positive experience of independent directors on national-level sports bodies. However, in the sport sector, 'independent' in reference to a board member is not uniformly defined. Another issue is to assume that 'independent' equates with competence or impartiality that may not be the case in practice. Further, an 'independent perspective' can be found within a board without the need to create a separate and distinct role.

CASE EXAMPLE: INTRODUCING APPOINTED DIRECTORS INTO BRITISH GYMNASTICS

The Sport and Recreation Alliance (SRA) note that introducing appointed directors to a board can be contentious. It can in practice mean that existing directors who are elected will need to vote themselves off the board and potentially reduce their influence in the sports organisation. Understandably, replacing elected directors with appointed directors raises questions about democratic processes in NPSOs. In the case of British gymnastics, introducing appointed directors formed part of a wider reform of the NGB. Other modifications included: the reduction in the number of directors; changing the responsibilities of directors to in effect devolve operational matters to professional staff; and reducing the number of home nation representatives to one per nation.

Independent learning task

Using the link, assess what difference appointed directors of the board made to British gymnastics as part of the wider package of reform: www.sportandrecreation.org.uk/sites/sportandrecreation.org.uk/files/web/British%20Gymnastics%20FINAL_0.pdf

Board responsibilities

Having identified the key roles of NPSO boards, a number of key responsibilities can be identified, including:

- complying with regulatory and legal requirements for the organisation;
- ensuring legal obligations including those on use of personal data are understood and implemented appropriately across the organisation;
- ensuring a clear set of key policies are in place and reviewed annually;
- putting in place appropriate financial controls;
- ensuring authority is delegated appropriately through committee structures;
- ensuring that checks and balances are in place to manage inappropriate use of decision-making responsibilities;
- ensuring effective systems and processes are in place;
- ensuring adequate mechanisms are in place for athletes, participants and members to feed in their thoughts and be involved with the organisation's development;
- assessing organisational risks and developing mitigation plans; and
- setting clear terms of reference, limits of authority and expectations whenever projects or tasks are delegated, be this to a committee or an individual.

Board–staff relations

It has been reported that the move towards professionalism at senior management level within NGBs has increased (Hoye and Cuskelly, 2007). Therefore the relationship between the board (volunteers) and the full-time senior staff is important as the level of trust, transparency and the quality of communication between the board and senior staff can shape the effectiveness of governance in NPSOs. Moreover, for the board to be able to effectively perform its role of supervision and oversight, it is clear that an NPSO requires: a clear definition of responsibilities; a coherent separation of powers; transparent election structures, processes and mechanisms; quality, accurate and timely information; and independent directors where there is a level of conflict that impacts on effectiveness and accountability.

It should be noted that the role of the board will vary from sport to sport and because of the size and resources of an organisation. Nonetheless, the critical issue is that the role of the board, and how it operates, is clearly defined and understood by its members (IOC, 2008).

In this context, it is important that senior board members seek to:

- establish a division of responsibilities between the chair of the board and CEO in writing, agreed by the board;
- recruit, appoint, monitor and support the CEO;
- facilitate effective board inductions;
- ensure senior members and senior staff are familiar with the governing document (e.g. constitution, articles of association, other documentation) and abide by the boundaries set;
- clarify the role of the board and the various functions it will fulfil;
- ensure the structure of the organisation is appropriate;
- put in place codes of conduct and terms of engagement for the board;
- review and update the governing documents;
- ensure board members understand their personal legal responsibilities;
- provide all board members with ongoing training and development to ensure they are adequately informed and effective in their roles;
- assist in appointing senior staff members and board members (elected, selected and independent);
- collectively review and initiate a board evaluation once per year;
- assume responsibility for the welfare of staff and volunteers;
- ensure each member of the board carries out a self-assessment and has an informal annual meeting with the chair; and
- ensure the chair receives an annual formal review from a designated member or members (two, maximum) of the board.

LIVERPOOL JOHN MOORES UNIVERSITY
LEARNING SERVICES

The role of the Chief Executive Officer (CEO)

The CEO's key role is strategic and includes establishing a vision, mission, values and reputation for the NPSO. Components of the role include:

- maintaining ethical standards and good governance in line with codes of practice (see Chapter 7);
- actively promoting and monitoring equality and diversity;
- ensuring the organisation is equipped to manage the safeguarding of children and vulnerable adults;
- supporting education and training of staff and volunteers;
- developing rules and regulations in cooperation with stakeholders, including participants, funders, sponsors, the local community, other governing bodies and others depending on the purpose of the NPSO;
- maintaining standards to foster appropriate development of the sport;
- promoting and communicating the interest of the sport, recreation, activity or area to a wider audience to raise its profile; and
- conducting a strategic review.

Policies and procedures

Policies drawn up by an NPSO usually relate to:

- the requirements for a person to become a member (e.g. their standard of play, or the nature of their contribution);
- the standards of conduct expected of members or officials;
- arrangements for protecting members and the general public from any potential danger arising through the use of the premises, facilities or equipment (where this applies);
- arrangements for protecting children, young people or vulnerable adults.

The range of policies and procedures will differ depending on the nature of the sport and the type of activities undertaken. For example, membership criteria and forms may vary, as might provisions for junior members. NPSOs are required to have:

- an equal opportunities policy;
- a code of conduct for fair play;
- child protection (safeguarding) measures;
- health and safety procedures, including duty of care, risk assessment, insurance, first aid and emergency procedures;
- club development policies; and
- a document relating to ethics in sport.

The constitution

A constitution sets out the purpose and rules of a sports organisation. Typically, the constitution will include:

- the aims and objectives for the organisation;
- the different forms of membership (e.g. adult, junior, social);
- the rules by which the NPSO will operate;
- subscription rates for members;
- how the affairs of the NPSO are to be managed (e.g. by the board and committees); and
- how the members control the NPSO, usually through an AGM.

General meetings

The main reasons for holding an AGM are:

- to elect officers;
- to consider the NPSO's annual report;
- to produce the chairman's annual report;
- to produce the annual accounts;
- to discuss and vote on amendments to the constitution or rules; and
- to recruit new members on to a committee (if applicable).

It is usual to publicise the AGM in advance to all members in order that decisions made at the meeting are accountable and representative of the organisation. An EGM can be called if at least one-third of the members (or some other proportion specified in the constitution) wish to amend a rule, amend the constitution or discuss urgent matters impacting on the NPSO, but which cannot be delayed until the AGM next takes place.

Committee meetings

Committee meetings are organised by the elected officers to manage operation of the NPSO. Regular meetings ensure that the NPSO is successfully planning, communicating and monitoring progress. The role of the officers on a *management committee* varies depending on the sport and the size or level of the organisation. Larger clubs usually employ a series of sub-committees to manage operations overseen by the *executive committee*.

Strategic governance

A key role for the board and CEO of an NPSO (if applicable) is to determine the strategic direction of the organisation. Although there are size and resource differences between NGBs, strategy development is a central issue for the board of all NGBs, particularly given the increasing pressure on NGBs. Following a period of reform, almost all UK NGBs have a strategy in place, although the strategy is not always developed by the board but tends to fall within the remit of senior staff. Strategic plans are commonly set for three to five years. More critical than the specific timescale is how coherently the strategy is defined and articulated to members and other stakeholders, including funders. An ill-defined and articulated strategy can impede the development of the NPSO. In terms of the content of strategies, it is a case of balancing a focus on overall objectives with a detailed action plan that includes reference to budgeted profit and loss accounts and cash flow forecasts; roles and responsibilities of those undertaking implementation; and marketing and sponsorship, for example. In recent years this latter component of a sport-related strategy has become central to NPSOs as each develops a 'business plan'. *Investing in Change* (UK Sport, 2003) notes that marketing and commercial advice was the second most important area in which NGBs required assistance. Further, negotiating sponsorship has become a key issue within the wider strategic approach of an NPSO.

Ferkins *et al.* (2005) found that a key issue in strategy development is the understanding of constraints on the development of strategic capability in NGB boards. Constraints are typically identified as a relative absence of resources to build capacity; an inability to commit the appropriate amount of time to develop the strategy; a lack of funding; uncertainty over sources of funding; and the competing allocation of time to dealing with operational issues. As stated, operational management is not an issue for the board, hence the need to operationalise a clear separation of responsibilities between the board and management staff. It is clear that NGB boards need to be able to delegate operational issues to NGB staff. However, this may be difficult for NGBs with very few or no full-time staff, in turn necessitating that board members facilitate the operation of the NPSO.

Board induction and professional development

Best-practice governance requires that organisations have formal and transparent procedures when appointing new board members. When new board members are appointed, an induction procedure is important. Research into the workings of NPSOs reveals that the majority of organisations have a formal induction procedure or training for new board members (UK Sport, 2004). NGBs usually provide new members with the terms of reference for board policies and procedures; a code of conduct and information relating to statutory duties; a formal contract that sets out the responsibilities of new members, although almost all board members are volunteers; a minimum standard of training within six months of appointment from a recognised authority; and training for their board members. Clearly these measures enable the board to perform more effectively. The ongoing programme of reform in the sector (see Chapter 1) is addressing aspects of professional development as some NGBs do not implement these measures in full (see Taylor *et al.*, 2009 for survey findings on sports clubs).

CASE EXAMPLE: BOARD REFORM AND PROFESSIONAL DEVELOPMENT IN HOCKEY WALES

Hockey Wales recently changed its articles of association to ensure a balanced board of elected and appointed directors. Importantly, the responsibility of appointing a chair was made into a board decision, not a membership one. With support from the government agency, Sport Wales, Hockey Wales prioritised a performance-related agenda and within a 'business model', the organisation rebranded itself. A number of governance changes were implemented:

- A board competency and skills framework was established to meet recruitment, training and behavioural expectations.
- A board skills analysis was conducted, utilising competency-based interviews, psychometric tools and a skills and experience chart.
- A recruitment policy and process was put in place resulting in the recruitment of four new directors to provide leadership, each with experience from outside of the sport sector.
- An independent chair was appointed for an initial one-year term and then a three-year term.
- A board evaluation and review was undertaken, led by the chair, that has proved a useful tool for the board and wider organisation.

The board now has a full complement of elected and appointed directors and the quality of communication between the two has improved significantly, as has the quality of support and guidance offered to the executive team and organisation. Also, the roles for the CEO, chair and board have been clarified, resulting in effective interaction within the organisation and external stakeholders. This case is an example of the reform or 'modernisation' of NPSO governance in the UK.

Election and appointment of board members

The underlying principles for nominating directors of the board are essentially the same in both corporate governance and for NPSOs. In both cases the nomination process involves identifying organisational needs and objectives identifiable in the strategy and matching them with competencies of prospective candidates. A mix of elected and appointed members can also assist in making decisions that benefit the organisation as a whole. Further, a diversity of views and opinions is arguably needed within a board as a plurality of opinions can make sure that the 'right decision' is made. The OECD (2004: 59) states: 'In carrying out its duties, the board should not be viewed, or act, as an assembly of individual representatives for various constituencies.' In other words, board members should, even if nominated or elected by a specific interest or group, act in the interests of all stakeholders and the NPSO as a whole. In practice, NPSOs tend to be more open to diversity and to accept promising nominees with limited or no board experience.

However, finding the right balance between representation and competence is always a challenge for NPSOs. By contrast with corporate governance, where it may be possible to acquire a competence-based board where corporate objectives are clear, for an NPSO the constituents and stakeholders are so varied, and the objectives so hard to define and measure, that a representative board can be seen as an essential part of ensuring that the organisation operates in the interests of its members. On the other hand, if the knowledge gap between elected members and those in the management is too wide, then problems can arise for the organisation. A two-board solution could be a way to address this issue by having a larger, more representative board above a smaller, more competence-based board. UK Sport (2004) suggest that there should be a maximum of three non-executive directors recruited from outside the sport sector that possess skills and experience of use to an NGB.

CASE EXAMPLE: TRANSFORMING THE BOARD OF DIRECTORS AT BADMINTON GB

As noted in a case study undertaken with the SRA with Badminton GB, transforming a board 'can be a journey with many obstacles'. Badminton GB engaged in a process of reviewing the organisation of the board and introduced independent non-executive directors. Lessons can be learned about facilitating change from this example that may be of value to other NPSOs. The aim of the 'transformation process' was to 'create and maintain an effective Governance Framework' and to 'ensure the effective working of the Service Level Agreement'.

Independent learning task

Identify the components of the 'transformation process' using the document at the link. What lessons can be learned that may be of value to other Non-Profit Sports Organisations? www.sportandrecreation.org.uk/sites/sportand recreation.org.uk/files/web/Badminton%20GB%20FINAL.pdf

CASE EXAMPLE: MAKING A BOARD FIT-FOR-PURPOSE AT SURF LIFE SAVING GB

As noted in a case study undertaken with the SRA with Surf Life Saving GB, a governance structure that is 'not fit for purpose' can result in poor decision-making, financial insecurity and a lack of accountability without checks and balances on lines of authority.

Independent learning task

Use the link to identify the governance issues affecting the governing body and analyse how these issues were addressed. www.sportandrecreation.org. uk/sites/sportandrecreation.org.uk/files/web/Surf%20Life%20Saving%20 FINAL_0.pdf

Size of the board

In practice, boards of NPSOs are often larger in size to accommodate representation from a range of stakeholders, whereas corporate boards are smaller in size (frequently fewer than ten members). The IOC (2008: 3) recommend that 'The size of the governing bodies should be adequate and consistent with the size of the sports organisations.' It is important that boards avoid being too large and unwieldy as this can result in ineffective decision-making. UK Sport (2004) recommends that the board of an NGB should consist of between five and ten directors, excluding the position of chair. However, UK Sport (2004) did not find a significant relationship between board size and a number of variables including turnover, number of full-time and part-time employees, number of member clubs and individual members. The way that boards are structured can have a significant impact on their ability to govern an NPSO effectively. However, organisational culture may be a factor here as, in Germany for example, a two-tier board structure with a higher number of board members overall is normal, whereas in the UK a unitary board is the main system.

Term limits and tenure issues

Term limits can be a useful mechanism to bring new ideas and experience to the board and to avoid an excessive concentration of power at executive level. However, it can be difficult for smaller NPSOs to acquire volunteers to serve on a board, especially over a long period of time. At the international level, IOC board members, for example, have a fixed two-term mandate limit, but nonetheless can return after a two-year 'sabbatical' (IOC, 2011). Transparency International (2011: 5) recommend a 'maximum of two terms for positions including the Executive Committee and the Finance Committee'. Irrespective of issues of power, NPSOs will normally benefit from new candidates with energy, additional competencies, perhaps specialist knowledge and ideas for innovation and improvement in governance.

However, the advantages of limiting tenure must be offset against the disadvantages. For new members there will be a period of adjustment as it takes time to understand governance in a specific context, to build relationships and enact reform. Strict term limits can therefore impede the successful functioning of a board. Also, it can be argued that term limits result in a loss of expertise, which can impact in particular on smaller organisations dependent on a few individuals. Further, it has been argued that term limits in fact reduce the value of holding office. On the other hand, some organisations such as FIFA tend to re-elect senior members over many years. 'FIFA does not match standards for rotation of top positions set by businesses or by other large organisations' (Transparency International, 2011: 3; also see Katwala, 2000: 27).

The length of tenure alone is perhaps not the key issue as an NPSO can be effective and accountable where there is: a properly functioning and effective board; an effective and independent administration; a selection system that attracts the right person to the post; open recruitment of board members; and avoidance of the power to decide the committee membership (and other potential political patronage systems). Nonetheless, there have been calls for a limitation of terms in office from outside the sports world (e.g. Council of Europe 2012; Transparency International, 2011). Of note is that high rates of re-election originate from the advantages incumbents enjoy over challengers because of the seniority of status. Hence, term limits are one check and balance in the system of governance. In fact, democracy within sport organisations may deepen through a continuous renewal of the board.

LEARNING ACTIVITY: QUESTIONS FOR THE BOARD

In investigating NPSO boards and the different components of administration, the following questions can be considered:

- How is it possible to find the optimal *balance* between the *political and administration* levels?
- What is the optimal board size (*number of members*)?
- Is it desirable/necessary to implement *a separation of powers* between the different parts of the organisation?
- How can a system of *checks and balances* best be set up in the overall organisational structure? What types of *checks and balances*?
- Should there be *term limits* or *rotation* for board members? If yes, how many and how long should such terms be?
- Should there be *term limits* for the chairperson? If yes, how many and how long should such terms be?
- How can the optimal balance be found between *representation* and *competence* on the board?
- To what degree should *stakeholders* be involved in decision-making processes? Which ones? And how?
- How best can members, board members, management and employees be *informed/educated/trained* on the governance standards?
- How best can *homogeneity of opinions* be avoided in the decision-making bodies?

- What mechanisms should exist to *review* or *appeal decisions*?
- How best should any *democratic processes* (e.g. elections) be organised?
- How should the board be *elected or appointed*? And by whom? And who should it be accountable to?
- Should there be *one or two boards* (or more) (e.g. supervisory board + management board)? If there are two (or more) boards, should they have the same or different members?
- Specifically, what *level of financial transparency* is needed/desirable?
- What should the *main principles of financial good governance* be? (For example:
  - Should there be internal and external auditors?
  - Should the accounts be reported according to certain norms?
  - What level of financial information should be made available? And to whom?
- What type of *internal control and/or compliance system(s)*, if any, should be established?

Source: based on CICA (2010a–2010h); see the study resources section

Board evaluation

A key role of the board is to evaluate board performance, both as a group and individually. This provides an opportunity for the board to evaluate its own effectiveness via an assessment of strengths and weaknesses, opportunities and threats; to set standards and performance expectations based on set criteria; and to evaluate individual member performance (Hoye and Cuskelly, 2007). The overall objective of board evaluation is to improve governance. Board evaluation is an action for NGBs to take at the early stages of any reform process and an annual evaluation of board performance is also considered 'best practice'. Moreover, an appraisal procedure for individual board members is usual in NPSOs.

LEARNING ACTIVITY: 'BEST PRACTICE' IN SPORTS BOARDS

Select three items from the criteria below (the list is not comprehensive) and assess to what extent 'best practice' is currently being met for any NPSO.

- The number of board or committee members is no more than ten.
- The board is involved in decisions on hiring senior staff.
- The appointment of at least one independent non-executive director from outside the sport to the board.

- The implementation of an induction procedure for new board members that sets out the role of the board, terms of reference, code of conduct, statutory duties and specific responsibilities.
- The provision of appropriate and relevant training for board members.
- The nomination of one individual with responsibility for evaluating annual board performance.
- The undertaking of annual appraisals of individual board members by the chair of the board in most cases.
- The development of a risk-management policy.
- The development of a marketing strategy.
- A delegation of operational issues.

Board culture

It is generally accepted that the sport and recreation sector in specific countries has its own distinct 'culture' and NPSO boards operate within the shared values, norms and assumptions that make up that culture (Hoye and Cuskelly, 2007). Therefore, if improvements are to be made, in board performance for example, then the values, norms and assumptions held by members need to be accounted for. How a board addresses issues and challenges and what it expects from its members are shaped by the culture of the organisation and the leadership of the board. In practical terms, this means that board members must provide formal induction and training to new board members; adopt a professional development approach to provision; and employ mentors, so that new members understand the 'culture' and can operate effectively within it. In recent years, the values, norms and assumptions within the corporate sector have entered the non-profit sector and this in turn has led to changes in the culture of sports organisations and the sector as a whole. NPSOs have responded differently to the challenges this shift presents (see Chapter 1 regarding the reform programme and Chapter 9 for the challenges ahead for sports boards).

Summary

This chapter has highlighted the administrative aspects of sport governance with a particular focus on the practices of the NPSO board and the governance challenges that board members face in a context of reform. It is clear that components of corporate governance are now employed by NGBs.

LEARNING ACTIVITIES

- Identify the key roles for the board of a non-profit sport organisation.
- How do the roles, powers and responsibilities of the executive differ from those of individuals responsible for implementing decisions?
- What are the key influences shaping decision-making by board members?
- Identify similarities and differences in terms of administration between larger and smaller NPSOs.
- Discuss the relative merits of term limits and tenure with reference to a sports organisation of your choice.
- Identify core board member skills and competencies required to govern a sports organisation. Of these, which are the most critical and why?

Bibliography

Andringa, R.C. and Engstrom, T.W. (2001) *Nonprofit Board Answer Book: Practical Guidelines for Board Members and Chief Executives*. Washington, DC: National Center for Nonprofit Bodies/Board Source.

Cannon, T. and Hamil, S. (2000) Reforming football's boardrooms. In Hamil, S., Michie, J., Oughton, C. and Warby, S., eds, *Football in the Digital Age: Whose Game is it Anyway?* Edinburgh: Mainstream.

Cornforth, C., ed. (2003) *The Governance of Public and Non-Profit Organisations: What Do Boards Do?* London: Routledge.

Council of Europe (2012) *Good Governance and Ethics in Sport*. Parliamentary Assembly Committee on Culture, Science Education and Media. Strasbourg: Council of Europe.

Enjolras, B. (2009) A governance-structure approach to voluntary organisations. *Nonprofit and Voluntary Sector Quarterly*, 38, 5: 761–783.

Ferkins, L. and Shilbury, D. (2010) Developing board strategic capability in sport organisations: the national–regional governing relationship. *Sport Management Review*, 13, 3: 235–254.

Ferkins, L. and Shilbury, D. (2012) Good boards are strategic: what does that mean for sport governance? *Journal of Sport Management*, 26, 67–80.

Ferkins, L., Shilbury, D. and McDonald, G. (2005) The role of the board in building strategic capability: towards an integrated model of sport governance research. *Sport Management Review*, 8: 195–225.

Ferkins, L., Shilbury, D. and McDonald, G. (2009) Board involvement in strategy: advancing the governance of sport organizations. *Journal of Sport*, 23, 3: 245–277.

Fishel, D. (2003) *The Book of the Board: Effective Governance for Non-profit Organisations*. Sydney: Federation Press.

Hoye, R. and Cuskelly, G. (2003) Board–executive relationships within voluntary sport organisations. *Sport Management Review*, 6, 1: 53–73.

Hoye, R. and Cuskelly, G. (2004) Board member selection, orientation and evaluation: implications for board performance in member-benefit voluntary sports organisations. *Third Sector Review*, 10, 1: 77–100.

Hoye, R. and Cuskelly, G. (2007). *Sport Governance*. Oxford: Elsevier Butterworth-Heinemann.

Hoye, R., Smith, A.C.T., Nicholson, M. and Stewart, B. (2014) *Sport Management: Principles and Applications*, 4th edition. London: Routledge

Ingram, R.T. (2003) *Ten Basic Responsibilities of Nonprofit Boards*. Washington, DC: National Center for Nonprofit Boards.

International Olympic Committee (2008) *Basic Universal Principles of Good Governance of the Olympic and Sports Movement*. Lausanne: IOC. www.olympic.org/Documents/Conferences _Forums_and_Events/2008_seminar_autonomy/Basic_Universal_Principles_of_Good_ Governance.pdf

International Olympic Committee (2011) *Olympic Charter*, Lausanne: IOC. Rule 1(2) www.olympic.org/Documents/olympic_charter_en.pdf

Katwala, S. (2000) *Democratising Global Sport*. London: The Foreign Policy Centre.

Organisation for Economic Co-operation and Development (OECD) (2004) *Principles of Corporate Governance*. Paris: OECD.

Sherry, E. and Shilbury, D. (2009) Board directors and conflict of interest: a study of a sport league. *European Sport Management Quarterly*, 9, 1: 47–62.

Shilbury, D. and Ferkins, L. (2011) Professionalisation, sport governance and strategic capability. *Managing Leisure*, 16, 2: 108–127.

Sport and Recreation Alliance (UK) (2011) *Voluntary Code of Good Governance for the Sport and Recreation Sector*. London: SRA.

Taylor, M. and O'Sullivan, N. (2009). How should national governing bodies of sport be governed in the UK? An exploratory study of board structure. *Corporate Governance: An International Review*, 17, 6: 681–693.

Taylor, P., Barrett, D. and Nichols, G. (2009) *Survey of Sports Clubs 2009*. London: CCPR.

Transparency International (2011) *Safe Hands: Building Integrity and Transparency at FIFA*. Berlin: Transparency International.

UK Sport (2003) *'Investing in Change': High Level Review of the Modernisation Programme for Governing Bodies of Sport*. London: Deloitte and Touche

UK Sport (2004) *Good Governance: A Guide for National Governing Bodies of Sport*. London: Institute of Chartered Secretaries and Administrators.

Yeh, C.M. and Taylor, T. (2008) Issues of governance in sport organisations: a question of board size, structure and roles. *World Leisure Journal*, 50, 1: 33–45.

4

LEGAL AND REGULATORY ASPECTS OF SPORT GOVERNANCE

LEARNING OBJECTIVES

At the completion of this chapter, students should be able to:

- outline the legal and regulatory context in which international, national and local sports organisations operate;
- understand how the European Union has impacted on sport governance;
- assess how legislation and regulatory guidance shapes sport governance in practice, including considerations of liability and risk;
- differentiate between legal forms of Non-Profit Sports Organisations;
- analyse the actions taken by sports organisations in response to the legal and regulatory context.

Introduction

A complex and changeable legal and regulatory environment poses many challenges for sports organisations. In a diverse and disparate sector characterised by legal uncertainty and raised stakeholder expectations, and in an increasingly litigious society, the Non-Profit Sports Organisation (NPSO) must steer a course through what can resemble a 'regulatory minefield'. Although this chapter will focus primarily on the national and local regulatory context, given that NPSOs in the UK and Europe are a core focus of this study text, this chapter will also include a section on how EU law, sports law and policy guidance shapes the context in which NPSOs operate. Clearly, different components of legislation and regulation will have variable impacts on different types of sports organisation operating at different levels. Therefore, this chapter will generalise across NPSOs unless otherwise stated.

The legal and regulatory context

As sport has become entangled with a range of legislation over the last 25 years, it is important for NPSO boards to have a grounding in legal and regulatory matters for the following reasons:

- The commercialisation of many sports.
- The professionalisation of the sport sector (and professionalism in sports organisations).
- The introduction of corporate governance practices into sport.
- Legal liabilities for board/committee members have increased.
- The management of risk has become an important aspect of working in the sport sector.

As Hoye and Cuskelly (2007: 22) observe,

> Increased professionalism in sport means the non-profit sport organisations are now engaged in a wider variety of revenue raising and commercial activities, the establishment of contracts with suppliers, sponsors, merchandisers and other business operations and in some cases employing paid personnel, even at the community level of sport.

In turn, these changes add pressures on board members that may involve upskilling volunteers and negotiating the challenge of recruiting and retaining suitably qualified volunteers. Moreover, volunteer board members have acquired additional responsibilities such as dealing with potential liability issues and implementing a number of legal duties. This has led to a significant escalation of organisations obtaining indemnity insurance, which in turn adds financial pressures on sports bodies.

With increased professionalism and commercialisation, the sources of regulation for non-profit organisations are similar to corporate bodies, namely:

- a government-determined set of legal rules supported by monitoring and enforcement;
- interpretations of statutory law made by judges;
- best-practice recommendations such as the *Code of Governance for the Voluntary and Community Sector* developed by the National Council for Voluntary Organisations (NCVO) in England; and
- accounting standards and auditing standards.

In response to changes in the regulatory environment over the last two decades in particular, NGBs must have a risk assessment strategy, accounting for legislative changes in areas where there is potential liability, such as:

- health and safety;
- child protection and safeguarding;
- disability discrimination;
- spectator safety.

Failure to meet legal duties may result in personal liability in the form of:

- statute – breaking the law;
- contract – breach or violation of a contract;
- tort – acts that cause injury or damage to another person or, more likely, a failure to act that leads to injury, for example. This can be viewed as neglect; and
- wrongful acts – decisions that harm others by having negative impacts on their rights, opportunities or privileges, or simply errors or omissions.

Therefore, the approach to fulfilling legal duties includes:

- *due diligence* – to act reasonably, prudently and 'in good faith' with the best interests of the organisation in mind;
- *loyalty* – to place the interests of the organisation before personal (private) interests; and
- *compliance* (obedience) – to act within the laws, rules, regulations and code of practice of the organisation.

These duties are considered to be the minimum requirements for board members.

In summary, sports organisations face several regulatory challenges and are required to enhance their capacity to govern an increasingly complex and potentially litigious operational environment. The following sections provide a fuller picture of the legal and regulatory context and raise issues and assess the challenges that NPSOs face.

Legal rules underpinned by government scrutiny and enforcement

Organisations in the non-profit sport sector are subject to a raft of legislation which an NPSO board will need to be familiar with and/or have legal support. In terms of the law, NPSOs should take account of: tax rules and regulations; financial liability; funding procurement methods; decision-making processes; and record-keeping rules. International sports organisations and major NGBs with a commercial arm will be affected by legislation that spans the regulation of sponsorship and marketing; control of anti-competition within the sports industry (EC Treaty

Article 81 concerning abuse of monopoly power); drug use in sport; and athlete contracts, for example. For the majority of NPSOs, areas of the law that have a more direct impact include: discrimination in employment and sports participation (the Equalities Act, 2010, inclusive of the Disability Discrimination Act, 1995); criminal and civil liability for injuries caused on a sports field; health and safety legislation; safeguarding of children; and spectator safety (e.g. for football clubs, the Football (Disorder) Act, 2000). Transgressing legislation may lead to enforcement and penalties.

Statutory requirements

Common law requires NPSOs to exercise reasonable skill and diligence in carrying out their duties and activities. Where an organisation is entrusted with powers that may be exercised for the benefit of others (e.g. participants), duties and obligations are imposed. This is termed a fiduciary relationship. Board members must therefore exercise their power for the benefit of the organisation. Within NPSOs there is a relationship of trust between the board and members that is underpinned by legal duties. Board members who fail to fulfil duties can be liable when the law (an Act or statute) is broken; when a contract is breached; or by an act that leads to injury to another person. In these circumstances, there may be financial implications that impact negatively on the organisation and possibly the individual board member.

Clearly, the legal status (or form) of the organisation determines the scope of statutory requirements. Each legal form imposes different statutes on the organisation. Board structures and requirements will vary according to the legal form. For those NPSOs with charitable status, the Charity Commission is the regulator, and for limited companies NPSOs are regulated by Companies House within the framework of the Companies Act 2006. This study text focuses primarily on the non-profit sector (national governing bodies (NGBs) and clubs run as non-profit organisations) as opposed to for-profit organisations, and therefore legal and regulatory aspects of governance impacting on limited companies is not a specific area included in this text. However, it is important to recognise that non-profit (or not-for-profit) organisations in the sport sector are subject to the same legal requirements as private/corporate sector organisations (for-profit), if the legal structure is the same.

In the case of unincorporated status, an NPSO does not have its own legal identity. Therefore members of the board (or governing committee) will enter into contract personally. Further, members of a board are joint and severally liable should legal action be undertaken by a claimant. The legal structure of an NPSO can therefore put board members at risk. NPSOs will therefore need to select the appropriate legal form and structure that fits with their purpose and objectives, size, resources and strategy.

Liability

NPSOs must take account of both occupiers and vicarious liability. In terms of occupier's liability, NPSOs that organise activities/events have a duty of care not only for any lawful visitor to the facility but also for trespassers. Premises must be 'reasonably safe' for participants, spectators, coaches, officials and others. What is 'reasonable' may be difficult to define, but in the case of delivering activities/ events, hazards can be accounted for in, for example, warning signs being located in 'unsafe areas'. In terms of vicarious liability, an NPSO is liable for a negligent act committed by a volunteer or staff member (during the course of their employment). In the case of services 'contracted out', this becomes problematic. NPSOs must of course avoid negligence. However, the Compensation Act (2006) protects sports organisations against 'false claims'. NPSOs need to do 'what is reasonable' and take precautions to limit risk. It is important nonetheless to make a distinction between 'reckless behaviour', which is a breach of the duty of care and is negligent, and 'careless behaviour', which is not a breach of the duty of care. Potential hazards include: school sport-related trips, outdoor recreation and swimming.

In terms of working with children, NPSOs need to refer to the legislation in place for the safeguarding and welfare of children and vulnerable adults and Disclosure and Barring Service (DBS) checks are required for staff and volunteers delivering sport-related activities. Additional provision (reasonable adjustments) must be made for young people with special educational needs (SEN) and any form of impairment or disability. Further, where sports clubs deliver activities in schools (e.g. after-school clubs), it is important that schools must undertake an assessment of risk in order that club volunteers can be confident that accidents will not result in litigation. Care should be taken with delivering activities within specific age groups in case of injury. Given the potential liability for clubs, it is important to educate and upskill volunteers (and/or staff) in expectations related to 'duty of care'.

Stadia safety, too, has become critical for sports organisations who own or hire a facility, particularly in association football (soccer). The Hillsborough case (Gardiner, 2009) was perhaps the 'tipping point' in the matter of spectator safety, although there had been many other tragedies before. Subsequently, the Taylor report (Hillsborough Independent Panel, 1990) resulted in all-seater stadia for top clubs. Safeguarding the interest of supporters is now paramount. Finally, the board of an NPSO will need to be aware of the UK Bribery Act 2010 (Wilkinson, 2010) and *whistleblowing* procedures in the case of volunteers or staff reporting matters that may be deemed unethical and/or illegal. The following section addresses the issue of risk for NPSOs in more detail.

Risk

Hoye and Cuskelly (2007) note that NPSOs must manage risk and ensure compliance with legislation, regulation and codes of practice. The challenge facing staff and volunteers in sports bodies is to implement legal compliance and risk management planning in a way that will protect the organisation from breach of the law while not adversely affecting volunteer enthusiasm and commitment.

In regard to compliance, questions that can be asked of sports organisations include:

- What would encourage the adoption of good governance principles?
- Why do some sports organisations adopt principles of good governance while others do not?
- Does compliance result from informal processes or legally imposed agreements?
- Do sports organisations possess the capacity to fully comply with codes of practice?

A key role for the board/committee of an NPSO is therefore the management of risk. Risk management can be defined as the process of managing an organisation's potential exposure to liabilities. UK Sport (2004) note that risk management has become important within NPSOs because an assessment of risk assists the board in making effective decisions within a broader strategy, in order to allocate resources with the objective of maximising impact, and to consider sustainability. Moreover, risk management is at the core of minimising the hazards and risks associated with participation in sport. Clearly, issues facing NGBs and clubs related to risk include: insurance for accidents, vetting of those working with vulnerable adults and with children and spectator safety, for example.

Managing risk can be challenging for sports organisations for a number of reasons, including:

- impact on the reputation of the organisation;
- acquiring income;
- retaining members and participants and other stakeholders;
- including board members; and
- maintaining an active volunteer workforce.

In sum, sports bodies need to reduce the probability, magnitude and unpredictability of risks in order to function effectively. This results in improved board confidence and optimism, in addition to facilitating the identification of opportunities and in preparing an organisation for future challenges (SPARC, 2004). Further, boards who undertake risk management develop a clearer understanding of responsibilities, roles and remit. In turn, the assessment of risk can improve organisational performance.

Hoye and Cuskelly (2007: 121) list the potential benefits for NPSOs of managing risk:

- more effective management of assets, events, programmes and activities;
- a safer environment for participants, officials, spectators and volunteers;

- a broader thinking about business objectives and outcomes;
- a greater ability to meet the needs of members and other stakeholders;
- flow-on benefits through the systematic identification of organisational deficiencies;
- improved communication, both internally and externally;
- improved compliance with the law, regulations and other formal requirements;
- lower costs and more budget certainty;
- enhanced image and reputation leading to increased interest in the sport and the organisation, greater participation and more financial support;
- better sporting outcomes;
- higher morale, more commitment and accountability;
- a better managed organisation able to support government objectives; and
- better quality experiences for participants.

An effective risk management strategy can therefore include an assessment of the nature and extent of the risks facing the organisation; the extent and categories of risk; the likelihood of the risks materialising; the organisation's capacity to reduce the incidence and impact of risks that do materialise; and the costs of operating particular controls in managing the related risks. The first task of an NPSO is therefore to write a risk-management policy.

One key aspect of risk management that has become increasingly prevalent is legal compliance. Ensuring that NGBs are fully compliant with the law is critical to minimise the risk of litigation. A more demanding legal and regulatory environment has been identified as an issue affecting sport boards (Ferkins *et al.*, 2005). With many NGBs lacking in resources to deal with legal issues, one way in which an NGB can minimise the risk of litigation is through *Sport Resolutions* (see the case study in this chapter). In this sense, 'good governance' can be considered as a form of risk management in itself (Monks and Minnow, 2011) and can be included in a good governance code (e.g. IOC, 2008: 5).

Risk assessment guidance is usually divided into a five stage process:

1. Identify the hazards.
2. Decide who might be harmed and how.
3. Evaluate the risk and decide on precautions.
4. Record your findings and implement them.
5. Review your assessment and update if necessary.

Recommendations found in codes of practice

In the last two decades there has been a proliferation of codes, guides and standards set out in a raft of documentation from national government departments and lead agencies with oversight for sport and organisations with a leadership role in the non-profit sector and from EU bodies such as the European Commission (EC). NGBs, regional and county-level bodies and clubs themselves have produced codes, guides and standards that members are expected to comply with, and international governing bodies such as the IOC have established codes that make recommendations for associated members. In the corporate sector, a company listed on a stock exchange receives a 'Good Governance Code' from the stock exchange which explains the criteria that companies must comply with. In the non-profit sport sector, similar codes have emerged in recent years as components of corporate governance have been adopted by NPSOs with more extensive financial resources and legal liabilities. In the absence of a higher level of regulation across the sport sector, by comparison with industries in the corporate sector, recommendations found in codes of practice are relied on to guide organisational behaviour.

Typically, a code includes consideration of the legal and regulatory context and principles of 'good governance' (see Chapter 7). For example, items included in a code include commitments to make transparent financial information that meets regulatory requirements and actions adhering to the fulfilment of legal duties. Codes therefore contain commitments to meeting legal, regulatory and ethical guidelines. Items found in codes of practice standardise and formalise practices if adopted and commit board members to applying recommendations, embedding the code over time in the organisation. Codes may also include reference to commercial rights. An example here is creating transparency in the awarding of commercial contracts, in awarding and hosting sports events, or other components of procurement.

A code of good practice in effect seeks to guide behaviour of the board/committee in respect of:

- conflicts of interest, including for example the voting rights of members with a personal interest;
- proper use and safeguarding of information;
- fair dealing with members and other stakeholders;
- facilitating payments, giving and receiving of gifts (probity);
- compliance with laws and regulations;
- reporting of unethical decision-making and/or behaviour; and
- communication of the code of ethics to members.

As noted in Chapter 7 on 'good governance', the *Voluntary Code of Good Governance for the Sport and Recreation Sector* (SRA, 2011) identifies the principles underpinning recommendations:

- Integrity – acting as guardians of the sport, recreation, activity or area.
- Defining and evaluating the role of the board.
- Delivery of vision, mission and purpose.
- Objectivity – balanced, inclusive and skilled board.
- Standards, systems and controls.
- Accountability and transparency.
- Understanding and engaging with the sporting landscape.

These principles shape engagement with and adherence to regulation and legislation.

However, there is a risk in relying wholly on recommendations in codes of practice for the delivery of effective and accountable sport governance, namely organisations 'paying lip service' to recommendations, rather than integrating recommendations into the culture and practices of the organisation. Further, organisations for which codes were designed may be the least likely in practice to implement recommendations. Therefore recommendations must be as specific as possible; feasible to implement; and underpinned by regulation where possible. The challenge facing those with a remit to produce a code is designing recommendations that are specific enough to be acted on in a sector with a multitude of sports organisations operating a different levels, with differences in purpose, resources and in legal form/status. Nonetheless, a generic set of recommendations offers a framework for identifying specific actions that a specific NPSO can take, in synergy with others delivering services in the same sport, for example.

Self-regulation

Given that the sport sector is not highly regulated and 'over-regulation' is resisted by governing bodies with a long history of self-determination, NPSOs will seek to regulate themselves while operating within the law. The concept and practice of self-regulation is contested, however. In brief, the arguments for and against self-regulation are identified as shown in Table 4.1.

NPSOs will assess the arguments for and against self-regulation in deciding what actions to take to stay within the law but retain a level of autonomy. Sports clubs will seek a level of local discretion in decision-making from national policy and governance guidelines and NGBs will also seek to regulate their organisations and

TABLE 4.1 Arguments for and against self-regulation

Arguments for	Arguments against
• It is more flexible than legal enforcement	• Lack of investigatory powers
• The rules can more easily be updated in a context of rapid change	• Diminishes public accountability
• Avoids potential conflict with regulatory bodies	• Does not account for non-compliant organisations
• Informal intervention in cases of non-compliance can avoid potentially costly sanctions	• Less certain and predictable outcomes
• Sanctions of disapproval and loss of reputation can be more effective than legal action	• Uncertainty can lead to inaction
• Avoids unnecessary litigation	• Self-regulation can be perceived as 'acting as judge and jury'
	• Imposes a burden on volunteers to resolve disputes with a legal course of action

sports without government intervention in addressing internal legal or financial matters, for example. At the international level, self-regulation is highly contentious in some resource-rich sports (see the case example of FIFA in this chapter). If an NPSO demonstrates the virtues of self-regulation, this should in itself deter legislative or regulatory bodies from direct or indirect intervention in the governance of the organisation or, at the very least, provide the NPSO with leverage in negotiations regarding the level of self-regulation that is desirable and achievable.

Specific actions that can be taken by the board of an NPSO to protect self-regulation include:

- meeting fiduciary responsibilities;
- acting within a duty of care;
- making decisions in the best interests of the organisation;
- developing a coherent strategy and monitoring performance;
- including stakeholders in aspects of governance (see Chapter 5);
- reporting back to members on matters of governance;
- monitoring CEO (where applicable) and organisation-wide compliance.

In summary, the sport sector has become entangled with a range of legislation over the last 25 years, and as a result legal liabilities and regulatory duties for board members have increased across many areas of operation. Boards are also increasingly expected to act within the parameters of codes of practice. Whether the sector is under- or over-regulated is a matter of debate. Clearly, legal and regulatory influences on NPSOs will vary across nation states and regions and for different sports. However, many of the same principles apply across nations with similar legal structures and a similar level of state or government involvement in sport.

Legal status of Non-Profit Sports Organisations

Governance challenges facing NPSOs may vary to some extent depending on legal status, but the fundamentals of good governance (both effective and accountable) apply to all NPSOs. The key point here for boards is that an organisation's legal status establishes the standard of care that a director must meet and certain duties that he or she is required to fulfil. It may also limit the powers, responsibilities and liability of the board if the organisation is a chapter or branch of a regional, national or international organisation. Many NPSOs are directed by volunteers on management boards rather than paid professionals responsible to shareholders. However, larger, resource-rich NPSOs employ paid professionals to manage the organisation. Rather than shareholders, NPSO boards are responsible to a range of *stakeholders*, including community partners, funders and, not least, the participants (members) engaged in sport and recreation and/or its administration. NPSOs can generate income and therefore 'profit', but any monies generated are invested in the operation of the organisation (apart from salaries, where this applies).

Corporate governance models cannot therefore be applied in full to the sport sector and modes of governance in the sport sector are varied by organisational type and legal status.

The legal structures of NPSOs in the UK can take many forms, from incorporated organisations (a company limited by guarantee, for example) or unincorporated forms of organisation (an association of members with unlimited liability) that can be charitable trusts or informal associations. In terms of the operational component of the NPSO, business formats include social enterprises and community interest companies. In the case of sports clubs or CASCs (Community Amateur Sports Clubs), if it is constituted as a not-for-profit (or non-profit) organisation, where members are not paid, and an open membership is promoted, then tax relief is available too.

Types of legal structure

Sports organisations can set up as an incorporated body with limited liability for members (a limited company), or an unincorporated association, or can be set up as a charity. Each option has advantages and disadvantages dependent on the purpose of the NPSO, its activities, goals, size, resources and expertise, among other factors (Governance hub, n.d.). Recently, a range of alternative types of organisation have emerged in practice, given difficulties in obtaining charitable status or the suitability of limited company options. This section provides an overview of the options for NPSOs and the challenges that each option presents.

Limited company

A limited company is an organisational structure which gives limited liability to its members. Limited company status can take the form of a company limited by shares or by guarantee. In the case of the former, shareholders each hold a share of the company. However, shares are not held by the general public and are not bought or sold (by comparison with public limited companies). New members are issued with shares but must transfer or redeem shares held on exiting membership status. Importantly, members holding over 50 per cent of the total shares can control the board. With a 75 per cent share of the organisation, the shareholder can change the constitution that sets out the purpose of the organisation. The key advantage of establishing a company limited by shares is that it facilitates investment with few difficulties, but the potential disadvantage is the political contest between shareholders for control of the board and its remit where it impacts on organisational effectiveness or accountability. Hence the competition for control of boards via share purchase in Premier League football (soccer) clubs in England, for example.

In the case of companies limited by guarantee, each member guarantees a sum of money towards the overall company finances. There are advantages and disadvantages for a sports organisation to consider in setting up this type of company.

Advantages of these arrangements include:

- As a distinct legal entity, it is easier for an organisation to enter into contractual arrangements, e.g. to borrow money, own buildings or stage events.
- Liability is reduced for individual members in the case of insolvency as each member will only be liable for the amount members have guaranteed. In other words, a sports club, for example, is liable rather than the individual members for the club's obligations and debts. This applies unless company law has been broken, e.g. where officers have acted negligently or fraudulently, in which case the individual is personally liable.
- Individual members can only be held responsible for any debts and obligations of the NPSO to the nominal value of their guarantee (SRA, 2015).

In order to qualify for this status, director details must be filed at Companies House, annual accounts must be filed and open for public inspection, and company directors (board members) acquire duties and responsibilities under company law. All companies require various legal instruments such as a Memorandum and Articles of Association, and acquire a duty to promote the success of the company (however defined) and a duty to act in the company's best interests (however defined). Some board members may potentially be prohibited from becoming a director because of their previous involvement with other companies or their financial status. Again, this has been an issue in English Premier League football and elsewhere in professional sport.

In summary, limited company status is usually sought by sports organisations where the following apply:

- The organisation owns high-value assets in the form of buildings, facilities or financial reserves. However, capital gains tax may be liable if an organisation owns considerable assets.
- The organisation is engaged in selling significant volumes of goods and services to non-members, such as training courses, accreditation, equipment and other materials.
- The organisation engages in planning major sports events where there is a potential risk of significant financial loss. However, the event itself could be set up as a limited company owned by the organisation.

A board therefore needs members with legal and administrative experience in order to operate effectively and within the law. Nonetheless, sports organisations tend to choose this model of governance because of the layer of protection it offers against financial and legal liability.

CASE EXAMPLE: FROM AMATEUR TO LIMITED COMPANY STATUS – AUSTRALIAN RULES FOOTBALL

The Australian Football League (AFL) oversees 'Australian rules' football that consists of 16 relatively wealthy clubs. The AFL is governed by an independent commission responsible for the sustainable development of the sport. It represents the clubs in governance matters such as brokering broadcasting rights, licensing and collective bargaining on behalf of players. The clubs are incorporated legal entities limited by shares and/or by guarantee, and are subject to Australian corporate regulations. The clubs were historically amateur sports bodies managed by volunteers, but today are businesses managed by professional administrators and governed by a board of directors. Boards feature independent directors recruited for their expertise in corporate governance.

Source: Foreman (n.d.)

Unincorporated association

Smaller sports organisations with limited resources and fewer members tend to be set up as unincorporated associations. An unincorporated association structure is most suitable for the majority of small local clubs without significant buildings, equipment or financial assets. This applies to a multitude of single-sport NPSOs in countries such as England, but less so in countries with many large multi-sport clubs with their own buildings, such as in Germany and the Netherlands. Unincorporated associations provide services primarily for their own members rather than the general public. In terms of advantages to establishing an unincorporated association, there are minimal or no costs incurred and no requirement to register at Companies House as the association does not have a legal status separate from individual members. In practice, individuals can create their own constitution and run their affairs within the rules in the constitution. Also of note for an unincorporated organisation is that a committee is democratically elected by its members to oversee the constitution and make decisions on behalf of members. Some sports organisations of this type employ sub-committees to enact decisions made by the board, usually reached in consultation with members.

Charitable status

Many sports organisations (both incorporated and unincorporated) register as a charity as there are significant tax advantages. More specifically, charitable status guarantees full exemption from tax on profits from membership fees, income from investment or bank interest. Further, gift aid can be claimed on donations from companies or the general public. However, in order to qualify, the organisation must have a charitable purpose as defined by the Charities Act 2006. Charitable purpose in the case of NPSOs relates to 'the advancement of amateur sport', which is defined as 'the advancement of any sports or games which promote health by involving physical or mental skill or exertion and which are undertaken on an amateur basis' (see Sport and Recreation Alliance resources: www. sportandrecreation.org.uk/smart-sport/board-new/structure/charity).

The 'advancement of amateur sport' is difficult to define more precisely but it can include the objectives of 'providing facilities', 'promoting education' or, commonly, 'promoting community participation'. Defining 'amateur' sport has also proven to be problematic. Engaging in activities for 'public benefit' is therefore the core identifiable purpose, but whether this can be quantified is problematic.

If assessing the possibility of becoming a charity, an NPSO will note that negotiating the registration process requires board member expertise as the process can be complex and lengthy. A sports organisation must take the following into account:

- Charity status is permanent and if acquired cannot be reversed.
- If the public benefit is not enacted then the regulatory body (the Charity Commission) can fine the sports organisation.
- Charity law applies, which can cause difficulties where funders require a sports body to prioritise specific objectives by contract and the Charity Commission expects the public benefit to supersede performance-related sport-specific objectives, for example.
- The charitable purpose ('the advancement of amateur sport') can be in conflict with other definitions of sport offered by Sport England or the European Commission (EC), for example.

Subsequently, some NPSOs applying for charitable status have been unsuccessful, which has led to a review by the Charity Commission. Professional sports clubs clearly cannot qualify, and if the 'public benefit' cannot be evidenced by amateur sports organisations it is unlikely that a club can become a charity. Where a club has separate functions, some functions charitable and some not, a club can in theory modify its legal structure to separate its charitable and non-charitable functions, but again this is complex and difficult to implement.

Of note are the different legal arrangements across countries. For example, in the UK the Charities Act 2006 applies to England and Wales, but in Scotland the Charities and Trustees Investment (Scotland) Act 2005 applies. NPSOs must therefore seek legal advice before applying for charitable status. In sum, charitable registration establishes an NPSO as a corporate body and legal entity (as distinct from the voluntary association of members in an unincorporated body). Charities benefit from more favourable tax treatment, including gift aid on donations, discretionary relief on rates and other tax benefits, but not all NPSOs will qualify. The main reason for this is the issue of charitable purpose. Further revisions to the qualifying criteria for charitable status are underway in the UK at the time of writing, which may have an impact of sport governance in and by NPSOs. It is generally understood that the benefits of charitable status are more attractive to the larger and/or wealthier sports organisations. Apart from the options cited (limited company, unincorporated association or charity), NPSOs have, in recent years, investigated other options.

Mutual societies

In recent years, a few sports clubs seeking to become incorporated and obtain the benefits of limited liability have explored the option of registration as a mutual society. The Industrial and Provident Societies Act (1965) was created to regulate organisations such as cooperatives, mutuals, housing associations and working men's clubs. One such example is the Rugby Football Union (RFU) in England (see the case study in Chapter 1). The advantages, particularly for larger membership sports clubs, include:

- The structure, management and governance of the club remains entirely unchanged by converting to mutual status.
- Control of the club remains with the members.
- This is a less expensive and more flexible route than incorporation as a company limited by guarantee (in most instances).
- Oversight and scrutiny from the Financial Services Authority (FSA) is not overly bureaucratic, although approval from the FSA is required for all rule changes and the FSA requires a copy of the annual accounts.
- Mutual status establishes the NPSO as a legal entity in its own right, capable of entering into contracts as a corporate body (members incur limited liability).

Business partnerships

Some sports organisations are registered as business partnerships. This type of organisation enables the members to operate as a legal partnership, creating a defined legal entity. The partnership can register for value added tax (VAT) and operate as a business employing other staff. The organisational type has limited liability partnership status (similar to limited companies).

Social enterprise

An NPSO can set up as a social enterprise if it has a social purpose (such as community cohesion, improved health, youth welfare) and it must operate for *all* of the community and not be operated as a 'private club' for specific members only. Many NPSOs are in effect a 'hub' of community activities. A social enterprise combines components of the public, private and voluntary (non-profit) sectors in its 'business model' in that it is an organisation for all (in parallel to a local authority remit); it operates as a business, generating income (like a private-sector body, although profits go back into the organisation and not to shareholders); and it is governed by a voluntary board (non-profit status). Social enterprises can legally procure outside investment, donations or grants, and use that funding to create new services, as long as this action meets a social need. A social enterprise aims to be self-funding within three to five years (but initially relies in part on government monies). It is intended to be sustainable (with longer-term goals) rather than operating as an NPSO that in many cases rely on short-term funding. Also, this type of organisation includes a wide range of stakeholders and sport-related services are delivered by the community itself. In summary, a social enterprise is an organisation established to meet social objectives within the parameters of a sustainable 'business model'.

Additionally, social enterprises can take different legal forms that can be aligned with the general principle of distributing (or re-distributing) any profit generated from business activities back into the enterprise in order to build the capacity of the organisation and scale the operation up. Therefore, social enterprises can be businesses owned and operated by charities in order to fund their operations. The legal form (status) and structure underpinning the sports organisation depends on the objectives (as set out in the constitution). As noted by the SRA, social enterprises have the legal options below; each has advantages and disadvantages depending on the purpose and resources of the NPSO:

- Sole trader. Liability and risk need to be assessed to avoid litigation.
- Limited company, by shares or guarantee.
- Community Investment Company (CIC). This is a limited company (usually by guarantee) that has special clauses in its constitution which ensure that the assets of the business will not be used to make a profit for the owners. A CIC is often used to create a 'trading arm' for an NPSO. A CIC has a constitution with strict rules on how investment and assets are to be managed.
- Cooperative. This is a group of equal members from a community seeking a common objective.

All of these legal structures are suitable for social enterprises. The choice of form/ structure depends on: the type of operations to be undertaken; how decisions are to be made; and how the organisation will be funded.

INDEPENDENT STUDY: SOCIAL ENTERPRISE AND SPORT

View the document at http://se-networks.net/downloads/Introduction%20 to%20Social%20Enterprise%20&%20Sport.pdf and identify three sport organisations that are operated as social enterprises. Assess the similarities and differences between them. Also view the following article for other examples: www.theguardian.com/social-enterprise-network/2013/jan/04/best-bits-social-enterprise-sport

Community Amateur Sports Club

For many NPSOs, especially smaller clubs, both limited company and charity status are not ideal. The legal aspects of setting up as a mutual society or business partnership can be prohibitive or unsuitable too. However, one option to emerge recently is registration with the Community Amateur Sports Club (CASC) scheme. It should be noted that CASC clubs are prohibited from applying for parallel charitable status. Advantages for smaller sports organisations include:

- CASCs can apply to be registered with the Inland Revenue to claim tax relief.
- Any club which registers is able to raise income exempt from tax up to a fixed amount per annum (specific financial allowances may change and this is not included in this text).
- Corporation tax on trading income does not apply up to a fixed amount per annum.
- Profits from rental income are exempt from tax up to a fixed amount per annum.
- Disposals of assets is exempt from capital gains tax.
- Gift aid on individual donations is allowable.
- Inheritance tax relief on gifts is allowable.

Sport England provide details of financial advantages of CASC and other details of the scheme (http://archive.sportengland.org/support_advice/cascs.aspx).

However, for a club to become registered as a CASC, it must be able to demonstrate that it is open to the whole community without discrimination, is organised on an amateur basis and provides facilities for, and promotes participation in, an eligible sport.

The European Union context

For NPSOs based within the boundaries of the European Union (EU), the last two decades have witnessed an increase in the regulation of sport. However, the influence of the EU has been felt by international-level governing bodies of sport too. In fact, decisions made at the supranational level have had an impact on the structures and governance of sport at national, regional and local levels. Although it is not necessary for NPSO boards to have a high level of expertise in EU law as it relates to sport, and independent legal advice can be sought where changes at the level of the EU impact on NPSOs, it is nonetheless important for board members to be aware of the key issues and challenges relating to legislation and regulation, in order to pre-empt potential litigation, for example. In turn, a basic level of competence in this regard will build the capacity of an NPSO and add organisational resilience given the potential for further intervention from EU institutions in the next decade.

This section explores the two key concerns of the EU in sport governance: the regulatory interest as a result of its commitment to protect the legal foundations of the single market (sport as an economic activity); and the political aspirations for sport, particularly in the field of the 'people's Europe' project (sport as a socio-cultural phenomenon). In this context, a discrete area of sports law has emerged (Parrish, 2003a) that has its roots in the post-*Bosman* political debate about the future of EU involvement in sport. The implications for governance of and by NPSOs are subsequently identified.

Rationale for EU intervention

Sport governance has sometimes come into direct conflict with the fundamental principles of the single European market (formerly known as the 'common market') and as a result a level of EU intervention has emerged. These four principles are free movement of people, goods, services and capital (sometimes known as the 'four freedoms' or four 'pillars' on which the EU was founded). The broad plan of the founding member states in establishing the EU was to both extend economic activity between member states and form a political union. The European Council (EC) as one component of the EU provided political guidance through the (non-binding) Amsterdam and Nice declarations on sport within broader treaties (European Council, 1997, 2000). However, two contrasting views of how sport should be governed emerged from these declarations: sport as an economic activity and therefore requiring regulation, and sport as a socio-cultural phenomenon, requiring legal protection (Parrish, 2003a, 2003b). The significance of these definitions for sport governance is discussed here.

The autonomy of sport

Governing bodies for sport were originally founded on the 'sacred principle' that there should be a separation of sport and state, as it was claimed that political matters would violate sport's integrity (Chappelet, 2010). However, the momentum of state intervention has expanded since the 1980s. As a result, there are three basic positions held on the autonomy of sport by groups (or coalitions) within the EU. First, the 'minimalists' do not perceive a greater role for the EU in sport than already exists. It is argued that treaty incorporation for sport would contradict the EU's claims of *subsidiarity* (this is where there is a preference to devolve powers to the most local level rather than powers being held centrally). It is also argued that sufficient flexibility already exists within the EU's legal framework for the EU to recognise the *specificity* of sport (that which is unique to sport). The IOC, for example, have argued that the governance of sport does not fall within the EU's competence (IOC, 2007: 2). This position has support within the EU from the European Council (EC), for example, who recognise the independence and autonomy of sports organisations and their right to govern themselves through appropriate associative structures.

Second, and at the opposite end of the spectrum, are the 'maximalists' who favour the development of a common sports policy through the establishment of a legal base for sport. It is argued here that an *article* for sport would stabilise the legal environment in which sport operates and provide a legal base for the development of sports funding programmes. In the middle of these two perspectives are the 'moderates' who do not support the development of a common sports policy but do want to see the legal environment clarified. This can be done via the adoption of a treaty protocol on sport which would place a legal obligation on the EU to recognise the specificity of sport within its legal framework (Garcia, 2011b; Parrish, 2003a, 2003b, 2003c).

As an outcome of there being two groups, *separate territories* exist for dealing with legal disputes involving sport: a 'territory' for sporting autonomy and a 'territory' for legal intervention. In practice, the EU facilitates an approach to sports governance and policy that allows the EU's regulatory and political interests in sport to co-exist. Future debates between sport and the EU will therefore be centred on the 'grey area' between the two 'territories'. By developing a particular legal approach to sport which treats sport differently to other sectors, the EU has in effect established a discrete body of sports law (Parrish, 2003a).

Given that the governance of sport in Europe is transforming from a hierarchical (or pyramidal and vertical) structure to more horizontal configuration of stakeholder networks, the European Commission that oversees sport (as one component of the EU) has opted for a supervisory role, offering governing bodies a degree of 'supervised autonomy' (see Chapter 2 for a theoretical analysis of sport governance). In this scenario, the specific role of sports federations is recognised (specificity) in exchange for organisations extending stakeholder representation within governing structures in line with the principle of subsidiarity.

Sport as economic activity

Sport started to become a significant economic activity in the 1990s (García, 2007b: 209) and as a result drew the attention of EU institutions. Dilemmas emerged surrounding the interaction between economic and non-economic sporting interests. For example, single ownership or financial control of more than one sports club entering the same competition in the same sport was viewed as potentially jeopardising fair competition; the significance of the sale of television broadcasting rights as a major source of income for certain sports and elite clubs; and rules legitimate in sporting competition but which may not be legitimate in other sectors of employment, such as limitations on the number of participants, the separation of men's and women's sporting competitions and methods of ensuring an uncertainty of outcome to maintain competitive balance.

However, it was in respect of the football transfer system impacting on freedom of movement that fully drew the EU into the regulation of sport – specifically, the *Bosman* ruling. Although the EU does not have a direct *competence* in sport, its institutions have been obliged to intervene mainly as a result of their duties to enforce the treaty's free movement and competition policy provisions. As a consequence, EU institutions have been active in the field of sport in recent years and, in particular, the European Commission has been one of the most active institutions in the area as a result of debates about whether different provisions of the EC Treaty apply to sport (García 2007a, 2007b, 2009a, 2009b, 2011b; Parrish, 2001, 2003a, 2003b, 2003c; Parrish and Miettinen, 2008).

CASE EXAMPLE: THE *BOSMAN* RULING

The *Bosman* ruling of the European Court of Justice (ECJ) in 1995 (Parrish and McArdle, 2004) increased the legitimacy of EU legal intervention in sport. In brief, the former footballer Jean-Marc Bosman challenged UEFA's use of nationality restrictions as these 'restrictions' were opposed to the EC Treaty on 'freedom of movement' and 'freedom of association'. The successful challenge resulted in 'nationality quotas' per club being ruled unlawful; it allowed players in the EU to move to another club at the end of their contract without the payment of a transfer fee; and it was the catalyst for a shift in control from clubs to players ('player power'). The European Commission considered the consequences of the ECJ ruling and also how to apply EU law to sport. A comprehensive approach to sport was initiated which led to the *European Model of Sport* 1998, the *White Paper on Sport* 2007, the granting of an express role for sport in the Lisbon Treaty 2009 and the *Communication on the European Dimension in Sport* in 2011 (see sections to follow).

Sport as a socio-cultural phenomenon

Since the 1984 Fontainebleau Summit, the EU has attempted to extend European integration beyond the economic field in order to create a 'people's Europe'. The European Parliament (1989) demonstrated a desire to balance the economic regulation of sport with the promotion of sport's socio-cultural and integrationist qualities. In effect, the EU used sport as a vehicle to implement a range of social, cultural and educational policy objectives. More specifically, the European Commission made claims that sports federations have a central role in ensuring mutuality between the various levels of sporting practice, from recreational to elite sport, where there could be equal access for men and women (Collins, 2008), alongside youth training, health protection and measures to combat doping, acts of violence and racist or xenophobic occurrences.

However, the growing commercialisation of sport combined with legal regulation could undermine these political objectives. Given that EU policy is subject to competing policy tensions between economic and political goals (where sport is a socio-cultural phenomenon), this can impact on NGBs, associations and clubs. For example, the commercialisation of sport has attracted litigation from stakeholders who used the treaty's free movement and competition provisions to challenge the regulatory choices made by the governing bodies.

The European model of sport

The European Commission first introduced the concept of a European model of sport (EMS) with its own characteristics in response to the Amsterdam Treaty (1997). The EMS preceded the *Helsinki Report on Sport* (EC, 1999) that sought to preserve sports structures and the social functions of sport. The Helsinki Report called upon sports organisations to more clearly define their 'missions and statutes' in order to demonstrate a rationale for special status. More specifically, the model explained:

- the 'organisation of sport in Europe';
- the 'features of sport in Europe'; and
- the 'importance' and the 'problems' of sport in Europe.

In respect of 'problems' with the EMS, a single comprehensive model is not advocated by the European Commission because of the great diversity of structures inherent in sport in Europe, and the fact that many of the features of the model are 'global' in reach rather than exclusively European (European Commission, 2007: 41). The model was therefore welcomed by powerful international sports organisations such as the IOC, FIFA and UEFA as pyramidal structures. Its focus on vertical solidarity was not opposed and the capacity of sports federations to justify their own policies and to avoid regulatory interventions by public authorities (e.g. national governments, EU institutions) or legitimacy challenges by stakeholders (e.g. clubs, athletes) remained unchallenged.

As Parrish and Miettinen (2008: 41–45) explain, the governing bodies argued for a 'sporting exception' to the application of EU law. European football's governing body, UEFA, is a clear supporter of the European model of sport, where it is argued that football is structured as a pyramid and a strong base is the only way to ensure a strong apex. Moreover, UEFA argue that elite, professional, semi-professional and amateur football are inextricably linked together through the pyramid and this 'keeps the football family together' (UEFA, 2005: 11, cited in García, 2007a). In terms of governance this means that UEFA locates itself in a central position of power. This view of the European model of sport is expressed in the *Independent European Sport Review* (Arnaut, 2006).

Subsequent to the establishment of the EMS, the provisions on sport in the EU Reform Treaty (commonly known as the Lisbon Treaty) in 2009 are worth noting. The Lisbon Treaty (Article 165 on the Functioning of the European Union) grants the EU an express role in the field of sport. It was agreed in the treaty that the EU will contribute to the promotion of European sporting issues, while taking account of its specific nature, its structures based on voluntary activity and its social and educational function. Further, developing the European dimension in sport by promoting fairness in sporting competitions and cooperation between bodies responsible for sports is highlighted.

However, following the Lisbon Treaty, the member states only granted the EU a 'supporting competence', the weakest type of the three principal types of EU competence. As a result, in 2011 the *Communication on the European Dimension in Sport* indicated that the European Commission's main policy tool in sport is 'structured dialogue' with leading international and European sport organisations and other sport stakeholders; and political dialogue with member states and other concerned parties. Thus, the EMS is not only difficult to define precisely (across many sports at many levels and many nation states), but difficult to operationalise.

Nonetheless, the significance of the model is that it underpins all debates concerning EU sport policy and governance. Within the EMS is a tension between sport as an economic activity and sport as a socio-cultural phenomenon and political instrument for integration. As noted, competing coalitions either seek minimal involvement of the EU in sport or seek to regulate practices. Although in practice sports bodies retain a high level of autonomy (at the international level), the legitimacy of the federations retaining 'special status' outside of the reach of the EU's legal and regulatory framework has been seriously challenged (notably that of FIFA) more recently (see the case example in this chapter).

Also of note is the ECJ's *Meca-Medina ruling* (Infantino, 2006) that signalled a new, 'market-friendly' approach to sports regulation. This decision means that a 'case by case' approach must be taken in the application of the EU's competition policy to sport. Governing bodies for sport favour legal protection from the application of competition law, where sport's 'specific characteristics' are recognised. However, the precise definition of what constitutes 'sporting rules' and 'commercial rules' is problematic. Nevertheless, the future of EU sports law will be concerned with exactly this definitional issue (Parrish and Miettinen, 2008).

In sum, the EMS remains a contested concept that can nonetheless have an impact on sport governance at a national level. In many ways, supranational (EU in this case) legal and regulatory issues and challenges mirror those within UK sport governance, namely: matters of definition and purpose; decision-making; collaboration across many organisations; implementation of policy; and compliance with rules and guidelines.

The White Paper on Sport

Following a period of intense debate and political activity around sport among the EU institutions as noted, particularly in football, the *White Paper on Sport* is the first comprehensive document on sport governance, although, critically, it is not legally binding (European Commission, 2007). The *White Paper*:

- analyses the societal, economic and organisational aspects of sport in Europe, at both amateur and professional levels;
- sets out the Commission's philosophy regarding sport's place in society;
- proposes a detailed action plan to promote the European aspects of sport; and
- summarises EU jurisprudence in this field.

The objectives of the *White Paper* are to:

- provide a strategic orientation on the role of sport in the EU;
- encourage debate on specific problems;
- enhance the visibility of sport in EU policymaking;
- raise awareness of the needs and specificities of the sector; and
- identify the appropriate level of further action at EU level.

In terms of implementation, the *White Paper* seeks to strengthen self-regulation where it promotes 'good governance'. This includes establishing basic rules on financial management and transparency, and a legal position on discrimination and the safeguarding of children, for example. Any restrictions of competition or 'free movement' must be compatible with the relevant EU provisions.

In effect, the *White Paper* is a compromise between the two competing coalitions of interests ('minimalists' and 'maximalists') that shape EU sports law. The territory of sporting autonomy (sport as a socio-cultural phenomenon to be utilised in meeting political objectives) and the territory of legal intervention (sport as an economic activity) are both acknowledged. As sports organisations become 'commercial' and operated within a business model underpinned by corporate governance practices, a degree of regulation by national and supra-national state bodies has emerged. The 'separate territories' approach is therefore legally fragile, but it offers a short-term settlement. A longer-term strategic view of EU sports law that includes clear guidelines on exemptions is the key challenge moving forward. In practice, the ECJ is likely to remain a venue for litigation, especially where a sport experiences a change in economic status, given increasing professionalisation and commercialisation.

The *White Paper* in effect implies that it is 'unrealistic' to define a single model of sport for Europe. However, European sports federations (e.g. those for football, basketball, handball, volleyball) have requested that the European Commission recognise the EMS by publishing clear guidelines on the application of EU law to sport, in order to avoid the possible consequences of ECJ rulings. In sum, the *White Paper on Sport* made a significant contribution to the debate on European sports regulation. The *White Paper* provides a foundation on which governing bodies across many sports (at both amateur and professional level) can be clear on their position in relation to EU law (at least in the short term).

CASE EXAMPLE: BROADCASTING AND SPORT GOVERNANCE

Gardiner (2009) discusses the 'rights to view' issue in the context of competition to broadcast sports events and the Broadcasting Act (1998) that protected certain events of 'national significance' or interest (including the Olympic Games, FIFA World Cup, FA Cup Final, Grand National, the Derby and

Wimbledon tennis). However, certain events were 'lost' including Test cricket and some 'Six Nations' rugby union. With the growth of subscription TV since the 1990s, sport has been a driving force behind the emergence of new media and interactive television services. TV rights are now a primary source of income for many sports in Europe, and their selling arrangements give rise to a number of issues, especially in the field of competition law. In brief, while 'joint selling' may in principle be problematic in competition law, the *White Paper* recognises its role in facilitating solidarity between amateur and professional sports as well as clubs of different sizes operating in the same league. This is an example of the 'special status' or specificity that can be afforded to sports organisations in EU law. In effect, the European Commission steers a course between competing visions of the regulation of sport. It is a policy that ostensibly restricts trade but if a legitimate sporting objective is sought, then regulation is minimal.

Models of sport regulation: where next?

Foster analysed three alternative 'models' of sport regulation by the EU (Foster, 2000: 43). First, the enforcement of private rights through the ECJ as seen in the *Bosman case*. Second, the regulation of sport by the European Commission through competition policy, which allows for exemptions to be granted in particular cases. A level of 'supervised autonomy' is implied. Third, a more political 'model' that accepts sport's self-regulation without the intervention of EU law (Foster, 2000: 60). Looking to the next decade, three alternative visions of sport governance emerge, each resulting in different roles for EU institutions.

- First, a regulatory approach in which EU institutions would be an essential part of sport governance. This approach would see an active role for the EU institutions in sport governance and implies that governing bodies' autonomy could be reduced. Governing bodies could in effect be responsible for implementation and not a strategic role or remit.
- Second, a level of 'supervised autonomy', where governing bodies for sport recognise the fundamental principles of EU law, with EU institutions enacting a supervisory role to ensure sport organisations behave within the parameters of EU law. In this 'vision', EU institutions do not have a pro-active role in directly regulating sport governance. Instead, self-regulation is the norm. It can be anticipated that sport governing bodies would seek to reduce supervision to a minimum by arguing that the specificities of the sport sector deserve a bespoke application of EU law.
- The third model would recognise the total autonomy of sport and sport would be granted an exemption from the application of EU law. In this approach, EU institutions would clearly have no regulatory role in sport governance. On

the contrary, EU institutions would endorse, support and facilitate sports governing bodies' initiatives (e.g. giving them political recognition or creating funding initiatives). EU institutions would work in partnership with sports bodies. Arguably, for many governing bodies this would be an ideal outcome where there is exemption from EU law, while retaining the option to procure funding through EU sports programmes. (However, the EU can only allocate funds to sport-related programmes if it has the legal competence to do so. The creation of such a competence might risk an expansion of regulatory functions for the EU in the area of sport.) Therefore, the 'supervised autonomy' model strikes a balance that many governing bodies and EU institutions can tolerate.

As noted, sport governance in the EU is composed of two coalitions. The *single market* coalition has a regulatory policy interest in sport, where stakeholders seek to ensure the legal foundations of the single market are protected. From this perspective, sport is recognised as a significant economic activity and sports rules can be aligned with EU law. The *socio-cultural* coalition pursues more political objectives for sport. In particular, the stakeholders within it want the specific characteristics of sport to be recognised in the application of EU law. As such, sport is seen less as an economic activity and more as a social and cultural pursuit. For example, amateur sport and 'sport for all' initiatives are viewed as offering fundamental social, educational and cultural values. Sport is seen as an instrument for integration, involvement in social life, tolerance, acceptance of differences and playing by the rules or 'fair play'. Further, the practice of physical and sporting activities and engagement in voluntary services are viewed as providing favourable conditions for the development of individual talent, rehabilitation and solidarity.

Arbitration

Where legal disputes emerge between NPSOs and athletes, for example, arbitration may be necessary. Two case examples follow.

CASE EXAMPLE: INTERNATIONAL LEGAL DISPUTES AND THE COURT OF ARBITRATION FOR SPORT

The Court of Arbitration for Sport (CAS) is a quasi-judicial body founded to settle disputes.

These disputes may be of a disciplinary nature (e.g. a case of doping) or commercial in nature (e.g. a sponsorship contract). CAS has a level of autonomy from governments and, critically, all the Olympic international federations recognise the jurisdiction of CAS in most cases. In doping cases, CAS is recognised as the legitimate body for resolving disputes, given its alignment with the World Anti-Doping Code. An International Council of Arbitration for Sport (ICAS) has also been founded so that there is limited influence over CAS from the IOC in financing and operational matters. In practice, many recent cases dealt with by CAS centre on transfer disputes in professional (association) football or soccer, or doping cases involving athletes across a range of sports.

Recommended reading: Reilly (2012).

CASE EXAMPLE: NATIONAL LEGAL DISPUTES AND SPORT RESOLUTIONS

Sport Resolutions provides independent dispute resolution for NGBs in the UK. The organisation is responsible for setting up panels of experts to offer arbitration, mediation and tribunal and administration services. In 2009, Sport Resolutions was responsible for organising panels to deal with legal issues relating to disciplinary matters, selection appeals, commercial issues and eligibility. Sport Resolutions is also responsible for operating the National Anti-Doping Panel, an independent body that determines anti-doping disputes in sport in the UK. The aim of Sport Resolutions is to make available to all sports in the UK independent, expert, timely and cost-effective resolution of all disputes and to provide information, education and training to prevent disputes arising.

Source: Sport Resolutions: www.sportresolutions.co.uk

Legal and regulatory challenges for sports organisations: summary

From this overview of sport governance at the level of the EU, a number of legal and regulatory challenges facing NPSOs can be identified, including:

- the impact on UK-based NPSOs of further ECJ interventions and changes in EU sports law and EC policy and guidance;
- how the *evolving* 'European model of sport' impacts on NPSOs in the UK (e.g. NGBs, clubs);
- where exactly the autonomy of sport as a 'separate' policy domain and 'special case' applies (exempt from aspects of EU sports law);
- whether most legal and regulatory challenges can be addressed through *self-regulation*, provided that EU law is respected;
- the implications of the *White Paper* where the emergence of new stakeholders (participants outside the organised disciplines, professional sports clubs, etc.) pose a challenge to the existing structures of sport governance;
- reform of or modifications to models of organised sport (hierarchical/vertical or network/horizontal) within EU law and good governance principles;
- the role of sport federations in sport governance;

- how NPSOs can *adjust to globalisation*. It can be argued that at the international level, given minimal regulation, powerful corporate sports organisations will increase their impact on government and governing bodies; and
- how NPSOs can initiate and build *good governance* within legal and regulatory frameworks (see Chapter 7).

INDEPENDENT LEARNING TASK

This chapter ends with a brief overview of an issue that NPSOs will have to fully address in the next decade, namely: match-fixing. Read the case example and undertake independent learning in order to identify and analyse the issue and assess to what extent, and how specifically, match-fixing may impact on NPSO governance. Also consider the likely effectiveness of national and supranational (EU) legislation and the wider creation of a regulatory environment in which sports organisations can address this issue. Finally, consider whether NPSOs are equipped to deal with this issue.

CASE EXAMPLE: THE REGULATION OF MATCH-FIXING

It is argued by many NPSOs that, in order to help combat match-fixing that is infiltrating some sports, a strong regulatory framework needs to be adopted by both sports organisations and legislative authorities. There is a general consensus that prevention and disciplinary procedures put in place by NPSOs must be supported within a coherent legislative framework. Recourse to criminal legislation may also be necessary, requiring national and supranational government agencies to enable investigatory powers and sanctions where appropriate. Betting laws in various jurisdictions must be taken into account as gambling has significantly evolved in nature in the last decade, which sports bodies recognise as contributing to match-fixing.

Summary

In many respects, the debates circulating in EU institutions and international sports organisations mirror the issues facing NPSOs operating at the national and local levels. NPSOs face many governance challenges in a context where the legal and regulatory environment is both complex and subject to change. UK–based NPSOs need to become familiar with aspects of both UK and EU law in order to modify policies, procedures and practices where required or appropriate. NPSOs seek to regulate behaviour and are subject to regulation and as a consequence face significant tests moving forward.

LEARNING ACTIVITIES

- To what extent should sport be regulated? Discuss.
- Why did EU institutions become involved in sport governance?
- How can EU law impact on the governance of UK sport? Provide examples.
- How did the outcome of the *Bosman case* affect sport governance?
- Identify the advantages and disadvantages of setting up a sports organisation as a limited company, unincorporated association or a charity.
- Undertake research to find out why some NPSOs have failed in their bids to acquire charitable status.
- What is negligence and how can NPSOs avoid it?
- How is the board of an NPSO subject to legal liability? Provide examples.
- How can a sports board address risk? Provide examples.
- Explain the 'European model of sport'.
- What is the significance of the *White Paper for Sport*?
- Identify and assess the level of regulation needed where sport is defined as economic activity or as a socio-cultural phenomenon.
- Explain the concepts 'specificity' and 'subsidiarity'.

Bibliography

Arnaut, J.L. (2006) *Independent European Sport Review.* www.independentfootballreview. com/doc/A3619.pdf

Barani, L. (2005) The role of the European Court of Justice as a political actor in the integration process: the case of sport regulation after the Bosman ruling. *Journal of Contemporary European Research,* 1, 1: 42–58.

Caiger, A. and Gardiner, S., eds (2000) *Professional Sport in the European Union: Regulation and Reregulation,* The Hague: TMC Asser Press.

Chaker, A.N. (1999) *Study on National Sports Legislation in Europe.* Strasbourg: Council of Europe Publishing.

Chappelet, J.L. (2010) *Autonomy of Sport in Europe.* Strasbourg: Council of Europe.

Collins, M. (2008) Public policies on sports development: can mass and elite sports hold together? In: Girginov, V., ed., *Management of Sports Development.* Oxford: Butterworth-Heinemann, pp. 59–87.

Cygan, A. (2007) Are all sports special? Legal issues in the regulation of formula one motor racing. *European Business Law Review,* 18, 6: 1327–1351.

Egger, A. and Stix-Hackl, C. (2002) Sports and competition law: a never-ending story? *European Competition Law Review,* 23(2), 81–91.

European Commission (1999) *The Helsinki Report on Sport: Report from the European Commission to the European Council with a View to Safeguarding Current Sports Structures and Maintaining the Social Function of Sport Within the Community Framework.* COM 644 final, 10 December.

European Commission (2007). *The EU and Sport: Background and Context, Accompanying Document to the White Paper on Sport.* SEC(2007) 935 final.

European Council (1997) *Declaration No. 29, on Sport, Attached to the Treaty of Amsterdam amending the Treaty on European Union, the Treaties Establishing the European Communities and Certain Related Acts*. EC: Nice.

European Council (2000). *Declaration on the Specific Characteristics of Sport and Its Social Function in Europe, of Which Account Should Be Taken in Implementing Common Policies*, Presidency Conclusions. EC: Nice.

European Parliament (1989) *Resolution of the European Parliament on Sport in the European Community and a People's Europe*, Rapporteur: Jessica Larive. OJ C 69/1989, 20 March, p. 234.

Ferkins, L., Shilbury, D. and McDonald, G. (2005) The role of the board in building strategic capability: towards an integrated model of sport governance research. *Sport Management Review*, 8: 195–225.

Forman, J.S. (n.d.) *Corporate Governance Issues in a Professional Sport*. Victoria, Australia: University of Technology.

Foster, K. (2000). Can sport be regulated by Europe? An analysis of alternative models. In: Caiger, A. and Gardiner, S., eds, *Professional Sport in the European Union: Regulation and Reregulation*. The Hague: TMC Asser Press, pp. 43–64.

García, B. (2007a) UEFA and the European Union: from confrontation to cooperation. *Journal of Contemporary European Research*, 3, 3: 202–223.

García, B. (2007b) From regulation to governance and representation: agenda-setting and the EU's involvement in sport. *Entertainment and Sports Law Journal*, 5(1).

García, B. (2009a) Sport governance after the White Paper: the demise of the European model? *International Journal of Sport Policy and Politics*, 1,3: 267–284.

García, B. (2009b) The new governance of sport: what role for the EU? In: Parrish, R., Gardiner, S. and Siekmann, R., eds, *EU, Sport, Law and Policy: Regulation, Re-regulation and Representation*. The Hague: TMC Asser Press, pp. 115–136.

García, B. (2011a) The 2001 informal agreement on the international transfer system. *European Sports Law and Policy Bulletin*, 2: 17–29.

García, B. (2011b) The EU and sport governance: between economic and social values. In: Groeneveld, M., Houlihan, B. and Ohl, F., eds, *Social Capital and Sport Governance in Europe*. London: Routledge, pp. 21–40.

Gardiner, S. (2009) Sport and the law. In: Bill, K., ed., *Sport Management*. Exeter: Learning Matters, chapter 14.

Gardiner, S., James, M., O'Leary, J., Welch, R., Blackshaw, I., Boyes, S. and Caiger, A. (2006) *Sports Law*, 3rd edition. London: Cavendish Publishing.

Governance hub (n.d.) *Governance and Organisational Structures*. London: Governance hub/NCVO.

Halgreen, L. (2004) *European Sports Law: A Comparative Analysis of the European and American Models of Sport*. Copenhagen: Forlage Thomson.

Henry, I.P. (2004) Sports structures in the United Kingdom. In: Tokarski, W., Steinbach, D., Petry, K. and Jesse, B., eds, *Two Players One Goal? Sport in the European Union*. Aachen: Meyer and Meyer, pp. 263–280.

Herman, M.L., Head, G.L., Jackson, P.M. and Fogarty, T.E. (2003) *Managing Risk in Nonprofit Organizations: A Comprehensive Guide*. London: Wiley.

Hill, J. (2009). The European Commission's White Paper on Sport: a step backwards for specificity? *International Journal of Sport Policy and Politics*, 1, 3: 253–266.

Hillsborough Independent Panel (1990) *Final Report of Inquiry by Lord Justice Taylor into the Hillsborough Stadium Disaster*. London: Home Office.

Holt, M. (2007) The ownership and control of elite club competition in European football. *Soccer & Society*, 8, 1: 50–67.

Hoye, R. and Cuskelly, G. (2007). *Sport Governance*. Oxford: Elsevier Butterworth-Heinemann.

Infantino, G. (2006). *Meca-Medina: A Step Backwards for the European Sports Model and the Specificity of Sport?* UEFA. www.uefa.com/MultimediaFiles/Download/uefa/KeyTopics/480391_DOWNLOAD.pdf

International Olympic Committee (2007) *The White Paper on Sport, Joint Statement with International Sports Federations*. IOC 10268/2007/mgy, 3 April.

International Olympic Committee (2008) *Basic Universal Principles of Good Governance of the Olympic and Sports Movement*. Lausanne: IOC. www.olympic.org/Documents/Conferences_Forums_and_Events/2008_seminar_autonomy/Basic_Universal_Principles_of_Good_Governance.pdf

Jarvie, G. (2006) Sport, law and governance. In: Jarvie, G., *Sport, Culture and Society: An Introduction*. London: Routledge.

Ko, L.M., Henry, I. and Tai, W. (2013) European models of sport: governance and organisational change in the EU. In: Henry, I. and Ko, L.M., ed., *Handbook of Sport Policy*. London: Routledge, pp. 117–138.

Lewis, A. and Taylor, J. (2008) *Sport: Law and Practice*. Haywards Heath: Tottel.

Monks, R. and Minow, N. (2011) *Corporate Governance*. Chichester: Wiley & Sons.

Parrish, R. (2001) Sports regulation in the European Union: a new approach? *Managing Leisure*, 6, 187–200.

Parrish, R. (2003a) *Sports Law and Policy in the European Union*. Manchester: Manchester University Press.

Parrish, R. (2003b) The birth of European Union sports law. *Entertainment Law*, 2, 2: 20–39.

Parrish, R. (2003c) The politics of sports regulation in the EU. *Journal of European Public Policy*, 10, 2: 246–262.

Parrish, R. and McArdle, D. (2004) Beyond Bosman: The European Union's influence upon professional athletes' freedom of movement. *Sport in Society*, 7, 3: 403–418.

Parrish, R. and Miettinen, S. (2008) *The Sporting Exception in European Union Law*. The Hague: TMC Asser Press.

Ravjani, A. (2009). The Court of Arbitration for Sport: a subtle form of international delegation. *Journal of International Media & Entertainment Law*, 2, 2: 267.

Reilly, L. (2012) Introduction to the Court of Arbitration for Sport (CAS) and the role of national courts in international sports disputes. *Journal of Dispute Resolution*, 1: 63–80.

Rogulski, A. and Miettinen, S. (2009) The EU and sport: the implementation of the White Paper on Sport and future prospects. *International Journal of Sport Policy and Politics*, 1, 3: 245–251.

Siekmann, R., *et al.* (2010) *The Lisbon Treaty and EU Sports Policy*. Report for the European Parliament (IP/B/CULT/IC/2010-028). www.europarl.europa.eu/activities/committees/studies/download.do?language=en&file=32471

Sport and Recreation Alliance (UK) (2011) *Voluntary Code of Good Governance for the Sport and Recreation Sector*. London: SRA.

SPARC (Sport and Recreation New Zealand) (2004) *Nine Steps to Effective Governance: Building High Performing Organisations*. Wellington, NZ: SPARC.

UK Sport (2004) *Best Practice Principles of Good Governance in Sport*. London: UK Sport.

Weatherill, S. (2009) The White Paper on sport as an exercise of 'better regulation'. In: Parrish, R., Gardiner, S. and Siekmann, R., eds, *EU, Sport, Law and Policy: Regulation, Re-regulation and Representation*. The Hague: TMC Asser Press, pp. 101–114.

Weatherill, S. (2011) *EU sports law: the effect of the Lisbon Treaty*. Oxford Legal Studies Research Paper No. 3/2011.

Wilkinson, P. (2010) *The 2010 UK Bribery Act: Adequate Procedures*. London: Transparency International.

5

STAKEHOLDING IN SPORT GOVERNANCE

LEARNING OBJECTIVES

At the completion of this chapter, students should be able to:

- define stakeholding in sport governance;
- assess the pressures to democratise sports organisations and the changing expectations of stakeholders;
- analyse how sports organisations are implementing measures to enhance stakeholding and how stakeholding can be extended for the benefit of sports organisations;
- understand the concept and practice of social responsibility in the sport sector.

Introduction

The governance of sport has evolved from a hierarchical or 'top-down' model of governance to a complex web of interrelationships between stakeholders (see Chapter 2). This shift has occurred as the growth of professional and commercial sport has emerged without a parallel shift in modes of governance to accommodate these changes (Katwala, 2000). Although non-profit sport organisations (NPSOs) are not public bodies, the principle of public participation and engagement established (to some extent) in the public sector can be applied to NPSOs, where the 'public' refers to stakeholders who have an interest (a 'stake') in the governance of the organisation. It has been argued that sport organisations need to develop their expertise in order to understand the needs of an increasing range of stakeholders and their expectations (Ferkins *et al.*, 2005). As a result, the recognition and management of stakeholder interests is considered a key element of good governance and best practice in contemporary sport governance.

In the corporate sector, 'stakeholders' are defined differently to the non-profit sport sector. Typical corporate stakeholders will be defined (sometimes by law) as creditors, employees and suppliers (OECD, 2004: 46). A broader definition of corporate sector stakeholders is provided by the *Global Reporting Initiative* (2011), who also include communities, civil society and shareholders/providers of capital as stakeholders. These stakeholders are considered to be worthy of greater involvement given changes in the corporate sector in the last decade, even if they are not fully recognised in the narrower definition or included in the governance of an organisation in practice. By contrast, in the non-profit sport sector, a wider range of organisations/groups or interests are recognised as stakeholders in many, but not all, cases in practice. 'Stakeholder' here can be defined as an individual or group or an organisation that has a direct or indirect interest or 'stake' in the governance of an NPSO and will usually be affected by the actions of the NPSO in question. For example, at the international level, UEFA specifically name leagues, clubs, players and supporters as stakeholders in their statutes (see Hindley, 2004, 2008). In some other NPSOs, however, there is no consensus as to the definition of a 'stakeholder' nor a named list of who is considered to be a stakeholder. Further, some organisations cite stakeholders as 'service providers' rather than organisations who are integral to governance. Moreover, in some countries a legal status is awarded to specific stakeholders in sport governance, such as referees/umpires, but not in other countries (such as the UK).

Stakeholders in the UK non-profit sport sector are those individuals or groups of people, of varying influence and involvement, who can affect or be affected by the actions, decisions and policies of an organisation. These stakeholders include service providers, funders and participants, for example, in addition to those responsible for decision-making. More specifically, NPSOs stakeholders can include:

- the participants: players, athletes, officials, members;
- leagues, clubs, associations (local, county, regional);
- governing bodies at other levels (international, national, regional, local);
- sponsors, business partners, other funders;
- central government departments and agencies;
- local government departments;
- supporters and fans (spectators); and
- the general public.

The following sections of this chapter focus on extending stakeholder participation, involving and including stakeholders, and addressing rising stakeholder expectations, so that NPSOs can evaluate stakeholder participation, build social responsibility and realise the benefits of extending stakeholder participation that may in turn strengthen the case for local autonomy. Good governance as related to stakeholding may therefore include a particular focus given to specific stakeholders in policy, strategy and resource allocation. Subsequently, this chapter will briefly address partnership working and collaboration in the sport sector, with a focus on NPSOs, given the emphasis placed on partnerships by government in the last decade, interoperability issues and any consequences for the governance of NPSOs. However, the chapter begins with consideration of the wider democratisation of sport within which the challenges of stakeholding, partnership working and collaboration are located.

Democratising sport

'Democracy' in NPSOs (ISCA, 2013) refers to: open and frequent access for members in order to influence the political and strategic direction of the organisation; equal rights of members to stand for election and vote for political leadership functions; and the opportunity to debate and influence the key decisions of the organisation. However, an issue raised concerning organisations in the non-profit sport sector, in respect of democratic processes, is the relative absence of stakeholder participation (Houlihan, 2013). Given the traditional hierarchic governance of sports, decision-making has rarely been in full consultation with participants/athletes or other stakeholders. The democratisation of NPSOs involves including the interests of athletes, coaches, officials, volunteers, managers and other internal stakeholders in the governance of sports organisations. However, organisations in the external environment (e.g. media/broadcasters, funders/sponsors, government agencies) are arguably also stakeholders in both the sport and its governance. The key issue is, however, to what extent stakeholders are a component of the governance of a sport or a specific NPSO and to what extent they should be.

For participants/athletes, in particular, a number of issues are pertinent and merit the input of participants/athletes. These issues include: team selection, resource allocation, programming priorities, competition schedules, training conditions and expectations, officiating concerns; athlete funding and doping infractions, for example. Therefore participant/athlete representation in sport governance is critical to ensure that their interests are included or 'voiced' in decision-making. A number of international governing bodies for sport have developed websites for their athletes that provides opportunities for input into the governance of the sport (such as the International Sailing Federation and the International Canoe Federation). Other sports organisations at the international level include elected athletes on the executive board (such as the International Triathlon Union) in a bid to be athlete-centred. In the UK, NPSOs have also taken steps to include participants/athletes in decision-making. However, very little research has been published to date on extending stakeholding to athletes in sports clubs or NGBs.

CASE EXAMPLE: ATHLETES AS STAKEHOLDERS – THE IOC ATHLETES' COMMISSION

The IOC has an Athletes' Commission which provides a 'voice' for athletes within the structures of the IOC. It is composed of 19 members, of which the majority are elected by the athletes themselves. Two elected members from the Commission represent athletes at the General Assembly level and have voting rights within the Assembly (IOC, 2001). Additionally, the IOC president has appointed several athlete representatives to serve on 23 different IOC commissions. Via these arenas, athletes can communicate their perspectives on issues such as: the media, the Olympic programme, ethics, women and sport and the Olympic Games. Also, the IOC's executive board is (at the time of writing) composed of five former Olympic athletes (four male; one female); one male serves as president, one male serves as vice-president and the remaining representatives hold member status. In this sense, the IOC is in effect driven by the 'voices' of athlete stakeholders, whether active or retired. This is not to suggest that all sports in the Olympic 'family' are represented equally, which may lack feasibility, or that men's and women's sport is fairly represented across sports.

Stakeholding and the reform of the non-profit sport sector

It should also be noted that NGBs in particular have been under pressure from the government agency for elite sport (UK Sport), via the 'modernisation' or reform agenda (see Chapter 1), to place an emphasis on stakeholding as a core component of their work.

CASE EXAMPLE: EXTENDING STAKEHOLDING – UK SPORT

One of the key recommendations made by UK Sport in the Modernisation Programme was the need for national governing bodies (NGBs) to communicate effectively with members, participants and wider stakeholder groups (UK Sport, 2003: 4). In the *Governance Guide for NGBs*, the four principles of good governance explicitly relate to stakeholders: accountability of decision-makers to stakeholders; participation so that all stakeholders are represented when decisions are taken; responsiveness of the organisation to its stakeholders; and transparency about the information on which decisions have been based, the decisions themselves and the way those decisions are implemented.

Pressures from UK Sport and Sport England (and the other sports councils in the UK) have in turn raised expectations among an array of stakeholders and potential stakeholders.

Stakeholder expectations

As Hoye and Cuskelly (2007: 28) observe, 'Sport governing bodies are ... confronting [an] environment of heightened expectations from organizational stakeholders for increased transparency and accountability.' In part this is because of high-profile failures in accountability and transparency in the sport sector. Given that NPSOs work in partnership across a range of stakeholders, there is scope for scrutiny from sponsors, funding agencies, delivery partners and service users and, not least, the members of sports organisations. Coupled with raised expectations among the public are pressures from government as noted. Cornforth (2003) argues that as a result of changes in legislation, government policy and pressures from stakeholders, for example, it is important for non-profit organisations to recognise the external context in which organisations operate. Equally, understanding the internal context is important when considering the capacity of a sports body to respond to external change. These capacities vary according to organisational size, structures, resources, management cultures, historical development, local priorities and so on.

For a single sports club, transparency and accountability become critical for stakeholders, given the range of potential and actual partner organisations that an NPSO might have, including:

- the NGB of the sport;
- government bodies (e.g. sports councils);
- local council departments;
- sponsors;
- funding agencies;
- schools and universities;
- local community organisations;
- residents groups;
- supporters groups; and
- the media.

Clearly, the nature, intent and extent of each partnership in this 'network' of stakeholders needs to be accounted for by the board of an NPSO. It can be argued that if sports were truly representative of their stakeholders on an international, national or local level then there would be little need for stakeholders to establish mechanisms for direct representation. Where representation is weak, in the case of lobby groups or specific interest groups, stakeholders are duty-bound by their own statutes to argue for change. For other stakeholder groups, without such statutes, there is a raised expectation nonetheless that NPSOs will include their voice in the governance of the organisation.

CASE EXAMPLE: SUPPORTERS GROUPS AND STAKEHOLDING

The emergence of issue-centred groups has contributed to a debate about the future governance of sports and one notable example is football (Hindley, 2005). An example of this is the campaign led by the Manchester United Supporters Trust to secure a 'stake' in their football club following the 'takeover' of Manchester United by the Glazer family. Parallel to this campaign was the formation of FC United of Manchester, a semi-professional football club set up by supporters. These developments raise questions about 'ownership' of a club, who should govern a club, the regulation and control of a club, participation and exclusion and the exercise of power in sport governance. Hindley (2005) identifies approximately 100 supporter trusts across England, Wales and Scotland that were founded as democratic, representative bodies with transparent decision-making processes. Critically, supporter representation at boardroom level is guaranteed through the collective ownership of shares.

LEARNING ACTIVITY

Review the UK government's position in 2015 regarding supporters as stakeholders: www.supporters-direct.org/press-release/supporters-direct-welcomes-government-sports-strategy. Additionally, access www.playthe game.org

Stakeholders and social responsibility

Stakeholding is one component of a 'social responsibility framework', defined broadly as where an organisation acts in line with societal responsibilities. Non-profit organisations can claim that this is their function or purpose, unlike corporate (private sector) bodies where profit maximisation can override societal responsibilities. It can be recognised that many sport organisations have been delivering social responsibility initiatives for many years, including philanthropy, community involvement, youth educational activities and youth health initiatives (Babiak and Wolfe, 2009). Further, as noted in Chapter 4, if an NPSO is a registered charity, then it must act in the wider public interest. In the case of sports organisations with different legal forms, a commitment to social responsibility objectives would need to be defined and assessed.

In terms of stakeholding specifically, actions NGBs or other Non-Profit Sports Organisations can take in order to enhance social responsibility include:

- undertaking a mapping exercise to identify their stakeholders according to the level of power they wield and the level of interest they have in governance;
- meeting with stakeholder groups to hear concerns and devise a way forward;
- seeking to implement stakeholder engagement and stakeholder participation strategies;
- including stakeholders in forums, offering committee membership and/or board membership if this assists in building representation within the organisation;
- developing a strategy towards managing different stakeholder organisations; and
- setting clear and coherent objectives for stakeholder inclusion and engagement in order to evaluate impact.

Enhancing stakeholder participation in NPSO governance can improve the quality and legitimacy of decisions. More specifically, Houlihan (2013) observes that involving stakeholders in decisions leads to informed decision-making and fewer disputes. Therefore NPSOs can benefit from including a wider range of voices into formulating the processes and procedures that underpin governance. However, the final (informed) decision will be taken by the board so as to retain authority and legitimacy in a context of many voices, interests and claims.

Corporate Social Responsibility

The concept of Corporate Social Responsibility (CSR) (Brassell, 2013) has entered the language and practice of sports organisations operating a 'business model'. This concept challenges the corporate sector to enact societal responsibilities beyond profit maximisation. This has resulted from failures in corporate governance and a subsequent desire for increased accountability and transparency. Applying CSR to professional sports with a commercial arm can be problematic as it can relate to many different aspects of a sports organisation's governance and activities. One key aspect of CSR is an organisation's interaction with stakeholders as it attempts to balance its commitments to relevant groups and individuals in its social environment. In fact, many sports organisations have come to realise that strong relations with the community are essential for a sport organisation to succeed. Further, CSR affects the organisation's ability to attract fans/spectators, secure corporate sponsors and also affects dealings with governments and other major stakeholders.

Smith and Westerbeek (2007) identify more specifically how CSR impacts on sport governance. For example, it is claimed that:

- the global reach of sport ensures CSR activities have mass media distribution and communication power;
- sport CSR has youth appeal;
- sport CSR can be used to deliver health through sport and physical activity programmes;

- sport CSR involves group interaction and can enhance social interaction;
- sport CSR can help improve cultural understanding and integration; and
- particular sport activities can enhance environmental and sustainability awareness.

NPSOs may adopt a CSR framework to improve their reputation for corporate governance in a non-profit context; differentiate themselves from competitors; develop brand loyalty; and improve financial performance. In turn, these changes may impact positively on stakeholder relations and engagement. For example, athletes as members of an NPSO may establish an Athlete Foundation. NPSOs have considered strategic philanthropy as a method for building a brand or organisational image or reputation. Also, professional sports clubs and leagues have established community schemes and other initiatives with social outcomes for similar purposes and potential benefits, not least stakeholder engagement. Further, some NGBs have used the concept of CSR to launch initiatives such as FIFA's *Football for Hope* movement. This involved a strategic alliance with partners involved in the delivery of street football for 'sport in development' purposes that can include goals linked to health promotion, peace building, children's rights and education, anti-discrimination, social integration and environmental activities. Moreover, some NGBs organise sports events linked to environmental benefits within the CSR ethos. The governance of sport manufacturers has also changed as a result of a focus on social responsibility. Babiak and Wolfe (2009) suggest sports organisations' CSR activities have a greater impact than commercial organisations and other industry sectors in part because some sport organisations have the expertise to deliver educational and social inclusion-based programmes that corporate sector organisations do not necessarily possess. In turn, a focus on social responsibility generally or CSR measures specifically can enhance stakeholding.

The implementation and evaluation of stakeholding

Within NGBs of sport the notion of stakeholding has raised a number of pertinent questions concerning how the interests of groups such as athletes, volunteers and supporters are articulated. Understanding and managing multiple stakeholder relationships is at the heart of good governance and is a critical consideration for NPSOs when planning and implementing strategy. The extent to which NGBs acknowledge and monitor the concerns of all stakeholders and take their interests into account in decision-making is a matter for further research. From the limited data available, however, it can be stated that the majority of NGBs do account for stakeholders, and stakeholder management is a significant issue among NGBs today.

Two main techniques that enable sports organisations to manage stakeholder relationships are: *stakeholder engagement*, which requires an organisation to meet and consult with stakeholder groups, but where those stakeholders have little influence on decision-making; and *stakeholder participation*, which involves a more inclusive management strategy, allowing stakeholder groups to be actively involved in decision-making and integrating them within the governance structures of an organisation. In practice, these two approaches overlap to a degree and may be thought of as positions on a continuum from low to high engagement.

The research on NGBs and stakeholding to date has found that:

- a very high proportion of NGBs provide information to stakeholders through their website and/or annual report;
- almost two-thirds of the NGBs reported that they sought feedback from stakeholders on particular consultations;
- almost one-third held focus groups involving stakeholders;
- a large majority of NGBs reported that these engagement initiatives did inform their decision-making processes;
- two-thirds of NGBs involved stakeholders within the governance structures of an organisation;
- two-thirds of NGBs have stakeholder representation on the main board or committee;
- two-thirds of NGBs have representation on the committee structure; and
- almost all NGBs provide stakeholders with the opportunity to attend the Annual General Meeting (AGM).

Stakeholder engagement can be seen as a necessary, but not sufficient, condition of stakeholder participation. In a pragmatic sense, full participation (however defined) may be constrained by the relative expertise or competencies of stakeholder representatives, organisational capacity, and/or internal conflict and competing agendas. However, these challenges can be overcome and therefore stakeholder participation as a component of a 'good governance' framework is achievable. It may therefore be the case that the choice of engagement or stakeholder strategies should be tailored to different stakeholder groups (Low and Cowton, 2004). It can be concluded that by combining a focus on the relative power of stakeholders with stakeholder engagement and participation strategies, a sports organisation can implement an appropriate strategy as part of its approach to governance.

In terms of stakeholder management, NPSOs can: undertake a mapping exercise and identify their stakeholders according to the level of power they wield and the level of interest they have in governance; seek to implement stakeholder engagement and stakeholder participation strategies appropriate to the position of stakeholders on a power/interest matrix; and invite key stakeholders to the board/committee to improve stakeholder representation. It can further be argued that 'best practice' in governance includes decisions made by board directors on the basis of competency, rather than an advocacy for specific stakeholder interests, so that directors can look at what is optimal for their sport rather than have a narrow interest or a conflict of interest. Approaches to stakeholder engagement vary in practice by frequency of engagement with stakeholder groups. Practices of 'engagement' include: surveys, focus groups, community panels, corporate advisory panels, written communication, management/union structures and other methods.

CASE EXAMPLE: ATHLETE INVOLVEMENT IN DECISION-MAKING BY SPORTS BODIES

A history of stakeholder distrust of the leadership of sports bodies exists wherein many elite athletes feel that their priorities and values are not being represented in key policy decisions (Hindley, 2007; Katwala, 2000). Houlihan (2004) criticised the IOC's Athletes' Commission as being micro-managed and the representation of athletes as being tokenistic (see case example above). Houlihan (2004) argued that sport policy is generally made *for*, or on behalf of, athletes, but rarely in consultation with athletes, and almost never in partnership with athletes. Houlihan further argued that the few governing bodies of sport that do provide a voice for athletes do so either through limited membership of the body's decision-making forum or through the formation of an 'athletes committee/commission' linked to the main forum, but safely quarantined from any significant decision-making opportunities. While many sport organisations have afforded opportunities for athletes to increase representation, a number of questions remain. For example, what processes are undertaken for the selection of representatives? How can sport organisations ensure that minority voices are not marginalised and their needs are met? To what extent are athlete voices evident in the decision-making process within international sport organisations? In addition, representation is a system where voting and bargaining are used to determine how athlete interests will be heard. There is no doubt that athlete representation on committees provides a platform for athletes to participate in decisions, actions and policies. It often depends, however, on their capacity for coalition-building, bargaining and influence, a process in which athletes can rarely afford to engage (particularly in terms of time, given their onerous training and competition schedules) (Houlihan, 2004).

Independent learning task

To what extent has athlete involvement in decisions affecting the governance of NGBs and clubs in the UK altered since Houlihan published this research? Provide examples.

Where a relationship has been established with stakeholders, in order to maintain quality relationships with each stakeholder, organisations must design a range of communication strategies that cater for each (increasingly including the use of NPSO websites, forums and social media). Clearly, information will need to be tailored to effectively communicate with, and sufficiently inform, different stakeholder groups. Using one single strategy to communicate to all stakeholders is therefore problematic and may lead to conflict between stakeholders with different aims and resources. In terms of evaluating stakeholder participation, Hindley (2007: 8) called for the evaluation of mechanisms for stakeholder participation, such as in coach/athlete associations and supporter groups, giving consideration to the representation of their views.

Partnership working, collaboration and interoperability

A raft of literature has emerged on partnerships and partnership working in sport over the last decade, although very little of this research has focused specifically on the non-profit sport sector. Nonetheless, an expansion of network governance in sport (see Chapter 2) has occurred. In the UK, partnership arrangements have involved NPSOs in certain initiatives such as those concerned with a closer working relationship between NGBs and clubs via the 'modernisation' programme (refer to Chapter 1). A key issue across the sector has proven to be interoperability or whether organisations have the capacity to function effectively in partnerships in order to address governance challenges. Another key issue has been coordination and cooperation. Green *et al.* (2013), in a case study in the USA, identify governance challenges in poorly coordinated systems, e.g. between school and non-school sport. The authors also note the influence of professional sport on the governance of some sports in the USA but not others, as is typical of governance in most countries.

INDEPENDENT LEARNING ACTIVITY

With reference to Green *et al.* (2013), assess the impact of a key challenge facing USA Football and the International Federation of American Football (IAF), namely coordination between agencies delivering American football. Focus in part on how the professional game shapes the governance of American football in educational establishments.

Summary

This chapter has provided an overview of stakeholding as one component of sport governance for NPSOs. In a context in which networks of relationships operate alongside or in parallel to hierarchical forms of governance, and where there has been increasing government pressure on the non-profit sport sector to work in formal partnerships or collaborations, and given raised stakeholder expectations (as part of a wider call for a 'democratisation' of sport), NPSOs can no longer work in isolation and must account for the views of members, athletes, supporter groups, the local community and, not least, funders, in sport governance. Looking forward, it is likely that the concept and practice of extended stakeholding will form one component of best practice and good governance in sports organisations. However, many NPSOs may resist or pay lip-service to the expectations and demands of stakeholders. The desirability and feasibility of stakeholder involvement or engagement remains an ongoing issue in the sector and a challenge for NPSOs to negotiate. For sport governance to be sustainable, stakeholding may have to become the norm (Bonollo De Zwart and Gilligan, 2009).

LEARNING ACTIVITIES

- How can sports organisations manage stakeholder expectations effectively?
- Identify the strengths and weaknesses of governing a sport via a multi-agency approach.
- Explain the differences between partnership working, collaboration and stakeholding with reference to sports organisations.
- What is the difference between stakeholding and *extended* stakeholding?
- How does stakeholding relate to social responsibility and CSR?
- How does the concept and practice of stakeholding impact on the governance of boards in NPSOs?
- Discuss how stakeholder theory relates to stakeholding practices by NPSOs.

Bibliography

Babiak, K. and Wolfe, R. (2009) Determinants of corporate social responsibility in professional sport: internal and external factors. *Journal of Sport Management*, 23: 717–742.

Bonollo De Zwart, F. and Gilligan, G. (2009) Sustainable governance in sporting organisations. In: Rodriguez, P., Késenne, S. and Dietl, H., eds, *Social Responsibility and Sustainability in Sports*. Oviedo: Universitat de Oviedo, pp. 165–227.

Brassell, M. (2013) Corporate social responsibility in the sports industry. In: Hassan, D. and Lusted, J., eds, *Managing Sport: Social and Cultural Perspectives*. Oxon: Routledge, pp. 1–16.

Brenner, S.N. and Cochran, P.L. (1991) The stakeholder theory of the firm: implications for business and society – theory and research. In: Mahon, J.F., ed., *International Association for Business and Society Proceedings*, 449–467.

Casini, L. (2009). Global hybrid public–private bodies: the World Anti-Doping Agency (WADA). Draft paper for the Global Administrative Law Conference on 'Practical Legal Problems of International Organizations', Geneva, 20–21 March.

Clarkson, M.E. (1995) A stakeholder framework for analyzing and evaluating corporate social responsibility. *Academy of Management Review*, 20, 92–117.

Cornforth, C., ed. (2003) *The Governance of Public and Non-Profit Organisations: What Do Boards Do?* London: Routledge.

Ferkins, L., Shilbury, D. and McDonald, G. (2005) The role of the board in building strategic capability: towards an integrated model of sport governance research. *Sport Management Review*, 8: 195–225.

Global Reporting Initiative (2011) *Sustainability Reporting Guidelines*. Amsterdam: GRI.

Green, B.C., Chalip, L. and Bowers, M.T. (2013) United States. In: O'Boyle, I. and Bradbury, T., eds, *Sport Governance: International Case Studies*. London: Routledge, pp. 20–36.

Hindley, D. (2004) Stakeholding and trusts: a framework for good governance within the football industry. In: Papapanikos, G.T., ed., *4th International Conference on Sports*, Athens Institute of Education and Research, Athens, Greece, 31 May–2 June.

Hindley, D. (2005) A matter of trust? How supporters are democratising football. In: *Play the Game Conference: Governance in Sport – The Good, the Bad and the Ugly*, Copenhagen, Denmark, 6–10 November.

Hindley, D. (2007) *Resource Guide in Governance and Sport*. www.heacademy.ac.uk/assets/hlst/documents/resource_guides/governance_and_sport.pdf

Hindley, D. (2008) Playing the game: the challenge of corporate social responsibility in English professional football. In: *The Social Impact of Sport Governance & Management*, University of Bocconi, Milan, 20–22 November. www.playthegame.org/upload/david_hindley_-_a_matter_of_trust_-_how_supporters_are_democratising_football.pdf

Houlihan, B. (2004) Civil rights, doping control and the world anti-doping code. *Sport in Society*, 7: 420–437.

Houlihan, B. (2013) Stakeholders, stakeholding and good governance in international sport federations. In: Play the Game, *Action for Good Governance in International Sports Organisations*. Copenhagen: Play the Game/Danish Institute for Sports Studies, pp. 185–189.

Houlihan, B. and Lindsey, I. (2008) Networks and partnerships in sports development. In: Girginov, V., ed., *Management of Sports Development*. Oxford: Butterworth-Heinemann, pp. 225–241.

Hoye, R. and Cuskelly, G. (2007). *Sport Governance*. Oxford: Elsevier Butterworth-Heinemann.

International Olympic Committee (2001) *Athletes' Commission Terms of Reference*. http://multimedia.olympic.org/pdf/en_report_712.pdf

International Sport and Culture Association (ISCA) (2013) *Guidelines for Good Governance in Grassroots Sport*. Copenhagen: ISCA.

Katwala, S. (2000) *Democratising Global Sport*. London: Foreign Policy Centre.

Kihl, L., Kikulis, L. and Thibault, L. (2007) A deliberative democratic approach to athlete-centred sport: the dynamics of administrative and communicative power. *European Sport Management Quarterly*, 7, 1: 1–30.

Kikulis, L. (2000) Continuity and change in governance and decision making on national sport organisations: institutional explanations, *Journal of Sport Management*, 14, 4: 293–320.

Low, C. and Cowton, C. (2004) Beyond stakeholder engagement: the challenges of stakeholder participation in corporate governance. *International Journal of Business Governance and Ethics*, 1, 1: 45–55.

Mackintosh, C. (2011) An analysis of county sports partnerships in England: the fragility, challenges and complexity of partnership working in sports development. *International Journal of Sport Policy and Politics*, 3, 1: 45–64.

Michie, J. (1999) *New Mutualism: A Golden Goal? Uniting Supporters and their Clubs*. London: Cooperative Party.

Organisation for Economic Co-operation and Development (OECD) (2004). *Principles of Corporate Governance*. Paris: OECD.

Senaux, B. (2008) A stakeholder-approach to football club governance. *International Journal of Sport Management and Marketing*, 4, 1: 4–17. http://dx.doi.org/10.1504/IJSMM.2008.017655

Sheth, H. and Babiak, S. (2010). Beyond the game: perceptions and practices of corporate social responsibility in the professional sport industry. *Journal of Business Ethics*, 91: 433–450.

Skelcher, C., Mathur, N. and Smith, M., (2004) *Effective Partnership and Good Governance: Lessons for Policy and Practice*. INLOGOV, University of Birmingham.

Smith, A.C.T. and Westerbeek, H.M. (2007) Sport as a vehicle for deploying corporate social responsibility. *Journal of Corporate Citizenship*, 25: 43–54.

Thibault, L., Kihl, L. and Babiak, K. (2010) Democratization and governance in international sport: addressing issues with athlete involvement in organizational policy. *International Journal of Sport Policy and Politics*, 2, 3: 275–302.

UK Sport (2003) *'Investing in Change': High Level Review of the Modernisation Programme for Governing Bodies of Sport*. London: Deloitte and Touche

Walters, G. (2012) Managing social responsibility in sport. In: Trenberth, L. and Hassan, D., *Managing Sport Business: An Introduction*. London: Routledge, chapter 23.

Wolfe, R.A. and Putler, D.S. (2002) How tight are the ties that bind stakeholder groups? *Organisation Science*, 13, 1: 64–80.

6

PERFORMANCE IN SPORT GOVERNANCE

LEARNING OBJECTIVES

At the completion of this chapter, students should be able to:

- define performance as it applies to sport governance;
- understand how sport governance relates to performance in sports organisations;
- assess how the performance of NPSOs is measured;
- examine the performance of the NPSOs.

Understanding performance

The published research on performance in and by NPSOs is limited in scope, from how it is defined to how it is measured (O'Boyle, 2013). Much of the literature on sport governance makes the assumption that better-performing boards will result in better organisational outcomes (Hoye and Cuskelly, 2007: 150). However, it can be problematic to quantify the performance of a board or committees within an NPSO and there is also an issue of defining the 'performance' of specific individuals such as board members, the CEO (if applicable), staff and volunteers. The performance of a sports organisation can also be assessed in terms of sporting success in competition; financial indicators; the number of participants; membership numbers; impact on the local community; or many other 'indicators of performance'. The purpose of the NPSO will clearly shape how 'performance' is audited and the resources of an NPSO may place constraints on meeting performance-related goals.

Performance in this context relates to:

- successfully modifying governance structures, processes and practices aligned to the 'modernisation' agenda for sport (see Chapter 1);

- functioning efficiently in an administrative capacity (see Chapter 3);
- operating within a legal and regulatory framework (see Chapter 4);
- extending the engagement of stakeholders (see Chapter 5);
- implementing 'good governance' guidelines and ethical codes of practice (see Chapter 7); and
- compliance with regulation and codes of practice or best practice guidelines in sport governance (see Chapter 8).

Clearly, evaluating or assessing performance is not solely an internal matter, as performance in terms of adherence to a reform agenda, for example, requires external audit.

Evaluation of performance

This chapter first centres on the governance of the NPSO and performance in terms of the board, board members, the CEO (where applicable) and the organisation as a whole.

The organisation

Studies of organisational performance for non-profit bodies have focused on: assessment of organisational effectiveness; what can be associated with effectiveness; and the effectiveness of assessment processes. However, the literature on the performance of sports organisations in the non-profit sector is scarce and few studies of national governing bodies (NGBs) or clubs in the UK, for example, are published. Nonetheless, from the literature available on non-profits, across many countries, the significance of the board is foregrounded. An influential board can procure resources and shape the direction of the organisation. Correlates of organisational effectiveness have been identified as:

- policy formulation;
- strategic planning;
- dissemination of the organisational mission or purpose;
- conflict resolution;
- the management of meetings;
- programme review;
- board development;
- resource development;
- financial planning and control; and
- engaging in shaping the operational component of an organisation (where this falls within the remit of volunteer board members).

However, the criteria to evaluate effectiveness will differ across multiple stakeholders who will value organisational objectives and outcomes differently. Further, board directors may value financial performance more than other aspects of performance, for example, or performance in terms of sporting success, or adherence to good governance guidelines (see Chapter 7), depending on the priorities of board directors and the purpose of the organisation. In this context it is unsurprising that given the multitude of NPSOs, with different legal forms, objectives, resources, relationships with government agencies and other differences, that establishing generic performance guidelines or criteria for all sports bodies is problematic. Simply put, 'one size does not fit all'. Hoye and Cuskelly (2007: 158) observe that a single definition of organisational effectiveness independent of the judgements of different stakeholders is not tenable or useful to sports bodies. Nonetheless, many professional bodies and government agencies with an oversight of the sport sector have produced guidance and guidelines on the different components of performance (e.g. Council of Europe, 2012; FIFA, 2009; ICSA, 2010; SRA, 2011; Sport and Recreation New Zealand, 2005; Sport England, 2005, 2011; UK Sport, 2004a, 2004b, 2008a; and many others).

The precise relationship between board performance and organisational performance may require an explanation derived from more than one theoretical perspective (see Chapter 2 for a theoretical analysis of sport governance). For example, Brown (2005) combined agency theory, resource dependency theory and an analysis of group decision processes to connect an understanding of the context in which boards operate, the political and strategic aspects of governance in a sector and the board's capacity to solve problems related to performance. In terms of problem-solving, the board may set expectations for other members, staff and other stakeholders in order to manage how performance is perceived by others. Further, the board directors may formalise processes and procedures in order to be able to benchmark performance and reduce issues that may arise from 'negative' interpersonal dynamics (conflict for status, personal preferences, judgements based on limited information or understanding). An agreed policy and strategy also enables an evaluation of performance to be gauged. However, 'positive' interpersonal dynamics may be a significant driver of board performance (consensus on organisational purpose, trust and mutual benefits, transparency in decision-making).

The board

The non-profit governance literature includes many examples of prescriptive guidelines for evaluating board performance. Examples of typical guidance include the recommendation that a board should:

- evaluate the effectiveness of the board annually;
- evaluate the performance of committees, sub-committees, standing groups, meetings and other decision-making forums;
- explicitly set standards and performance expectations according to pre-agreed criteria derived from the organisation's policies;

- set time aside each year to assess individual member performance;
- use an independent facilitator (or consultant) to assist in designing an appropriate evaluation process;
- assess individual performance in confidence;
- conduct peer and self-appraisal of all board members including the board chair (and the CEO where this applies);
- utilise the outcomes of the evaluation process as the basis for organisation, board and board member developmental goals; and
- conduct a bi-annual review of the process by which performance is evaluated and make changes if necessary.

The purpose of board evaluation is clearly to enhance organisational performance. However, the outcome of the evaluation process cannot be fully understood without locating the findings in the institutional context (objectives, organisational resources, external pressures), past performance, the investment in staff and volunteer learning and, potentially, a range of other factors. Arriving at a judgement about board performance is therefore not straightforward and the outcomes can be contested even where set criteria are used to steer the evaluation process. 'Performance' in many cases may be a subjective judgement more than an impartial outcome arrived at through a transparent process where the assessment criteria are fully understood and shared by the assessor and the assessed. In fact, some research (see Hoye and Cuskelly, 2007: 154) found that different groups such as athletes, coaches, sponsors and funding agency staff used different criteria to conceptualise and evaluate 'effective' board performance. The authors also note that more effective boards had motivated board members who had a strong identification with the organisation and its purpose.

In sum, the effectiveness of board and organisational performance are interdependent. The key four board roles – monitoring and control, strategising, providing access to resources and providing advice and counsel – if successfully executed, will enhance both board and organisational performance. Clearly, organisational size/resources and the competencies of board directors will also impact on how effectively these four board roles are undertaken. Key attributes of the board can be identified as: human capital/intelligence; structural capital (processes, procedures that facilitate positive interaction between members/directors); and social capital (relationships between key personnel within an NPSO for example, and between the board and external stakeholders). These three sources of 'capital' are usually combined to form 'intellectual capital' which, when it is channelled through the NPSO's four key roles, shapes board and organisational effectiveness (Nicholson and Kiel, 2004).

The board member

In Canada, CICA (2010c) consider how performance of individual directors can be assessed. CICA note that that boards are usually responsible for assessing the quality of their own performance but have traditionally been reluctant to do this in a formal manner. This is in part because board directors are unpaid volunteers and therefore do not see performance assessment as part of their role and/or may not welcome criticism and/or may not be confident undertaking assessments of others. Moreover, board directors may become discouraged if they feel that their performance and contribution are not appreciated or believe than board morale will fall if assessment identifies 'poor' performance. Hoye and Cuskelly (2004: 96–97) concluded that 'evaluating the performance of the board members who are elected by their general membership, in addition to subjecting them to regular re-elections, may deter many members from standing for election to the board'. Evaluating individual board member performance raises issues concerning: the relevance of evaluation criteria; the evaluation process utilised; reporting mechanisms or who the outcomes are for; and what action should be taken post-evaluation.

However, in the context of the reform of the non-profit sport sector in recent years (see Chapter 1), board performance is considered too important to be absent from any review process. CICA argue that, if properly and sensitively handled, assessments of the board, committees and individual directors can be valuable for the organisation and its continuous improvement in terms of performance (however defined or measured).

The CEO and staff

The performance evaluation of the CEO has attracted more attention than board member performance in the governance guidelines of sport agencies (Hoye and Cuskelly, 2007: 163). It is the board that is responsible for evaluating the performance of a CEO. It is good practice to use agreed criteria by which to make an assessment based on the goals of the NPSO. Criteria are usually related to the use of authority, the extent of compliance with board directives and whether strategic objectives were attained within a timescale. These strategic objectives can be related to building organisational capacity (finances, human resources, expertise, partnerships) and/or sport-specific goals (performance, participation, membership and so on) or other areas under direct operational control. It is usual for a sub-committee of the board to conduct the performance appraisal rather than the board chair. Care is needed if making a distinction between the performance of the CEO and the performance of the organisation as a whole, which can be problematic in practice, where the CEO has a remit to lead across many aspects of the NPSO.

Where an NPSO employs staff, the board's stewardship responsibilities include appraising (at least annually) the performance of employees who report directly to the board. This may be done in a number of ways:

* The chair of the board conducts the appraisal on behalf of the board.
* The board appoints a committee of one or more directors to conduct the appraisal.
* The board conducts the appraisal as a committee of the whole.

The appraisal process can be uncomfortable, particularly in an informal culture where there are friendships between the individual and members of the board. An appropriate approach to the issue is to begin by establishing a clear understanding between the board and the employee of the requirements of the position and the basis on which performance will be evaluated. This can include: meeting measurable targets, conforming to the organisation's ethical standards and maintaining good relationships with stakeholders. It may also be appropriate to obtain input from employees and other stakeholders in any assessment of performance.

A closely related and key issue is succession planning. The board must make sure that the organisation is prepared to keep operating when key staff members resign or are away for extended periods of time. It is usual for NPSOs to pre-empt this issue by drawing up a list of potential successors to positions such as executive director. Further, procedures are usually established by an NPSO to ensure that copies of critical records or information are maintained and located in a way that ensures confidentiality and anonymity.

The volunteer workforce

Volunteers are a valuable and often essential resource for NPSOs. Hence the investment by NGBs and government agencies in volunteer recruitment, training, retention and volunteer management. Building volunteer loyalty and commitment reduces the cost of high turnover and unreliable or inconsistent performance. However, assessing the performance of volunteers has proved to be a contentious issue. Nonetheless, to ensure quality standards are met, a number of actions can be taken, including:

- screening prospective volunteers who will be in positions of trust (e.g. handling funds, working with children and other vulnerable people);
- ensuring descriptions of duties are clear, coherent and appropriate;
- conducting periodic reviews of volunteer performance (e.g. on committees);
- delivering appropriate orientation, supervision and training;
- requesting feedback from volunteers on organisational and board performance;
- encouraging peer assessment and open dialogue as part of a wider shift towards greater transparency;
- mentoring volunteers in critical positions via annual evaluations of their performance based on agreed goals.

Governing bodies of sport

A periodic review of performance may be undertaken internally and via external scrutiny. In the UK, NGB performance has become a central component of sport governance (Sport England 2008, 2013) as NGBs seek success for their sports in line with government strategy to raise the performance of athletes in international competition as part of the 'modernisation' programme (UK Sport, 2003), which is audited (NAO, 2005, 2008) and the performance of which is explicitly linked to securing funding for the sport (UK Sport, 2008a; 2008b). Further, NGBs must raise participation (Sport England, 2004) although many authors have concluded that the emphasis of UK sport policy has been on elite athlete success (Green, 2009; Green and Houlihan, 2005: also see Chapter 1) and this is increasingly the case in other countries such as Canada and Australia (Houlihan and Green, 2008). Apart from governments, international sports organisations such as the IOC have had significant influence on the focus on elite sport at the national level (Houlihan, 2009). In a study in New Zealand, Sam and Macris (2014) investigated 'performance regimes' and noted that performance measurement in elite sport is relatively unproblematic by comparison with measurement of performance in community sport. The medals table in the Olympic Games is a simple method of demonstrating performance through comparison between nation states, albeit contested. However, demonstrating evidence of meeting goals to raise or widen participation in community or 'grass-roots' sport is more problematic due to differing methods of measurement, comparing data in isolation from context, acquiring representative samples and proving causality between actions by the NPSO and outcomes. For example, the annual *Active People* survey conducted in England has drawn much criticism.

For the year 2011/2012, Sport England assessed the performance of 46 NGBs within the broader 2009–2013 *Whole Sport Plans* framework (Sport England, 2005). Of relevance for this study text are the criteria used to assess performance in terms of governance. Aspects of performance assessed by Sport England have included: participation and performance targets; the level and quality of accreditation; quality of facilities; and coaching standards. However, the components of *governance* of note in these assessments relate to:

- new modes of governance, from restructuring of the board to organisational mergers;
- a shift towards a business/commercial development 'model';
- the effectiveness of partnerships and collaboration;
- strategic development;
- knowledge development;
- the level of influence of the board or NGB as a whole;
- the introduction of methods for measuring performance (e.g. commissioned outcomes);
- the introduction of a CEO to lead the NGB;
- the relationship with Sport England or other government bodies; and
- other aspects of *corporate* governance introduced into the non-profit sport sector (e.g. commissioning and procurement).

CASE EXAMPLES: NGB PERFORMANCE ASSESSMENTS

Independent task: compare the facets of governance highlighted in the following brief reviews of specific sports.

Angling

The impact of recently-formed County Angling Action Groups could be increased and links with other local partners, in particular CSPs, needs to be improved. The ADB is targeting a date within the next six months for merger with the Angling Trust (the membership body) and we are encouraging the governing body to set in place a long-term strategic vision which focuses on the wider needs of the sport. Close monitoring of the impact of the merger and progress toward a strategic vision is required over the next six months.

Archery

The NGB has focused on improving its knowledge and understanding of the sport to help build strong foundations for future development. Archery GB's insight and knowledge of the sport is continually improving and the NGB has a clearer understanding of priorities moving forward.

In the next year, it is anticipated that Archery GB will engage further in the commercial archery environment.

Basketball

England Basketball still needs to demonstrate that it is up to the job of delivering growth outside its traditional structures, in a market with significant potential. The development of measurable, strategic relationships with external delivery partners will be important for England Basketball if it is to maximise the resources at its disposal. Qualitative evidence is now being gathered to demonstrate ... effectiveness.

Bowls

The newly established Bowls Development Alliance has responded to the challenge to develop the sport of bowls. The governing body's capacity has increased significantly, with a number of new appointments. A key strategic area for development over the next six months is health and inactivity; this area offers a significant opportunity for the Bowls Development Alliance to diversify its funding sources and to enhance links at a local level.

Goalball

Following a number of resignations from the governing body in February 2011, good progress has been made to stabilise Goalball UK. Key to this has been the appointment of an Executive Chairman who has brought substantial momentum and focus. Whilst there is still considerable work remaining and further improvements to be made, Goalball UK is no longer viewed as a high governance risk. Goalball UK has appointed a National Development Officer, who is providing much-needed delivery capacity.

Lacrosse

English Lacrosse remains a good example of a relatively small governing body with clear, targeted plans to expand its sport from a limited participation base. Following a strong performance, English Lacrosse has received additional investment to deliver a new product, 'INTO Lacrosse', which will target the informal sports market and provide a range of competitive and social playing opportunities for students leaving university. The governing body has also had success in its work to improve links between schools and clubs and to engage young people in volunteering.

Modern pentathlon

Since the arrival of a new chief executive in April, Pentathlon GB has focused on developing a clarity of purpose owned by the whole organisation, and underpinned by more robust operational standards for staff and volunteers. The governing body has made positive progress clarifying the principles of its England Talent Pool programme.

Rounders

Rounders England has made a step change in the last six months, helped by market insight from the Women's Sport and Fitness Foundation. It is using this to clarify which consumers to target in order to grow the sport with the help of a substantial marketing and PR programme. The appointment of a new Development and Competitions Director has had a significant impact on delivery, and extended the number of County Sport Partnerships being commissioned to deliver rounders.

Triathlon

Triathlon England continues to perform well and is on track to deliver against all of its commissioned outcomes. The sport is benefiting from an ever-increasing profile through elite success, television coverage and celebrity participation. Triathlon stands apart from the traditional sporting landscape as growth is being driven by events in partnership with the commercial sector. The strength of the governing body lies in its ability to influence this sector, which is being bolstered through its event accreditation programme.

Wheelchair Basketball

British Wheelchair Basketball continues to make good progress and is on track to achieve its commissioned outcomes. British Wheelchair Basketball has numerous successful local partnerships and, in the absence of a regional staffing infrastructure, it will need continued support from local partners such as County Sports Partnerships to ensure success.

Wheelchair Rugby

Great Britain Wheelchair Rugby has gone through a significant transformation in the past two years and is now an efficient and well-managed organisation. The organisation has been very successful at brokering partnerships to aid its sustainability and support delivery which has been crucial given the relatively small Sport England investment.

Source: Sport England: http://archive.sportengland.org/funding/ngb_investment/ngb_progress_reports_2011-12.aspx

Performance of international sports organisations

Assessing the governance of NGBs is not significantly different from assessing how international sports bodies perform. Below is an example of a more detailed performance review of an international governing body.

CASE EXAMPLE: PERFORMANCE REVIEW OF THE INTERNATIONAL CRICKET COUNCIL

In reviewing the performance of the ICC, it was found that there was:

- strong governance led by an independent chairman supported by a streamlined board containing independent directors;
- fair representation on the board, providing diversity of interests and experience;
- ICC executive management empowered to implement the strategy of the ICC;

- decisions taken in the best interests of the game, not individual members;
- all directors exercising their fiduciary duty first and foremost for the benefit of the ICC;
- equality of voting at the board and the full council; and
- fair rotation of the ambassadorial role of president between all members.

However, areas in which to improve performance were recommended:

- There needs to be clarity over its remit and objectives to ensure good governance.
- The board requires an independent chairman to lead it, who is appointed solely on merit.
- The board needs to embrace diversity and independence of view.
- An equitable voting structure should apply of 'one person, one vote', removing the current power of veto that sits with the full members.
- The role of president should become an ambassadorial role.
- The ICC needs to ensure that an effective ethical code, covering both on- and off-field activities, is developed, embedded, policed and consistently enforced, with all members being expected and required to adopt similar standards within their own member bodies. This needs to be embedded in a pragmatic and effective manner rather than being seen as merely aspirational.
- Remove discrimination against associate and affiliate members. It also deprives them of fair and appropriate representation on the board of the ICC. It prevents them receiving commensurate funding which would enable cricket to be developed.
- Moving from the present subscription-based funding mechanism for the ICC, to one where the ICC is self-funding is essential.
- Promote the embedded values of cricket in the governance of the sport (fair play, integrity, trust and transparency) within a binding code of ethics.

Source: Woolf and PricewaterhouseCoopers (2012).

Performance and good governance

Board members are responsible for ensuring that the organisation operates in compliance with both its 'legal purpose' (which must be compatible with the government regulations for non-profit organisations, and, if applicable, charitable status) and 'good governance' standards (see Chapter 7). The process of reviewing governance in line with 'good governance' standards can help to re-energise, refocus and renew the organisation (CICA, 2010b). Specifically, board directors will need to:

- read and understand the organisation's legal purpose(s) as stated in the incorporation documents;
- understand why the organisation exists and its core values and purpose;
- ensure that the current strategy is compatible with the legal purpose;
- regularly review and approve the strategy; and
- clarify what the organisation is legally authorised and entitled to do.

Good governance practices can usually be made comprehensible and explicit through policy and strategy, which would usually include a determination of long-term goals (i.e. mission, vision and values) and objectives which reflect the relationship that the organisation has with its different stakeholder groups, and how the organisation intends to meet stakeholder needs (see Chapter 5). Furthermore, a *Code of Conduct* can be advocated by those in leadership positions, in order to:

- set the boundaries of acceptable behaviour;
- reduce the risk and associated costs of fraud, conflicts of interest and other ethical lapses;
- help introduce new employees and volunteers to the organisation's standards;
- attract and retain high-calibre employees, volunteers and business partners;
- provide employees, volunteers and others subject to the *code* with parameters;
- inform contractors, suppliers and others doing business with the organisation of its expectations regarding acceptable behaviour;
- establish the basis for sanctions against those who deviate from the *code*.

Board members should demonstrate *leadership* by monitoring the organisation's processes for assessing the integrity and ethical behaviour of its volunteers and staff and for measuring compliance with the organisation's values.

Financial performance

The sustainability of an NPSO (defined here as its ability to fund its activities year after year) is a major responsibility of the board. Ideally, one or more directors should understand accounting and financial statements, but boards should not rely wholly on internal expertise but seek advice from the Sport and Recreation Alliance (SRA) (in the case of England) or a similar body with oversight of the sector in other countries, or an independent financial adviser. Board directors need to understand: the sources of the organisation's funds; how funds are used; the operating and capital budgets; methods of procuring external funding; fundraising methods; membership fee structure; charges for services; merchandising; annual budgets; bidding processes; and the wider funding context for sport (access to and changes in central and local government grants, National Lottery monies, commercial sources).

The board's treasurer is responsible for: maintaining accurate accounting records; assigning responsibility and targets for each category of funding; budgeting; and funding distribution aligned to organisational objectives, and aspects of planning and strategy, for example, although in practice these duties might be delegated to paid staff. Funding in the sport sector is often conditional upon meeting performance-related targets as one aspect of effective governance or 'best practice'. How funds acquired are subsequently spent may also be determined by the funding body, who may also require reports that account for the use of the funds. NPSOs must exercise care in complying with funding restrictions and requirements, to avoid the risk of losing the confidence of the funders and the additional risk of 'claw-back', where funds are returned to the funder if a 'breach' occurs. The board of an NPSO must therefore build the trust of funders in order to sustain a positive relationship for the longer term. Funding in the sport sector is often short term and the funding cycles of different funding agencies may differ, leading to the challenges of sustaining a programme, for example, and coordinating an in-house funding strategy where more than one funding source (and funder) is the norm. Further, some funding requires 'match funding' before it is awarded to the NPSO.

The funding environment is therefore complex and the governance of finances for larger sports clubs and most NGBs, for example, requires expertise. Although unrestricted funds may be used for any purpose, such an arrangement is increasingly rare, and furthermore, some NPSOs create their own internal restrictions on funding allocation by matching receipts from certain sources to expenditures on specific activities or projects. This is undertaken in order to manage uncertainties in revenues. Financial performance is therefore dependent on a number of factors that the board must negotiate in order to build organisational capacity for the longer term.

Strategic performance

In Canada, CICA (2010b) raised a number of questions regarding the strategic performance of the board of non-profit organisations. CICA emphasise that the performance and success of an organisation often depends on having beneficial relationships with stakeholders and meeting their expectations, although in practice this can be challenging when the expectations vary among stakeholders or are not compatible with the interests of the organisation (see Chapter 5). Stakeholder expectations should, however, inform the development of a strategic plan. This usually takes the form of a written document which describes the organisation's vision, mission and values, the strategic objectives, and it will usually include an action plan with designated roles and responsibilities for those who will operationalise the strategy. This 'plan of action' will be set within a timeframe agreed upon via consultation with stakeholders (members, partner organisations, funders and so on). The board's governance responsibilities include approving the strategy. In NPSOs with professional staff, the CEO and senior staff will usually be responsible for delivering the action plan and assessing the outcomes against the objectives. In organisations with few or no staff, the board may develop the strategic plan itself or appoint a board committee that will provide the board with the material it needs to discuss and approve the plan.

The key steps in the strategic planning process are typically:

1. Review the organisation's internal strengths and weaknesses and the opportunities and threats in the external environment (SWOT analysis).
2. Define the planning assumptions.
3. Consider strategic alternatives and record the reasons for accepting or rejecting them.
4. Select and describe the rationale for any proposed changes in strategy.
5. Develop an implementation plan that aligns activities with the strategy and assigns accountabilities for all strategic initiatives.
6. Develop performance objectives (quantitative and qualitative) that will be used to monitor strategic progress.
7. Create a system for progress review and schedule regular reviews of performance.
8. Build the strategic document on the previous strategy (if there is one) where the focus is on learning in a cycle of continuous improvement.
9. Disseminate the outcomes of the strategy/action plan to stakeholders, including key funding agencies.

Measuring performance

Good strategic and operational planning includes identifying measurable objectives that build on results and achievements. This can be difficult for those NPSOs whose legal purpose is expressed in terms of meeting a social need. There are, essentially, two types of measurement, namely, quantitative and qualitative. Quantitative measures record activities that can be quantified in numbers such as participation data, membership and other factual information, including financial results. Funding agencies often ask for quantitative information in their grant application forms. NPSOs operating within a model of corporate governance will usually set short-, medium- and long-term targets. Qualitative measures record address aspects of the work of NPSOs that are more difficult to quantify, such as stakeholder perceptions, opinions and viewpoints, or the meanings conveyed in documentation, or the values and beliefs held by board members, for example. Qualitative measures can be expressed in numbers by using such techniques as surveys. Additionally, interviews, with board members for example, or an analysis of documentation, or an observation of performance may be applied.

NPSOs with a charitable or social purpose may have to demonstrate effective performance where anecdotal evidence is not sufficient to either 'make the case' for good governance or to access funding. Nonetheless, innovative approaches to demonstrating performance in regard to social outcomes and impacts is possible via social accounting methods and the use of instruments such as Social Return on Investment (SROI) that has been used to assess the social value and impact of charities and other non-profit organisations (King, 2014).

In order to enhance performance, the board can:

- monitor a manageable number of quantitative and qualitative objectives that indicate the organisation's strategic progress;
- set organisational objectives that are appropriate for monitoring its performance;
- produce regular reports that compare actual performance results to targets;
- identify where actual performance varies from the target set and understand the reasons for a 'performance gap', and seek solutions before setting new targets.

Leadership

In this short section leadership is defined, the qualities of leaders identified and the issue of dual leadership discussed as a particular concern in sport governance for the non-profit sector.

Defining leadership

To distinguish leadership from management, it has been argued that leaders create and change organisational cultures, while managers and administrators work within them. Although the extensive body of literature on leadership is not reviewed in this study text, the salient findings of research on leadership applicable to NPSOs in the UK are extrapolated for the purposes of analysing organisational performance. In brief, it is noted that impactful leadership by the board chair and/or Chief Executive Officer (CEO) motivates volunteers and staff to lead themselves (enhance ownership and responsibility) and in this sense leadership is shared among members and employees (where applicable). Leadership is therefore needed at all levels of an NPSO and is not wholly the preserve of the senior personnel.

Effective leadership is transformational, bringing positive change to a sports organisation, whereas management is transactional, involving specific tasks or actions such as: setting and achieving goals, objectives and targets; managing inputs, outputs and outcomes; measuring impact; managing people (human resources); managing budgets; managing transactions (contracts) and so on. It has therefore been claimed that 'A manager must be a successful leader in order to be effective' (Taylor, 2011: 334). Nonetheless, a distinction can be made between management (operational) roles and responsibilities, and those in a leadership position. Here, the leader is responsible for strategic planning and development, commissioning, procurement and setting a vision for the NPSO to motivate volunteers and staff alike.

Leadership qualities

In addition to their technical abilities and experience, the organisational leadership must possess personal qualities that inspire others to action and improvement in performance. Therefore, in selecting a prospective leader, a selection panel (of board members if appointing a CEO) will consider looking for individuals with the following qualities:

- Integrity – the leader must have personal integrity and insist that the organisation behaves ethically.
- Courage – possessing the courage to ask 'tough questions' and to advocate for support or opposition to proposals and actions. Loyalty to stakeholder interests may demand that leaders express dissent and persist in demanding answers to their questions. In this sense, the position is in part political.
- Good judgement – a focus on the important issues in decision-making processes. In the 'modernised' NPSO, the leader employs sound business practice in any options analysis.
- Perspective – a leader would have a broad knowledge and experience of working in the sport sector ideally, although many boards employ leaders from outside the sport sector with expertise in governance.
- Commitment to learning – leaders tend to remain up to date with the issues and challenges facing NPSOs. They tend to take responsibility for their own education in areas of their contribution to the board. The culture of a board is arguably as important as the skills, experience and knowledge of its members and therefore the incoming leader (e.g. CEO) would understand how to mould an organisational culture towards achieving its goals and other more specific organisational objectives.
- The CEO (or board directors in the case of a volunteer-run NPSO) should have the behavioural skills needed to function and work effectively together with the members and wider range of internal and external stakeholders. Skills may include:
  - An ability to present opinions – they are articulate and able to present their views clearly, frankly and constructively.
  - A willingness and ability to listen – they listen respectfully and make sure they understand what they have heard.
  - An ability to ask questions – they know how to ask questions in a way that contributes positively to debates.
  - Flexibility – they are open to new ideas and responsive to the possibility of change.
  - Dependability – they do their homework and attend and participate in meetings.

(CICA, 2010a).

As stated by the SRA (Sport Wales/SRA, 2015), leadership is not only to do with strategy, risk management, controls and processes, but is also a matter of culture, values and integrity. The leader sets the tone for the organisation and inspires and motivates members and other stakeholders towards attaining certain standards of good governance and best practice. The leader in effect creates and shapes the culture of the organisation. More specifically, the NPSO leader:

- inspires others;
- offers a vision, leading to a goal, supported by strategic insight;
- sets the example;
- provides both challenge and support;
- strives to improve the organisation;
- invests in the continuing professional development of volunteers/staff;
- communicates effectively; and
- builds trust.

CASE EXAMPLE: GOVERNANCE AND LEADERSHIP FRAMEWORK FOR WALES

In 2014, Sport Wales (government agency) and the SRA began to facilitate a move by Welsh governing bodies to create a structured programme of leadership and governance development. The *Governance and Leadership Framework for Wales* was the outcome (SRA, 2015). The approach taken to governance emphasises both systems, policies, procedures and regulations, on the one hand, and behaviours, values and ethics, on the other. It is argued that a balance between these core aspects of governance is needed to develop high-performing organisations.

Independent learning task

How has the development of this framework made a difference to the governance of sport in Wales? Provide examples.

Dual leadership

The introduction of professional (salaried) staff into NPSOs has resulted in dual leadership roles, with many UK NPSOs now effectively led by a CEO alongside the board chair. Organisational leadership has therefore become critical, as one aspect of governance, in the performance of an NGB of sport or sports club, for example. The once clearly demarcated boundary between 'amateur' and 'professional/commercial' in the sport sector has become 'blurred', as with the separation of non-profit and corporate governance. Overlapping roles and responsibilities can emerge in these circumstances as the dynamic of an NPSO changes. Although there are few studies of dual leadership in NPSOs, this section will highlight the key issues and challenges facing organisations that transformed from a volunteer-run body to one in which professionals deliver services led by a CEO (or person with a similar title and leadership role).

In practice, NPSOs may be governed by a small group (or coalition) rather than two individuals (chair and CEO), that usually includes senior staff – the (executive) board members – but this core group govern in a network of partnership arrangements with representatives of funders, regulatory agencies and a lead government agency, for example. However, each NPSO differs to some extent in its governance arrangements as each NPSO will vary in size, scope and resources, including the level of leadership expertise. Organisational leadership can therefore be understood in broader terms than simply two individuals in formal leadership positions. However, the board chair and CEO do set the expectations of the organisation, make the key decisions and create and communicate a 'vision' for staff and members to engage with via 'mission statements', strategic documentation and, critically, in person.

Of note for NPSOs is the importance of the relationship between the board chair, CEO and board members. Hoye and Cuskelly (2007: 144–145) highlight the leader–member exchange theory that has been utilised by researchers in exploring the dynamics of these relationships. Clearly, the quality of relationships here will in part determine organisational and individual performance. 'High-quality' exchange relationships are founded on mutual trust, reciprocity, respect and a level of obligation. However, developing successful relationships depends on three conditions being met: mutual respect for the capabilities of the other; the anticipation of deepening reciprocal trust with the other; and the expectation that obligation will mature over time as a partnership forms. Where this is the case, there tends to be positive organisational outcomes, such as:

- extended organisational commitment;
- higher morale and motivation;
- positive performance evaluations; and
- higher frequency of staff progression and lower staff turnover.

To summarise, leadership in NPSOs is critical to organisational performance (however defined).

Summary

This chapter has provided an overview of the core components of sport governance performance: the organisation, board, board member, CEO and staff, volunteer workforce and leadership. Performance can be viewed as financial performance and/or achieving 'good governance' standards or in other ways, depending on the purpose of the NPSO. Leadership can be transformational in creating a 'vision' for the NPSO and setting the tone for behaviour, decisions and actions. For an NPSO to be successful, performance has to be defined, goals and outcomes agreed on across the board and between the board and paid staff (where applicable) and across stakeholders. A method for measuring performance needs to be agreed on too. Once achieved, the CEO and/or board directors can successfully lead the organisation, its volunteers and staff. The performance of the NPSO in meeting standards set by government, as in the case of NGBs in England, is also a facet of sport governance. However, differences in relations between the non-profit sector and government (or state) across countries shapes the way in which performance is defined, implemented and assessed.

LEARNING ACTIVITIES

- Performance can be understood differently by stakeholders of an NPSO. Explain this statement.
- Identify specific ways in which sports organisations can evaluate organisational performance.
- How does professionalisation impact on sport governance? Provide examples.
- How can performance appraisal be introduced for board members and the volunteer workforce without damaging morale?
- Assume you are a board director seeking a new CEO to lead the organisation. Identify the key qualities and expertise you require from candidates.
- How can a review of governance assist in building organisational performance?
- Discuss who should define performance in or by NPSOs.
- Independent task: compare how and why understandings of performance are similar or different between two countries. Account for the relationship between the NPSO and government.

Bibliography

Berry, B.W. (1997) *Strategic Planning Workbook for Nonprofit Organizations*, revised and updated. St Paul, MN: Wilder Foundation.

Brown, W.A. (2005) Exploring the association between board and organisational performance in non-profit organisations. *Nonprofit Management and Leadership*, 15: 317–339.

Canadian Institute of Chartered Accountants (CICA) (2010a) *20 Questions Directors of Not-for-profit Organizations Should Ask about Governance*. CICA: Toronto.

Canadian Institute of Chartered Accountants (CICA) (2010b) *20 Questions Directors of Not-for-profit Organizations Should Ask about Strategy*. CICA: Toronto.

Canadian Institute of Chartered Accountants (CICA) (2010c) *20 Questions Directors Should Ask about Building a Board*. CICA: Toronto.

Coalter, F. (2004) Stuck in the blocks? A sustainable sporting legacy. In: Vigor, A., Mean, M., and Tims, C., eds, *After the Gold Rush: A Sustainable Olympics for London*. London: IPPR/Demos, pp. 93–108.

Cornforth, C. (2001) What makes boards effective? An examination of the relationships between board inputs, structures, processes and effectiveness in non-profit organisations. *Corporate Governance*, 9: 217–227.

Council of Europe (2012). *Good Governance and Ethics in Sport*. Parliamentary Assembly Committee on Culture, Science Education and Media. Strasbourg: Council of Europe.

Eadie, D. (2001) *Extraordinary Board Leadership: The Seven Keys to High-Impact Governance*. Gaithersburg, MD: Aspen Publishers.

FIFA (2009) *FIFA Code of Ethics*. Zurich: FIFA. www.fifa.com

Foster, A. (2004) *Moving On: A Review of the Need for Change in Athletics in the UK*. London: UK Sport/Sport England.

Green, M. (2009) Podium or participation? Analysing policy priorities under changing modes of sport governance in the United Kingdom. *International Journal of Sport Policy and Politics*, 1, 2: 121–144.

Green, M. and Houlihan, B. (2005) *Elite Sport Development: Policy Learning and Political Priorities*. London: Routledge.

Houlihan, B. (2009) Mechanisms of international influence on domestic elite sport policy. *International Journal of Sport Policy and Politics*, 1, 1: 51–70.

Houlihan, B. and Green, M. (2008) *Comparative Elite Sport Development: Systems, Structures and Public Policy*. Amsterdam: Butterworth-Heinemann.

Hoye, R. (2002) Leader–member exchanges and board performance of voluntary sport organizations. *Nonprofit Management and Leadership*, 15, 1: 55–70.

Hoye, R. (2006) Leadership within voluntary sport organisation boards. *Nonprofit Management and Leadership*, 16, 3: 297–313.

Hoye, R. and Cuskelly, G. (2003) Board power and performance in voluntary sport organisations. *European Sport Management Quarterly*, 3, 2: 103–119.

Hoye, R. and Cuskelly, G. (2004) Board member selection, orientation and evaluation: implications for board performance in member-benefit voluntary sports organisations. *Third Sector Review*, 10, 1: 77–100.

Hoye, R. and Cuskelly, G. (2007). *Sport Governance*. Oxford: Elsevier Butterworth-Heinemann.

ICSA (2010) Good governance: a code for the voluntary and community sector. www.governancecode.org/wp-content/uploads/2012/06/Code-of-Governance-Full1.pdf

King, N. (2014) Making the case for sport and recreation services: the utility of social return on investment (SROI) analysis. *International Journal of Public Sector Management*, 27, 2: 152–164.

National Audit Office (NAO) (2005) *UK Sport: Supporting Elite Athletes*. London: HMSO.

National Audit Office (NAO) (2008) *Preparing for Success at the London 2012 Olympic and Paralympic Games and Beyond*. London: HMSO.

Nicholson, G.J. and Kiel, G.C. (2004) Breakthrough board performance: how to harness your board's intellectual capital. *Corporate Governance*, 4: 5–23.

O'Boyle, I. (2013) Managing organizational performance in sport. In: Hassan, D. and Lusted, J., eds, *Managing Sport: Social and Cultural Perspectives*. Oxon: Routledge, pp. 1–16.

Robinson, L. (2012) Contemporary issues in the performance of sports organisations. In: Robinson, L., Chelladurai, P., Bodet, G. and Downward, P., *Routledge Handbook of Sport Management*. New York: Routledge, pp. 3–6.

Robinson, M.K. (2001) *Nonprofit Boards That Work: The End of One-Size-Fits-All Governance*. London: Wiley.

Sam, M.P. and Macris, L.I. (2014) Performance regimes in sport policy: exploring consequences, vulnerabilities and politics. *International Journal of Sport Policy and Politics*, DOI: 10.1080/19406940.2013.851103

Sport and Recreation New Zealand (2005) *Nine Steps to Effective Governance: Building High Performance Organizations*, 2nd edition: www.sportnz.org.nz/Documents/Sector Capability/Web_PDF_11.10.06.pdf

Sport England (2004) *Driving Up Participation: The Challenge for Sport*. London: Sport England.

Sport England (2005) *Whole Sport Plans: Key Performance Indicator Manual.* London: Sport England.

Sport England (2008) *Sport England's Partnership with National Governing Bodies of Sport.* www.sportengland.org/sport_englands_partnership_with_national_governing_bodies_of_sport.htm

Sport England (2011) *Good Governance Guidance.* London: Sport England.

Sport England (2013) *2013–17 Whole Sports Plan Investments.* www.sportengland.org/our-work/national-work/national-governing-bodies/sports-we-invest-in/2013–17-whole-sport-plan-investments/

Sport Wales/SRA (Sport and Recreation Alliance) (2015) *Governance and Leadership Framework for Wales: Developed by the Sector for the Sector.* Cardiff: Sport Wales.

SRA (Sport and Recreation Alliance (UK)) (2011) *Voluntary Code of Good Governance for the Sport and Recreation Sector.* www.sportandrecreation.org.uk/sites/sportandrecreation.org.uk/files/web/GovernanceCodeFINAL.PDF_.easyprint%20Version.pdf

Taylor, P. (ed.) (2011) *Torkildsen's Sport and Leisure Management,* 6th edition. London: Routledge.

Thibault, L., Slack, T. and Hinings, B. (1991) Professionalism, structures and systems: the impact of professional staff on voluntary sport organizations. *International Review for the Sociology of Sport,* 26: 83–97.

Thibault, L., Slack, T. and Hinings, B. (1993) A framework for the analysis of strategy in non-profit sport organizations. *Journal of Sport Management,* 7, 25–43.

UK Sport (2003) '*Investing in Change': High Level Review of the Modernisation Programme for Governing Bodies of Sport,* London: Deloitte and Touche.

UK Sport (2004a) *Best Practice Principles of Good Governance in Sport.* London: UK Sport.

UK Sport (2004b) *Good Governance: A Guide for National Governing Bodies of Sport.* London: Institute of Chartered Secretaries and Administrators

UK Sport (2008a) World class governance. www.uksport.gov.uk/pages/world_class_governance/

UK Sport (2008b) No compromise funding strategy. www.uksport.gov.uk/pages/no_compromise/

Winand, M., Rihoux, B. and Qualizza, D. (2011) Combinations of key determinants of performance in sport governing bodies. *Sport, Business and Management: An International Journal,* 1, 3: 234–251.

Woolf and PricewaterhouseCoopers (2012) *An Independent Governance Review of the International Cricket Council.* February.

7

GOOD GOVERNANCE

LEARNING OBJECTIVES

At the completion of this chapter, students should be able to:

- define 'good governance';
- understand why sports organisations adopt a good governance framework;
- identify and explain the key principles underpinning good governance;
- analyse the methods by which good governance measures are implemented;
- assess the extent to which sports organisations have applied good governance principles in practice;
- critically reflect on the issues and challenges, opportunities and constraints facing sports organisations seeking to achieve or maintain good governance.

Introduction

The expansion of literature focused on 'good governance' resulted from a series of high-profile failures in corporate governance from the 1980s onwards. A series of inquiries tend to follow such failures. One notable example is the 1993 *Cadbury Committee on the Financial Aspects of Corporate Governance* that recommended changes in management structures and compliance mechanisms. Subsequent inquiries across a variety of corporate bodies led to an emphasis on the rights and interests of stakeholders, and subsequent government regulatory bodies developed corporate governance standards. Given a corporate governance ethos and associated practices have gathered momentum in the sport sector, non-profit sport organisations (NPSOs) are increasingly subject to criticism regarding the governance of sport, and in some cases corruption has been cited, resulting in calls for good governance (Transparency International, 2009a, 2009b). In the UK, NGBs have also been subject to a 'modernisation programme' aimed at improving governance (see Chapter 1) as has been the case in Australia and Canada, for example. Pressure to reform has emerged, most notably in association football (soccer) from stakeholders including the sponsors, supporters, participants, local communities and many clubs, in addition to the media and government (Transparency International, 2011). Not least, pressure for change has gathered momentum from the general public. Critically, good governance in sport has gathered support at the European level too. As stated by the Council of Europe (2005),

> Good governance in sport is a complex network of policy measures and private regulations used to promote integrity in the management of the core values of sport such as democratic, ethical, efficient and accountable sports activities; and that these measures apply equally to the public administration sector of sport and to the non-governmental sports sector.

However, in comparison with a large body of literature on corporate governance in general, publications on good governance in the sport sector were relatively few in number until recently. The reasons for this include:

- pressures on organisations to adopt good governance models in the corporate sector emerged a decade or more before similar pressures surfaced in the sports sector;
- generic theories of governance (see Chapter 2) do not fully explain the complex and diverse sport sector at international, national or local levels; and
- sports organisations constitute a specific type of organisation which is not easy to classify or categorise, unlike, for example, stock-exchange-listed corporations, unlisted corporations, charities and so on. Lacking a clear categorisation, it has proved harder to describe/prescribe what is/should be 'good governance'.

Nonetheless, both practitioner-based literature including codes, guides and recommendations and a small body of academic literature have emerged as debates around 'good' and 'poor' governance in sport have become regular topics in the media. For example, since 1997 *Play the Game* has worked to raise awareness about good governance in sport, and has established a conference and a communication platform (www.playthegame.org.) Subsequently, in 2011, following the European Commission's Sports Unit call for a preparatory action in the field of the organisation of sport, momentum was gained for the study of good governance in sport. Play the Game forms partnerships with six European universities and the European Journalism Centre, and acquired EU funding for a project entitled *Action for Good Governance in International Sports Organisations* (AGGIS). Given the difficulties of implementing good governance principles, Play the Game has also developed a tool for measuring the quality of governance – the *Sports Governance Observer*.

Definition of good governance

There are many definitions of 'good governance' that are applicable to the sport sector. In this study text, the following definition captures the essence of what good governance is about from an administrative perspective, namely: 'The process by which the board: sets strategic direction and priorities, sets policies and management performance expectations, characterizes and manages risks, and monitors and evaluate organizational achievements in order to exercise its accountability to the organization and owners' (Sport New Zealand (formerly SPARC), 2004). ISCA (2013) claim that good governance is part of the 'hardware' and 'software' of sport organisations in the sense that it is manifested in the fundamental documents of a given organisation and the mechanisms and principles underpinning decisions and actions. The OECD (2004) observe that good governance should provide proper incentives for the board and management to pursue objectives that are in the interests of the organisation. However, good governance in a normative sense is associated with ethical practice, accountability to stakeholders and a transparency of decision-making, not only effectiveness and efficiency. In this sense, good governance can be viewed as political as it is defined by powerful sector organisations such as the IOC and by governments, and is not only an organic concept originating within NPSOs, especially where sanctions may be applied to NPSOs that do not meet guidelines set out in codes of practice or which behave unethically or in some cases illegally.

Good governance in sport

Sports organisations, in particular those with international reach, have traditionally been autonomous or semi-autonomous of the state or specific government intervention (Geeraert et al., 2013). As a result, these organisations are able to choose the optimal regulatory context for their operations. In Switzerland, FIFA, for example, is embedded into a legal system that gives them protection against internal and external examination. However, due to the increasing commercialisation of sport and European legislation, government bodies have sought to challenge the 'exceptionalism' of sport and its hierarchical self-governance. However, governments often grant the sports organisations special treatment (see Chapter 4 on the legal and regulatory context). Debates around good governance are therefore closely bound-up with issues of autonomy and regulation.

From the perspective of the European Union (EU), autonomy does not equate with independence from the rule of law, democracy, transparency and accountability in decision-making, and inclusiveness, in the representation of interested stakeholders (European Commission, 2011). It is only recently that a call for good governance has finally reached the traditionally closed sporting world (e.g. Council of Europe, 2012; European Commission, 2012a, 2012b; IOC, 2008; Katwala, 2000; Pieth, 2011; Sugden and Tomlinson, 1998). Attention has begun to focus on sport in the context of the increasing level of commercialisation of sport;

high-profile cases of governance failure involving corruption and bribery (Numerato *et al.*, 2013); and sport becoming subject to the more avaricious and predatory aspects of global capitalism (Andreff, 2000; Henry and Lee, 2004; Sugden, 2002). Moreover, it is claimed that sport can contribute positively to society through enhancing public health through physical activity, conveying positive values, contributing to integration and social cohesion and, not least, contributing to the economy (European Commission, 2007). Therefore a lack of good governance in the sport sector has the potential to have substantial negative repercussions. Furthermore, public perception of international sport governance and to some extent at a national level tends to focus on an inertia towards the achievement of better governance (Play the Game, 2011).

CASE EXAMPLE: A RATIONALE FOR GOVERNANCE REFORM – THE WADA REPORT INTO CORRUPTION WITHIN THE IAAF

Play the Game cites a report by WADA's independent commission that revealed extensive corruption, nepotism and abuse of power in the IAAF as well as an undermining of the anti-doping structure in the association. A previous report in 2015 had cited a need for the IAAF to ban Russian athletes from international competition. This later report in 2016 found that the IAAF management had 'covered up' knowledge of athlete doping. Therefore the corruption is viewed as 'embedded' within the organisation. Recommendations of the report include: a review of governance structures and principles; safeguards for whistle-blowers; a separation of anti-doping work from the political work of the IAAF; an investigation into athletes that were extorted; and the establishment of an independent compliance committee. Clearly, reputational damage to the governance of the IAAF has been an outcome. However, there is also an opportunity for reform that could benefit athletics and its governance.

Source: www.playthegame.org/news/news-articles/2016/0140_corruption-embedded-in-the-iaaf-second-wada-report

Inertia in regard to delivering good governance can at least in part be attributed to knowledge gaps in how to achieve good governance. The absence of codes and frameworks for implementation and assessment is one factor in this regard. Notwithstanding that good governance principles must take account of the specificity of the relevant organisation and that codes from other sectors or from corporate organisations cannot be applied without modification, a core set of principles is required for non-profit sports bodies operating at the national and local levels. Generalised good governance principles have been identified at the international level. The International Olympic Committee (IOC) created a narrative of 'good governance' via the *Basic Universal Principles of Good Governance of the Olympic and Sports Movement*. These principles were subsequently incorporated into the IOC Code of Ethics and the Olympic Charter. Further, the Council of Europe (COE, 2005) published the *Recommendation Rec on the Principles of Good Governance in Sport* that impacts on 47 countries and their national sports organisations. Adapting these principles for local-level non-profit sports bodies is the challenge facing administrators.

At the national level, in the UK, given increasing government concerns regarding governance standards in sport, arising in part from the fact that the government invests public monies into the sector, pressure has been brought to bear on NGBs and other sports bodies to produce guides for their membership. This has taken the form of the *Good Governance Guide for National Governing Bodies* (UK Sport, 2004b) and the *Voluntary Code of Good Governance for the Sport and Recreation Sector* (SRA, 2011). Of importance here is that although most non-profit sports bodies are governed with the principles of good governance in mind, implementation and assessment can be problematic, in part because members of NPSOs can be elected into the governing structures without an appropriate skill-set or experience.

Rationale for good governance

There are a number of reasons why non-profit sports bodies engage or seek to engage in good governance. The International Sport and Culture Association (ISCA, 2013) identify these reasons as:

- Strategic thinking and direction-setting are fundamental to success.
- The sport environment is complex and the demands on leaders are significant.
- Management can thrive when supported by strong governance.
- Organisations need to be accountable to their members and stakeholders.
- Organisations want to be recognised as credible by the public.
- Funding partners expect results and accountability.
- Participants in sport have high expectations of their organisation and its leaders.

Additionally, existing principles and mechanisms to deliver good governance have proved inadequate. This led to a proposal to establish a *Global Code for Governance in Sport* (Play the Game, 2011). Critically, at a time of financial austerity, government funding support has become conditional upon sports bodies delivering not only a high level of organisational performance, but a higher standard of governance. ISCA (2013) also note that good governance is a prerequisite for grass-roots sport organisations' legitimacy, autonomy and survival. In this sense, good governance centres on safeguarding an organisation's assets. Nonetheless, despite the many reasons to establish good governance principles and practices, ISCA (2013) argue that introducing a set of rules and regulations does not ensure good governance. Moreover, good governance depends on the organisational context, competencies and capacity of board members, among other factors. However, the alternative to self-administered good governance is increased external regulation and a compromised level of autonomy, which may, ISCA (2013) observe, demotivate volunteers and employees.

Principles of good governance

International institutions have developed and distributed criteria that indicate good governance for both the corporate, public and non-profit sectors at the national and international level (e.g. European Commission, 2001; OECD, 2004). Key principles include accountability, transparency, efficiency, effectiveness and prudent financial management. It is argued by organisations such as the OECD that good governance principles will become embedded in a 'democratic environment' over time. These principles have in turn been adapted to the sport sector. For example, *The Good Governance in Grassroots Sport* project (ISCA, 2013) is based on the core principles of good governance as detailed in the 2007 *White Paper on Sport* and the 2011 *Commission Communication on Sport*, namely: democracy, transparency, accountability in decision-making and inclusiveness in the representation of interested stakeholders (associations, federations, players, clubs, leagues, supporters, etc.). Representation and inclusiveness can take the form of the involvement of under-represented groups in decisions, the access of these groups to activities and the inclusion of external stakeholders in decision-making processes.

Key sports organisations have also identified good governance principles. For example, the FIA (motor sport) and EOC (European Olympic Committees) have produced a statement of good governance principles that included democracy, elections and appointments; transparency and communication; decisions and appeals; conflicts of interests; solidarity; and recognition of other interests. Beyond the UK and EU context, the Australian Sport Commission (2009) has also produced a statement on good governance principles and guidance for organisations. In sum, the core principles across corporate and non-profit sector governance are accountability, democracy, transparency and solidarity, and this applies irrespective of geography. Each of these core principles is addressed in the following sections.

Accountability

The IOC (2008) states that all sports bodies shall have adequate standards and processes for accountability and these should be consistently applied and monitored. However, in practice, levels of accountability, however defined, have been variable in the sport sector. At its simplest, mapping accountability entails identifying *who is accountable, for what, how, to whom* and *with what outcome* (Bovens, 2007; Mulgan, 2000). However, the concept of 'accountability' is difficult to define precisely. Accountability clearly involves a relationship between those who call for modifications to existing practices and those with oversight for existing practices and who are in effect 'held to account'. A distinction can be made here between accountability (providing an answer) and responsibility (liability). Accountability is perhaps best understood in relation to other components of good governance defined in this chapter, such as transparency. Houlihan (2013) adds that accountability also relates to: efficiency in the pursuit of organisational objectives; a culture of trust, honesty and professionalism; and organisational resilience.

In terms of implementing accountability, the pursuit of accountability in isolation from the history, culture and objectives of an organisation may only serve to undermine efficiency and capacity-building. However, the pursuit of efficiency in isolation might weaken trust, transparency and professionalism. Further, pursuing high levels of professionalism in isolation may impact negatively on establishing and implementing measures to support accountability. Good governance, therefore, needs to permeate all aspects of a sports organisation in order that accountability becomes embedded and normalised practice.

Consequently, achieving a level of accountability that impacts on organisational practices must involve an extended role for multiple stakeholders in decision-making as opposed to a single board or executive. In other words, formal mechanisms for checks and balances on the use of power may not be sufficient for understanding accountability. In fact, traditional understandings of accountability may constrain how organisations are held to account. Therefore, a concept of 'extended accountability' can be applied by non-profit sports bodies in order to align stakeholder interests with those of the board. Boards of non-profit sports bodies can extend accountability by:

*   establishing reporting mechanisms to enhance transparency;
*   monitoring and evaluation of actions on a regular basis;
*   including stakeholder representation on boards;
*   building trust in a two-way communication between board members and stakeholders;
*   disclosing any information pertaining to the board's understanding of accountability;
*   consulting with key partners, funders, participants and other stakeholders as part of its strategic and operational planning cycles;
*   publishing key information online: the Strategic Plan, annual reports, policy documents, programme reports, research results, evaluations and media releases;
*   reporting financial information;
*   presentation of management forecasts where applicable;
*   participation in conferences and fairs;
*   engagement with stakeholders through social media;
*   collating feedback from stakeholders on accountability; and
*   explaining confidentiality clauses.

In regard to confidentiality, an 'Access to Information Policy' for NPSOs can be based on generic principles such as those cited for the corporate sector by the World Bank (2003), namely: maximising access to information; setting out a clear list of exceptions; safeguarding the deliberative process; providing clear procedures for making information available; and recognising a 'right to appeal' process. Failing to implement these types of measures could result in stakeholders using statutory powers to challenge existing practices or calling for personnel change at board level. However, conflict can be avoided via a recognition by the board of the benefits of being accountable for the sports organisation. Benefits include:

- developing the good reputation of a sports organisation, as perceived by stakeholders including funders or sponsors;
- acquiring political support from government bodies;
- building legitimacy as a lead agency and authority in a particular sport;
- assimilating stakeholder perspectives into core objectives and practices;
- improving organisational performance; and
- enhancing learning capacity, flexibility and adaptability in an ever-changing sector context.

Therefore, accountability is important to provide a democratic means to monitor and control conduct ('the democratic perspective'); for preventing the development of concentrations of power ('the constitutional perspective'); and to enhance the learning capacity and effectiveness of administration ('the learning perspective').

To extend accountability beyond introducing or changing formal mechanisms, accountability can be viewed as three inter-related components, including: an NPSO being obligated to inform stakeholders about policy and practice; the opportunity for stakeholders to question the board regarding, for example, the adequacy of the information; and the opportunity for stakeholders to pass judgement on the conduct of the board or wider sports organisation. Extending accountability can also be manifested in the scope and content of reports or other means of disclosure. Typically, a report, where accountability has been a core concern in its construction, includes: the NPSO mission and values; governance structure and processes; sources of funding and financial data; and objectives and outcomes achieved.

In the final analysis, at the core of the concept and practice of 'extended accountability' is stakeholder engagement and involvement in the policy and delivery of objectives. Although sports organisations can deliver accountability by contract, grant or substantive terms, for accountability to become a permanent feature of an organisation, a relationship based on trust needs to be embedded. Therefore, the extent of accountability in practice can change over time, adapting itself to the organisation's evolving activities and actions and to the requirements of the stakeholders.

In moving forward, sports organisations can learn from non-governmental organisations in other sectors. Many organisations use the *International Non-Governmental Organisations Accountability Charter*. Organisations such as Amnesty International, Oxfam International and Greenpeace International recognised the need for an international, cross-sectoral code of ethics that would reflect the core values and priorities of the non-government sector. Charters produced by organisations such as these codify practices in the areas of: respect for universal principles; independence; responsible advocacy; effective programmes; non-discrimination; transparency; ethical fundraising; and professional management. At the heart of this initiative is accountability to stakeholders.

Transparency

Transparency is closely related to accountability (Hood and Heald, 2006). Transparency can be conceived as an intrinsic component of democratic, accountable organisations, and a safeguard against corruption. As accountability requires institutions to inform their members of decisions, it follows that organisations must have procedures that ensure transparency in decision-making. The central issue is therefore the extent to which NPSOs release information, which information to release and to whom. However, as Pound (2011) observes, sports organisations have been deficient with regard to transparency and many have resisted any suggestion that its governance should be transparent.

Unlike in corporate governance, where national and European Union legislation imposes disclosure requirements on public companies, such as financial reporting, many sport bodies have operated via a business model that does not necessarily meet the expectations of corporate governance by legislators. However, as both amateur and professional sport is in part resource dependent on public–sector funding, public expectations of sports organisations have changed. The growing pressure for increased transparency is also driven by the new communication technologies, i.e. the internet and social media, which allow for a greater flow of information and an increased public participation. Transparency is also an important principle in contemporary public relations, where it is often regarded as a precondition for trust, collaboration, dialogue, insight, accountability and rational governance. In fact, transparency in communication is central to organisational transparency in governance and is essential in particular for the good reputation of the NPSO among its main stakeholders.

Given this changing context, and in order to operationalise transparency in a meaningful and impactful way, sports organisations can undertake the following actions:

* Adhere to disclosure requirements, including financial reporting on an annual basis.
* Present financial statements in a clear, concise and coherent manner in order to be understood.
* Produce regular narrative accounts for stakeholders and the general public that seek to justify decisions, actions and results.
* Engage in a constructive dialogue with those who contest decisions, actions and results in addition to an open dialogue on the values of the organisation.

In terms of communicating transparency, a list of recommendations can be drawn up that apply to sports organisations. For example, publicly accessible documentation via a website can include the following:

- Basic biographical information about its board members and senior officials.
- Remuneration of its board members and senior officials on its website, if applicable.
- Contact details of board members and senior officials.
- Statutes or constitution.
- Organisational chart.
- An annual financial report.
- An annual record of activities.
- Strategic plan.
- The agenda and minutes of its statutory meetings.
- Reports of its standing committees on its website.

Achieving transparency requires that organisations build a capacity for full implementation and this may require resources, in order to become embedded practice over time. It is possible that a shift in management culture or change of leadership may be required to drive the transparency agenda in some sports bodies, implying a process of review and revision or, in other cases, a wholescale re-organisation. A push for increased transparency may fail where this capacity is absent, resulting in misinformation, information overload and unjust blaming. As an unintended consequence, a push for full transparency may result in resistance, less transparency and secrecy, and therefore progress towards full transparency (however defined) may be incremental. In short, sports organisations are required to reveal relevant information about values, decisions, processes, structures, procedures, functioning and performance. In turn, this builds confidence among stakeholders (including the public) that they are treated in a responsible and equitable manner.

Finally, apart from considering which information should or can be made publicly available, there are also considerations of (a) the completeness of information, (b) the 'colouring' of information and (c) the usability of information, including its timeliness. Another challenge when operationalising transparency is how to make information available where organisations can adopt a model of 'real-time transparency' (there is continuous surveillance by stakeholders, for example) or a model of 'retrospective transparency' (where information is released in a reporting cycle). Also of note is the frequency of communication with members on policy decisions, elections and other matters (executive, legislative, judicial, commercial) and the process of two-way communication between the board and organisational stakeholders.

Also of note in terms of transparency are principles of financial good governance. The OECD (2004: 54–56) highlight the standards required for financial good governance. This includes: the need for an independent auditor's report to the board and any stakeholders to make recommendations on cost accounting, budgeting, forecasting, power of signature, written process descriptions and any other relevant business, and the distribution of information to stakeholders concerning the organisation's finances including monies distributed to members of other organisations (Transparency International, 2011: 58). A minimum standard is expected in line with International Accounting Standards. Larger sports organisations operating within a framework of corporate governance are also expected to adhere to International Financial Reporting Standards.

Democracy

Democracy in NPSOs means the open and frequent access for members of the organisations to influence the political and strategic direction and leadership of the organisation. It entails both the equal right of members to run and vote for political leadership functions, as well as the possibility to debate and influence the key decisions of the organisation (ISCA, 2013). One of the main issues with regard to democratic processes in international non-governmental sports organisations is a lack of stakeholder participation (see Chapter 5). Indeed, due to the traditional hierarchic governance in sports, sports policy has rarely been carried out in consultation with athletes and almost never in partnership with athletes (Houlihan, 2004). This seems paradoxical, as sporting rules and regulations often have a profound impact on athletes' professional and personal lives. Moreover, hierarchic governance in sport is a major source of conflict, since those that are excluded from the decision-making process may want to challenge the federation's regulations and decisions (García, 2007; Parrish and McArdle, 2004) and failure to consult stakeholders increases the potential for rifts in sport governance (Henry and Lee, 2004).

The relation between a board/executive and members can be defined in accordance with the principal–agent model, where members bestow their sovereignty to the board and expect its executive body members to act in their best interest. Since NPSOs are membership organisations, they have a membership-based control structure which entails that the Annual General Meeting (AGM) controls the activity of the board, which they elected to oversee organisational management and to hire personnel and in which ultimate authority is vested (Hoye and Cuskelly, 2007). Democratic processes in Non-Profit Sports Organisations tend to include the following:

- There are elections of the president and the governing bodies and standing committees.
- The elections are on the basis of secret ballots and clear procedures detailed in its governing document(s).
- The organisation offers to the candidates standing for election opportunities to present their programme/manifesto.
- The decisions on allocation of major events are made through a democratic, open and transparent process.

- The organisation's major policy decisions are taken by ballot in the general assembly/congress or similar.
- The organisation defines a quorum in its governing document(s) for its decision-making bodies.
- The organisation's elected officials have a term limit.
- The organisation's general assembly meets at least once each year.
- The organisation's governing body meets regularly.
- The organisation has gender equity guidelines for its leading officials.
- The criteria for a bid for major events are communicated to its members in good time.
- The organisation provides opportunities for stakeholders to be represented within the organisation.

In considering athlete involvement in democratic processes, elements to be included are: the right of athletes to participate in sports competitions at an appropriate level should be protected; sports organisations must refrain from any discrimination; and the voice of the athletes should be heard in sports organisations.

Fairness

Fairness is commonly understood as a moral obligation regarding rule adherence, or at least as a norm pertaining to an agreed upon interpretation of the rules. NPSOs strive to maintain a fair compromise between public and private interests. In cases of scandal, conflict or crisis, organisations are expected to present their stakeholders with balanced information. An organisation's policies on information-sharing can be deemed fair if it provides equal access to all stakeholders. In practice, sports organisations may implement separate communication policies when dealing with different stakeholders. The question is whether NPSOs meet standards of fairness in treating stakeholders differently in specific circumstances.

Another facet of fairness is equity. In this regard, it can be argued that:

- resources should be distributed equitably;
- the equity in sport should be reinforced;
- the right to participate in competitions should be encouraged and secured for those at an appropriate level for the athletes concerned;
- the opportunity to organise large sports events should be open; and
- the criteria for choosing venues for events should be fair and transparent.

Gender inequality is also an issue related to the concept and practice of fairness. Equity issues in terms of positions within the organisation have been raised within a number of sports bodies with regard to gender (Henry and Lee, 2004). Consequently, there have been calls for greater diversity within the executive bodies (Council of Europe, 2012).

A further consideration related to fairness is voting procedures. Arrangements within an NPSO at the national or local level may differ from those at international level, but the principles are much the same. In FIFA, each nation represented via an association has one vote in the Congress, yet each association represents very different membership sizes. In view of the differences in size and financial support between FIFA members, a system that recognises the power and contribution of larger members while preserving some influence for relatively poorly resourced members can be problematic to establish. NPSOs therefore face the challenge of engaging those most affected by political decisions in the governance of the organisation. A sense of 'ownership' is required for members to agree to the decisions and actions of the board or CEO, for example. The extent to which members shape governance in practice is often contested, as boards are elected to lead, make key decisions and influence outcomes.

Separation of powers

The separation of powers is also a good governance practice in NPSOs. For example, the separation of power between the management of an organisation and the board entails a system of checks and balances that necessitates the implementation of internal control procedures. Indeed, a checks and balances system is paramount to prevent the 'concentration of power' that in turn may undermine the principles of good governance. Further, separating the disciplinary bodies from the political and executive arms of a sports body means that active officials are usually excluded from the disciplinary body. The separation of powers or the lack of separation has been a core issue in international sport, leading to a concentration of power and the lack of democracy in some organisations.

In principle and practice, sports bodies can structure their operations by dividing legislative, executive and judicial powers. The legislative power of making laws, the executive power of carrying them out and the judicial power of judging whether laws have been enacted are usually treated as separate. The concept of a separation of powers in the sport sector normally implies separating the disciplinary bodies from the political and executive arms of an NPSO, but regardless of which types of separation exist, there is a need to understand, disclose and communicate an explanation of why such separation of powers exist in sports bodies, and this is also good governance practice in line with corporate governance (e.g. OECD, 2004). In sum, sports organisations must weigh up organisational performance, efficiency and effectiveness with considerations of fairness, democratic processes, transparency and accountability. Conflicting negotiations and bargaining processes might be necessary until such a time that the core principles of good governance are a sustainable feature of an organisation.

Ethics in sport governance

The study of ethics as it applies to sport has gathered momentum in recent years in reaction to unethical practices in some professional sports and sports organisations (De Leon, 2003; Vanden Auweele *et al.*, 2015). At the international level, the establishment of the IOC Ethics Commission following the Salt Lake City scandal in 1999 (Mallon, 2000) set the tone for other sports organisations to establish ethics committees. Subsequently, codes of ethics have been introduced by many sports bodies, and organisations such as Transparency International (2011: 4–6) offer specific recommendations on the content of a code of ethics. As the OECD (2004: 60) note: 'An overall framework for ethical conduct goes beyond compliance with the law, which should always be a fundamental requirement.' In other words, actions may be legal but not necessarily ethical and of course the law can be open to interpretation. Issues such as conflicts of interest, receiving gifts and the difficulties of identifying and reporting unethical practices suggests that NGBs would benefit from having a code of ethics and benchmarking standards across the sector.

In establishing an Ethics Committee, the process for selecting members is critical for sports organisations in order to ensure the requisite quality and integrity of members. A key issue is the relative independence of the ethics committee membership from the board and CEO, so as to facilitate constructive criticism and enable improvements to occur. Further, an Ethics Commission should have the power to initiate investigations autonomous of board direction and offer whistle-blower protection where more serious issues arise. The employment of a member independently accountable to any organisational audit and operating outside of a 'chain of command' is a tactic used in the corporate sector that sports bodies might benefit from. NPSOs can also establish a code of ethics. It is suggested that the process of drawing up an ethics code can be valuable in itself for an NPSO, as a reflection on current practices can lead to change that benefits stakeholders and organisational reputation. In turn, reputational benefits can result in an expanding membership base and increased income. In practice, drawing up an ethics code forms part of a series of measures, which, taken together, can form good practice. Other components might include the introduction of a disciplinary code for addressing cases of unethical behaviour and, additionally, establishing a code could lead to undertaking a review of the transparency and accountability measures already in place.

An ethics or integrity code could include: conflict of interest rules; guidelines for receiving/giving gifts; rules concerning betting on its sports; an independent body to monitor the application of all these rules; recognition of the World Anti-Doping Code; integrity awareness/education programmes for its major stakeholders; and collaboration with government agencies on integrity issues.

Good governance codes

In corporate governance, a company listed on a stock exchange receives a 'Good Governance Code' from the stock exchange which explains the criteria that companies must comply with. Similar codes have emerged in recent years for the non-profit sport sector. Although the absence of a code of good governance does not necessarily mean there is 'bad governance', it does imply that the challenges of good governance have not been fully addressed to date. Typically, a code (e.g. NCVO, 2005) includes consideration of the key principles of good governance such as accountability, transparency, fairness and a separation of powers. Ethical behaviour (however defined) can become standardised and formalised in contracts and in any written expectations of behaviour by board members, officials, players or spectators, for example. Codes of good governance may also include reference to commercial rights. An example here is transparency in awarding of commercial contracts or other components of procurement. The selection process in awarding and hosting sports events can feature in a code too, ensuring that events are chosen in a transparent, rigorous and accountable manner. Both the non-profit sport sector (SRA, 2011) and government agencies (e.g. UK Sport, 2004a, 2004b) have produced guidance or specific codes of practice as a result of concerns regarding unethical practice.

In the UK, in a *Voluntary Code of Good Governance for the Sport and Recreation Sector*, the SRA (2011) identify seven principles of good governance as:

1. Integrity – acting as guardians of the sport, recreation, activity or area.
2. Defining and evaluating the role of the board.
3. Delivery of vision, mission and purpose.
4. Objectivity: balanced, inclusive and skilled board.
5. Standards, systems and controls.
6. Accountability and transparency.
7. Understanding and engaging with the sporting landscape.

Beyond the UK, many organisations have produced similar codes and toolkits for boards of NPSOs to implement (e.g. Sport and Recreation New Zealand, 2005; Vicsport, 2010). The next section assesses the scope for implementing good governance codes.

Implementation of good governance

Attempting to implement a single code across many different sports, different countries, from the local to national to international level, and across professional and amateur sport clearly presents challenges. Sports organisations must therefore adapt a generalised code to specific contexts and organisational objectives, size, resources and capacity. In addition to this, most good governance codes are implemented on a voluntary basis or on a 'comply and explain' basis where an organisation is dependent on external funding sources. Realising good governance in practice is therefore much more difficult than writing a code or agreeing principles to underpin a code. For example, the IOC's (2008) *Good Governance Principles* may not fully account for organisational capacity issues, with the outcome being few of the principles being enacted. Hence the need for a phased approach to implementation in many cases as new practices may take several years to become the 'new normal' within an organisation.

In order to implement good governance principles stated in codes of practice, sports organisations can take specific actions based on cooperation, coordination and consultation with those organisations who are stakeholders in the sport (partner agencies, funders, participants) or who have oversight for the sport (government, international body) while retaining a level of autonomy and discretion in decision-making. Inevitably, this is a 'balancing act' that requires skilled negotiation, brokering and lobbying. To achieve successful implementation of the principles, members of the board or executive body should be chosen on the basis of their ability, competence, quality, leadership capacity, integrity and experience. However, where board members have little experience in respect of delivering good governance, expertise in specific fields may need to be procured. Alternatively, where new board members are appointed to oversee implementation, candidates should have professional competency and a professional history. Further, the selection process should be based on objective criteria that are set out clearly to candidates.

As a first step towards the effective implementation of good governance, the following steps can be taken:

- Present good governance as a focus area at a board meeting and discuss how it may benefit the organisation.
- Present a self-assessment tool and encourage board members to commit to the undertaking of a self-assessment process.
- Deliver a good governance workshop for the board.
- Discuss the results (scoring), differences, challenges and solutions.
- Feed the results into a good governance 'framework' (agreed principles and practices) that the board can agree to.
- Allocate roles and responsibilities for implementation.

In establishing and developing a framework for implementation, a code of ethics needs to be at the core. For example, based on IOC documentation, sports organisations can: develop, adapt and implement ethical principles and rules; follow ethical rules which should refer to and be inspired by the IOC code of ethics; and monitor the implementation of ethical principles and rules.

Another important component in the implementation of good governance is the power of signature. In this respect:

- Good governance implies proper financial monitoring.
- In order to avoid any abuse of powers of representation (in particular signing), adequate rules should be set up, approved and monitored at the highest level.

- Precise, clear and transparent regulations should be established and applied, and effective controlling systems and checks and balances should be put in place.
- As a general rule, individual signature should be avoided for binding obligations of an organisation.

With a code of ethics and power of signature in place, the next consideration is internal management, communication and coordination. Here,

- Good internal communication reinforces the efficiency of sporting organisations.
- Good information flow inside sporting organisations ensures good understanding by membership of activities undertaken and allows managers to make timely and informed decisions.
- Good working conditions and atmosphere, as well as motivation and incentive policies, are essential for the smooth functioning of the organisation.

A further component of implementation is risk management, where a clear and adequate risk-management process should be put in place. This could include: identification of potential risks for the sports organisations; evaluation of risks; control of risks; monitoring of risks; and disclosure via transparency.

The successful implementation of good governance may therefore necessitate a fundamental review or audit of the rationale, organisational structures and capacity to deliver principles in practice. Two key challenges therefore face non-profit sports bodies in the UK today, namely building capacity for good governance and building compliance (see Chapter 8) among stakeholders in order to realise goals that at first may appear aspirational rather than feasible. Building capacity for good governance in NPSOs implies that organisations identify their key challenges in the overall management of their organisations inside the broad definition and principles of good governance. This requires stakeholders to exchange and learn from each other. The method to do so is primarily the identification and valorisation of organisational 'good practices'. Also required is the board's acknowledgement that good governance is fundamental to strategic and organisational management decisions. Finally, successful implementation requires compliance with good governance principles and practices (see Chapter 8).

CASE EXAMPLE: COMPLIANCE WITH GOOD GOVERNANCE PRINCIPLES – IOC OLYMPIC AGENDA 2020

Recommendation 27 of the IOC Olympic Agenda concerns compliance with basic principles of good governance. This recommendation states that all organisations that belong to the Olympic Movement must comply with the *Universal Principles of Good Governance* of the Olympic and Sports Movement.

Compliance is to be monitored and evaluated by the IOC, who offer supporting tools to encourage compliance and build organisational capacity. Sports organisations within the IOC 'family' are responsible for managing a self-evaluation process, with the IOC overseeing outcomes. Therefore sports bodies must report on their progress and the IOC can request evidence of evaluation. Recommendation 29 specifically insists on transparency in financial statements that are audited according to International Financial Reporting Standards (IFRS), as with corporate bodies, even though these standards are not legally required from the IOC. Other actions relating to compliance include a recommendation to strengthen the ethical framework of the IOC itself. Specifically, the IOC Ethics Commission created a *Code of Ethics* aligned with the *Olympic Agenda 2020* agenda that centres on transparency, good governance and accountability.

Benefits of good governance

There are a number of benefits for sports organisations adopting good governance principles and practices. Critically, the implementation of good governance principles should assist sports organisations to fulfil their objectives more effectively. Second, given that stakeholders and the general public, via media outputs, for example, have a general perception that the sports sector as a whole has poor governance (Play the Game, 2011), implementation should help to counteract this negative perception. Third, implementation can help justify calls for increased autonomy where funders consider good governance a minimum *quid pro quo*, both at the European level (European Commission, 2011a, 2011b) and national level (see Chapter 1 in regard to the modernisation of the UK sport sector). Fourth, and related to the other points raised here, adopting good governance also builds reputation that in turn may attract participants, membership, funding and political support. However, the benefits of implementation may not be tangible in the short term, especially where sports bodies have been subject to criticism regarding failure to operate within an ethical framework or, occasionally, a legal framework. Resistance to change can also be anticipated in some sports organisations and skilled management practices will be required to build good governance. As observed by Play the Game (2011) in the document *Action for Good Governance in Sport*, achieving better governance in sport requires NPSOs to revise their internal and external mechanisms to cope with the ongoing commercialisation, professionalisation and globalisation of sport.

In theory at least, implementing good governance can be approached in stages. An ideal model of implementation would consist of the following:

- Circumstances external to the sports organisation do not impose significant constraints on change to working practices.

- There is a single implementing body responsible for delivering good governance with the consensus of partner agencies.
- There is complete understanding of, and agreement upon, the objectives to be achieved by all stakeholders.
- The relationship between good governance principles and practices is coherent, concise and clear to all stakeholders.
- Adequate time and sufficient resources are available to the sports organisation.
- At each stage in the implementation process (however designed), the required combination of resources is accessible.
- Dependency on external resources is minimal and/or autonomy and self-determination is high.
- In moving towards agreed objectives it is possible to specify, in complete detail, the tasks to be performed by each participant.
- There is effective communication among, and coordination of, the various elements or agencies involved in the programme.
- The outcomes and impact of any changes to existing practices can be assessed and understood by stakeholders.
- Learning capacity is enhanced and further modifications to practices do not pose a significant challenge or extensive additional resourcing.

In practice, however, sports organisations are unlikely to establish or develop good governance practices in isolation from the wider economic, political and socio-cultural context in which each organisation operates. Therefore, skilled practitioners are needed to traverse a complex sector characterised by multiple agencies pursuing similar or differing agendas across the public, non-profit and corporate sectors.

Evaluating good governance

It is more difficult for sports organisations than corporations to set and measure objectives, since NPSOs have both general and abstract objectives. A corporate (private) enterprise embodies a central objective of generating and maximising profit which can be quantified and benchmarked against all other corporations in similar markets. In the sport sector, there can be disagreement on core principles, definitions and mutual benefits, voluntary codes are unclear or ambiguous, and organisational objectives are wide-ranging. Further, tools for assessment are not standardised and their relative merits are disputed. Moreover, there is little history of measuring 'best practice' for good governance and the skills or incentives to do so cannot always be evidenced. Nonetheless, self-assessment tools have recently become a fixture of good governance. The *AGGIS Sports Governance Observer* provides a means to these ends. In particular, the tool is comprised of four dimensions, which are all of paramount importance in relation to good governance (see www.goodgovsport.eu/selfassessmenttool).

Effective measures of good governance in sport need to be founded on:

• democratic structures based on clear and regular electoral procedures open to the whole membership;
• organisation and management of a professional standard based on a code of ethics and procedures for dealing with conflicts of interest;
• accountability and transparency in decision-making and financial operations, including the publication and auditing of yearly financial accounts; and
• fairness in dealing with membership, including gender equality and solidarity.

(Council of Europe, 2005)

In sum, if there is an ambition to define 'good' practices, there is also a requirement to establish parameters towards which practices can be measured or evaluated. Due to the non-binding nature of good governance principles and because good governance principles have to be implemented on a 'good will basis', and adapted to each organisation, NPSOs need to assess their decisions and actions on a regular basis. Sharing the outcome of assessment with all stakeholders will in turn safeguard the organisation's legitimacy and sustainability.

Summary

This chapter has addressed the principles and practice of good governance. This required that 'good governance' be defined and explained. The concern of the chapter was to highlight how good governance can be implemented and assessed by NPSOs in order to benefit a sports organisation. More critically, this chapter problematised the challenge facing NPSOs in delivering good governance in a complex political and administrative context.

LEARNING ACTIVITIES

• Why was a reform of the governance of sport necessary?
• In fewer than 100 words, define 'good governance'.
• Implementing good governance presents challenges for NGBs and clubs. Identify those challenges and suggest potential solutions.
• How can good governance be assessed?
• With reference to an NGB of your choice, explain how the principles of good governance have been applied or are being applied.
• Who is accountable, for what, to whom, for whom, by what means and with what expected outcome?
• How much accountability is required to maintain and demonstrate integrity without impairing organisational efficiency?
• How do we avoid accountability being seen solely as adversarial and a punishment?

- How do we make accountability processes a set of activities that NGBs and clubs want to be involved in?
- How do we design an accountability system that does not simply encourage 'blame avoidance', but rather as a positive and welcome management resource?
- Identify three reasons why accountability is important for sports organisations.
- How can accountability be defined? Provide examples.
- Make a list of recommendations you would offer to a sports organisation regarding the implementation of accountability principles.
- What do we mean by transparency?
- What are the aims of increased transparency?
- Identify the actions a sports organisation might take to improve transparency.
- Review a number of NGB websites to determine the current level of transparency. In a group, decide what should be transparent and what does not need to be.
- With reference to Persson (2013), assess the key challenges facing NPSOs in Scandinavia.
- With reference to Dorsey (2016) assess the key issues impacting on good governance in the Middle East.

Bibliography

Agere, S. (2000) *Promoting Good Governance: Principles, Practices and Perspectives*. London: Commonwealth Secretariat.

Aguilera, R.V. and Cuervo-Cazurra, A. (2009). Codes of good governance. *Corporate Governance: An International Review*, 17, 3: 376–387.

Andreff, W. (2000) Financing modern sport in the face of a sporting ethic. *European Journal for Sport Management*, 7: 5–30.

Arnaut, J.L. (2006) *Independent European Sport Review*. www.independentfootballreview. com/doc/A3619.pdf

Australian Sport Commission (2009) *Governance Principles: A Good Practice Guide*. www. goodgovsport.eu/files/GGGS_WEB/Files/3_Governance_principles_-_a_good_ practice_guide.pdf

Babiak, K. (2010). The role and relevance of corporate social responsibility in sport: a view from the top. *Journal of Management & Organization*, 16, 4: 528–549.

Babiak, K. and Wolfe, R. (2009) Determinants of corporate social responsibility in professional sport: internal and external factors. *Journal of Sport Management*, 23: 717–742.

Bovens, M. (2007). Analysing and assessing accountability: a conceptual framework. *European Law Journal*, 13, 4: 447–468.

Burger, S. and Goslin, A.E. (2005) Best practice governance principles in the sports industry: an overview. *South African Journal for Research in Sport, PE and Recreation*, 27, 2: 1–14.

Chaker, A.N. (2004) *Good Governance in Sport: A European Survey*. Strasbourg: Council of Europe.

Charity Commission (2010) Initiative of several English organisations, *Good governance – A code for the voluntary and community sector*. www.charitycommission.gov.uk/index.aspx

Council of Europe (2005) *Recommendation Rec (2005)8 of the Committee of Ministers to Member States on the Principles of Good governance in Sport*. https://wcd.coe.int/ViewDoc.jsp?id=850189&Site=CM

Council of Europe (2012) *Good Governance and Ethics in Sport*. Parliamentary Assembly Committee on Culture, Science Education and Media. Strasbourg: Council of Europe.

De Leon, L. (2003), On acting responsibly in a disorderly world: individual ethics and administrative responsibility. In: Peters, B.G. and Pierre, J., eds, *Handbook of Public Administration*. London: Sage, pp. 569–580.

Dorsey, J. (2013) *A Decade of Defiance and Dissent: A Wake-up Call for Sports*. Singapore: RSIS.

Dorsey, J.M. (2016) The Middle East. In: O'Boyle, I. and Bradbury, T., eds, *Sport Governance: International Case Studies*. London: Routledge, pp. 156–166.

European Commission (2001) *Promoting a European Framework for Corporate Social Responsibility*. Green Paper COM (2001) 366 final.

European Commission (2007). *The EU and Sport: Background and Context, Accompanying Document to the White Paper on Sport*. SEC(2007) 935 final.

European Commission (2011a). *Developing the European Dimension in Sport*, COM (2011) 12 final, January. http://eurlex. europa.eu/LexUriServ/LexUriServ.do?uri=COM:2011: 0012:FIN:en:PDF

European Commission (2011b), Expert Group 'Good Governance', Report from the 1st meeting (6 December 2011). http://ec.europa.eu/sport/library/documents/b24/xg-gg-20111206-final-rpt.pdf

European Commission (2012a) Expert Group 'Good Governance', Report from the 2nd meeting (13 March 2012). http://ec.europa.eu/sport/library/documents/b24/xg-gg-201203-final-rpt.pdf

European Commission (2012b) Expert Group 'Good Governance', Report from the 3rd meeting (5–6 June 2012). http://ec.europa.eu/sport/library/documents/b24/xg-gg-201206-final-rpt.pdf

Geeraert, A., Alm, J. and Groll, M. (2013) Good governance in international sport organizations: an analysis of the 35 Olympic sport governing bodies. *International Journal of Sport Policy and Politics*, 6, 3: 281–306.

Henry, I.P. and Lee, P.C. (2004) Governance and ethics in sport. In: Chadwick, S. and Beech, J., eds, *The Business of Sport Management*. Harlow: Pearson Education.

Hindley, D. (2003) Good governance: an ethical approach to sport? In: *31st Annual Meeting of the International Association for the Philosophy of Sport*, Centre for Ethics, Equity and Sport at the University of Gloucestershire, Cheltenham, 18–21 September.

Hood, C. and Heald, D. (2006) *Transparency: The Key to Better Governance?* Oxford: Oxford University Press.

Houlihan, B. (2004). Civil rights, doping control and the world anti-doping code. *Sport in Society*, 7: 420–437.

Houlihan, B. (2013) Accountability and good governance. In: Play the Game, *Action for Good Governance in International Sports Organisations*. Copenhagen: Play the Game, pp. 22–24.

Hoye, R. and Cuskelly, G. (2007). *Sport Governance*. Oxford: Elsevier Butterworth-Heinemann.

International Olympic Committee (2008) *Basic Universal Principles of Good Governance of the Olympic and Sports Movement*. Lausanne: IOC. www.olympic.org/Documents/ Conferences_Forums_and_Events/2008_seminar_autonomy/Basic_Universal_ Principles_of_Good_Governance.pdf

International Olympic Committee (2009) *Codes of Ethics and Other Texts*. Lausanne: IOC.

International Olympic Committee (2011) *Olympic Charter*. IOC: Lausanne, July 2011. www.olympic.org/Documents/olympic_charter_en.pdf

International Sport and Culture Association (ISCA) (2013) *Guidelines for Good Governance in Grassroots Sport*. Copenhagen: ISCA.

Katwala, S. (2000) *Democratising Global Sport*. London: The Foreign Policy Centre.

King, N. (2014) Questionable ethics: good governance or terminal decline for FIFA. In *Governance and Compliance*. London: ICSA.

MacAloona, John J. (2011) Scandal and governance: inside and outside the IOC 2000 Commission. *Sport in Society: Cultures, Commerce, Media, Politics*, 14, 3: 292–308.

Mallon, B. (2000) The Olympic bribery scandal. *Journal of Olympic History*, May: 11–27.

Mulgan, R. (2000), 'Accountability': an ever-expanding concept?' *Public Administration*, 78, 3: 555–573.

National Council for Voluntary Organisations (NVCO) (2005) *Good Governance: A Code for the Voluntary and Community Sector*. London: NVCO.

Numerato, D., Baglioni, S. and Persson, H.T.R. (2013) The dark sides of sport governance. In: Hassan, D. and Lusted, J., eds, *Managing Sport: Social and Cultural Perspectives*. London: Routledge, pp. 284–300.

Oliver, R.W. (2004) *What is Transparency?* New York: McGraw-Hill.

Organisation for Economic Co-operation and Development (OECD) (2004). *Principles of Corporate Governance*. Paris: OECD.

Parrish, R. and McArdle, D. (2004) Beyond *Bosman*: the European Union's influence upon professional athletes' freedom of movement. *Sport in Society*, 7, 3: 403–418.

Persson, H.T.R. (2013) Scandinavia. In: O'Boyle, I. and Bradbury, T., eds, *Sport Governance: International Case Studies*. London: Routledge, pp. 167–183.

Pieth, M. (2011) Governing FIFA. Concept paper and report, Universität Basel.

Play the Game (2011). Cologne Consensus: towards a global code for governance in sport. End statement of the conference, Play the Game conference, Cologne, 6 October.

Pound, R. (2011) Responses to corruption in sport. Presentation to Play the Game Conference, 3 October.

Salcines, J.L.P., Babiak, K. and Walters, G. (2013) *Routledge Handbook of Sport and Corporate Social Responsibility*. London: Routledge.

Sawyer, T.H., Bodey, K. and Judge, L. (2007). *Sport Governance and Policy Development: An Ethical Approach to Managing Sport in the 21st Century*. Champaign, IL: Sagamore Publishing.

Smith, A.C.T. and Westerbeek, H.M. (2007) Sport as a vehicle for deploying corporate social responsibility. *Journal of Corporate Citizenship*, 25: 43–54.

SPARC (Sport and Recreation New Zealand) (2004) *Nine Steps to Effective Governance: Building High Performing Organisations*. Wellington, NZ: SPARC.

Sport and Recreation New Zealand (2005) *Nine Steps to Effective Governance: Building High Performance Organizations*, 2nd edition. www.sportnz.org.nz/Documents/Sector Capability/Web_PDF_11.10.06.pdf

Sport England (2011) *Good Governance Guidance*. London: Sport England.

SRA (UK) (2011) *Voluntary Code of Good Governance for the Sport and Recreation Sector*. London: SRA.

Sugden, J. (2002) Network football. In: Sugden, J. and Tomlinson, A., eds., *Power Games*. London: Routledge, pp. 61–80.

Sugden, J. and Tomlinson, A. (1998). *FIFA and the Contest for World Football: Who Rules the People's Game?* Cambridge: Polity Press.

Transparency International (2009a) *Business Principles for Countering Bribery: A Multi-Stakeholder Initiative led by Transparency International*. Berlin: Transparency International.

Transparency International (2009b) *Corruption and Sport: Building Integrity and Preventing Abuses*. Berlin: Transparency International.

Transparency International (2011) *Safe Hands: Building Integrity and Transparency at FIFA*. Berlin: Transparency International.

UK Sport (2004a) *Best Practice Principles of Good Governance in Sport*. London: UK Sport.

UK Sport (2004b) *Good Governance: A Guide for National Governing Bodies of Sport*. London: Institute of Chartered Secretaries and Administrators.

Vanden Auweele, Y., Cook, E. and Parry, J., eds (2015) *Ethics and Governance in Sport: The Future of Sport Imagined*. London: Routledge.

Vicsport (2010) *Good Governance Tool Kit*. www.vicsport.asn.au/Assets/Files/FINAL_Good_Governance_ToolKit_Update.pdf

Walters, G., Trenberth, L. and Tacon, R. (2010) *Good Governance in Sport: A Survey of UK National Governing Bodies of Sport*. London: Birbeck University.

World Bank (2003). *Toolkit: Developing Corporate Governance Codes of Best Practice*. Washington, DC: World Bank.

8

COMPLIANCE IN SPORT GOVERNANCE

LEARNING OBJECTIVES

At the completion of this chapter, students should be able to:

- identify the causes of non-compliance with the regulatory framework for sport governance;
- analyse the approaches and methods employed to encourage or enforce compliance;
- evaluate the extent to which sports organisations comply with guidance relating to best practice and good governance.

Introduction

Non-profit sport organisations (NPSOs) seek compliance from stakeholders and are themselves required to comply with legislation and a raft of regulation, policy guidance and codes of practice. Hence, compliance is not unidirectional. More specifically, on the one hand, NGB boards seek to gain compliance from county or regional bodies and local-level clubs, and these organisations in turn seek compliance from members and other stakeholders in achieving their own objectives. On the other hand, *Whole Sport Plans* have required national governing bodies (NGBs) in the UK to meet specific criteria in order to access funding (see Chapter 1). However, it is important to differentiate between policy and legal compliance, where the former relates to the question of how extensively the normative standards are being met through implementation, while the latter usually relates to the question of the formal compliance with agreements. For example, 'good

LIVERPOOL JOHN MOORES UNIVERSITY
LEARNING SERVICES

governance' is largely dependent on NPSOs self-administering changes in line with good practice codes or guides. This differs from NPSOs complying with the law (see Chapter 4).

This chapter primarily focuses on the compliance of NPSOs with regulatory requirements and good governance guidelines or codes of practice. The causes of non-compliance and the methods that can be employed to encourage compliance are foregrounded. This chapter also considers the compliance of sports organisations operating at the international level through a series of case examples. Parallels can be drawn between the local, county, regional, national and international levels, where compliance issues and standards suggest that sports organisations face some similar challenges despite differences in scale, size and resources. For NPSOs, it is not always clear whether complying or not complying with plans to reform the sport sector provides any significant relative advantage or whether the costs associated with compliance are too high. Nonetheless, the 'modernisation' of the sport sector has in practice impacted on the governance of sport to varying degrees across sports and across countries.

Compliance with legislation

A raft of legislation (see Chapter 4) requires compliance by NPSOs from the Bribery Act to the Equalities Act to safeguarding and health and safety legislation, for example. This short section takes the example of the *Companies Act* as its reference point. Although legal status differs in the non-profit sport sector, where an NPSO is registered as a company, the Sport and Recreation Alliance (SRA) cite areas of the Companies Act (2006) that can impact on NPSOs. These are listed as:

- setting out in statute directors' duties;
- allowing companies to indemnify directors;
- confidentiality of directors' home addresses;
- shareholder rights including setting out in statute the right to bring a claim on behalf of the company in certain circumstances;
- raising share capital and takeovers;
- auditor liability and offences;
- company formation and administration including the responsibilities of Companies House and greater use of electronic reporting and filing;
- political donations;
- corporate governance rules implementing EU directives; and
- new rules to allow company law to be updated more regularly.

As with many pieces of legislation, designed in reference to the corporate sector, the Companies Act was not designed with NPSOs in mind and therefore in 2010 the SRA adapted *Articles of Association for NGBs*, for example. Again, this is an example of how corporate governance has influenced non-profit sector governance. This chapter, however, focuses on compliance of NPSOs with the regulatory context rather than legislation. Given self-regulation has been a feature of the non-profit sport sector, and NPSOs have a level of autonomy from government, the chapter commences with consideration of non-compliance with regulation, policy guidance and codes of practice.

Causes of non-compliance with regulation

The causes of non-compliance can be many and variable in nature. Non-compliance may be a choice on the part of an organisation or board member, where there is no intent to comply, or a matter of capacity, where the intent is to comply, with a code of practice for example, but the NPSO cannot implement guidelines given existing resources, including the level of staff and/or volunteer expertise. An NPSO may lack the necessary financial or administrative resources to enact compliance, or there may be a lack of expertise at board level, or a poor understanding of codes of practice, policy guidelines or legal requirements. Further, measuring the extent to which NPSOs are achieving compliance criteria can be difficult without the necessary expertise, and employing external consultants to undertake an assessment can be expensive for organisations with limited resources. However, in regard to choice, resources needed for compliance may be knowingly diverted elsewhere or obligations evaded. In practice, the benefits of compliance may have low organisational salience or there is simply no history or culture of working within parameters set by external agencies. Also, organisations can choose a 'free-rider' strategy, where benefits are acquired from the compliance of others, but costs are avoided. Any or all of these reasons can result in partial or selective compliance.

When considering whether conditional funding, monitoring and sanctions are the optimal instruments for ensuring compliance, the reasons for non-compliance need to be assessed. In other words, non-compliance may be due to factors beyond the scope of sanctions. A focus on building the capacity of NPSOs to implement actions in line with codes of practice, for example, would therefore more likely result in compliance with guidelines or targets, with sanctions used sparingly and only in those cases where 'good governance' is evaded. Alongside building capacity, the board of NPSOs must be convinced that the benefits of compliance with good governance guidelines outweigh any vested interest in preserving the status quo.

Approaches to achieving compliance

The academic literature on the subject of compliance starts by identifying two assumptions at opposite ends of a spectrum. At one end is the assumption that organisations must be coerced into change and as a result sanctions can legitimately be applied to ensure compliance. At the other end of the spectrum, the focus is on systems design, where the assumption is that non-compliance is usually the result of ambiguity and resource limitations rather than choice (Chayes and Chayes, 1995; Chayes et al., 1998). Therefore, 'coercive enforcement is as misguided as it is costly' (Chayes and Chayes, 1995: 22). In other words, coercive enforcement can result in conformity (or partial conformity) for a period of time, but it cannot result in willing compliance, especially if the level of autonomy is high, such as in the non-profit sport sector. As a result, 'non-compliance is best addressed through a problem solving strategy of capacity building, rule interpretation, and transparency, rather than through coercive enforcement' (Tallberg, 2002: 613).

Compliance can also depend on the degree to which NPSOs are expected to change and what aspect of their work needs to change in order to meet compliance criteria. In other words, some changes will not require any significant modification to governance practices, attitudes or the culture of an organisation. Administrative changes are relatively simple to implement, such as the frequency of elections, maximum length of terms of office, the reporting of meetings, publication of financial data and so on. However, making modifications to the culture of an organisation would clearly require a longer time period and possibly a re-organisation and re-direction of the organisation and/or new board members.

Organisations often rely on a limited range of instruments to achieve compliance, such as inducements, information and sanctions. Inducements and information include educational efforts and financial transfers that may induce compliance. Sanctions may be applied where these approaches are ineffective. In practice, inducements, education and sanctions tend to be used in response to perceived problems in the sport sector, such as inequity, falling participation and declining relative performance standards. A more pro-active and pre-emptive approach places the emphasis on the design of the compliance system. Acquiring and embedding effective and sustainable agreements between government agencies and NPSOs and agreements between NPSOs and their stakeholders therefore require a mix of methods to achieve compliance that recognise NPSO modes of governance (historically and today) and future planning.

However, NPSO boards seeking compliance from members, for example, need to be aware of the many methods of non-compliance. Oliver (1991) developed a typology of responses to pressures requiring compliance. Organisations such as NPSOs have the option to:

- conform or acquiesce;
- compromise;
- comply symbolically, but in practice conceal non-compliance, such as by minimising scrutiny;
- engage in active resistance; and
- attempt to manipulate the pressures being applied.

In practice, NPSOs can choose to enact a strategy of non-engagement with the compliance measures; retrenchment; the establishment of parallel structures or organisations that bypass the authority of those seeking compliance; and/or acquire new resources to increase autonomy and/or reduce resource dependencies. Given the difficulties to acquiring a level of compliance, the next section investigates the specific strategies and tactics that could be employed by sports organisations.

Strategies and tactics for achieving compliance

This section identifies a range of strategies and tactics that NPSOs can utilise in order to encourage compliance with organisational objectives and codes of practice. It also considers ways in which NPSOs may be required to comply by external agency objectives and codes of practice.

In terms of achieving good governance, methods for ensuring compliance include extending transparency, moral disapproval and positive leadership behaviour. First, the introduction of an agenda to increase transparency in decision-making by NPSOs is related to a perceived and actual lack of accountability in international sport (see Chapter 7). Compliance with regulation or guidance is more readily achieved in 'transparent organisations', it can be claimed. For example, if the majority of NPSOs are making transparent their policies, strategy, modes of governance, financial data and the identity of board members, for example, then those organisations not complying with a shift towards greater transparency will need to justify why specific information should not be made visible to stakeholders and other organisations. Hence the 'comply or explain' methodology used by regulators and funding agencies. There may be legitimate reasons for the confidentiality of data and an anonymity of personnel, but this in itself can be made transparent to ensure accountability to stakeholders.

Second, moral disapproval may be considered by regulators of NPSOs or the sports organisation itself. The sport sector embodies rules, norms and values such as fair play and respect, and therefore there is a general disapproval of 'cheating'. Off the field of play, organisations are expected to be accountable to players, spectators and other stakeholders. Where this is not the case, moral disapproval can follow, marginalising the organisation that does not conform. Compliance with a code of practice, for example, in part relies on a consensus in the sport sector that 'good governance' should at least be an aspiration where it is not already a norm. In terms of moral disapproval, sports organisations may also comply due to external pressure and the fear of reputational damage (Wymeersch, 2006). Third, positive leadership behaviour is a strategy where code compliance is ensured by board members and management, who take responsibility for applying the code, under the overall guidance of members and stakeholders. In this approach, an 'ethical tone' must be set by key personnel (Bonn and Fisher, 2005). This tone tends to emanate from the moral values of an organisation's culture (Wieland 2005).

A second approach to ensuring compliance is via extending the level of scrutiny of a sport or specific organisation. This can be achieved via external monitoring and assessment or an internal audit. In terms of external scrutiny, in general the extent of compliance is positively associated with the size and resources of a sports organisation. This is because larger organisations, especially those that operate a business model with commercial sponsors, for example, and paid directors, tend to attract more attention from regulatory bodies and may be more closely scrutinised by the media. Although greater scrutiny does not necessarily result in a high level of compliance with codes of practice, the likelihood of such an outcome increases over time. Nonetheless, the non-profit sector for sport is not highly regulated and therefore extending scrutiny may not be an effective tool for achieving compliance unless it is combined with other strategies and tactics. The trend, however, is towards increasing regulation as a component of the wider 'modernisation' agenda, at least in some nation states.

Where limited regulation remains, self-assurance and on-site audit is an option to increase compliance. In England, core-funded NGBs are required by Sport England to complete a self-assurance assessment that is intended to be a valuable tool in developing the capacity of NGBs to improve their governance. This provides Sport England with an indication of whether the NGB can manage public funds. The self-assurance assessment is then reviewed by independent auditors followed by a report to Sport England and the NGB. In the 2013–2017 funding cycle, there is an expectation that NGBs meet specific standards in relation to equality, diversity, safeguarding and anti-doping. NGBs are expected to demonstrate continuous improvement in all matters concerning governance. This can be evidenced via an in-depth on-site review of practice. The government agency can then advise on areas for governance change. This advice tends to relate to components of management and administration, such as: organisational policy; strategic planning; financial management; human resource management; and risk management. It can be noted that failing to meet recommendations or conditions can result in the loss of funding support.

Further, compliance can be more readily achieved where there are 'realistic contents' and relatively low compliance costs. Code compliance is clearly more likely to be achieved where the internal norms and values of an NPSO do not deviate too much from the code to be adopted. Given the limited scope of regulation in the sport sector, code compliance becomes a matter of negotiation between a government agency and an NGB, for example, or in the case of the *Voluntary Code of Good Governance for the Sport and Recreation Sector*, between the SRA (2011) and its members. Across a range of organisations, internal norms and values will differ, resulting in differing degrees of compliance. If the costs of making changes in order to comply are relatively low for an NPSO, then compliance is more likely. Therefore, there is a positive relationship between organisational resources and compliance costs. In the sport sector, many changes can be made towards good governance without incurring significant costs that might impact negatively on an NPSO.

Finally, as a strategy to acquire or extend compliance, an emphasis can be placed by regulators on 'inside–outside interaction'. Here, the NPSO board is critical in establishing compliance both within the organisation and with the demands or expectations of external stakeholders, funders and regulators. It is this interaction between organisations that is a condition for the effectiveness of governance codes. Therefore, the interaction between an NGB and its stakeholders or government agencies shapes the level of compliance with a code of practice, for example. At the hub of this interaction is the board chair and/or CEO, who is responsible for stimulating the adoption of and compliance with governance codes (Aguilera and

Cuervo-Cazurra, 2009). 'Inside–outside interaction' centres on the relationships between organisations within networks governing sport. Therefore, compliance becomes a matter of negotiation that may take varying levels of resources to achieve. There is always the danger that codes of practice become too vague, post-negotiation, for implementation to be practicable or meaningful. Moreover, recommendations for change originating from negotiation can be avoided or evaded, whereas 'conditions' generally cannot. Therefore, achieving code compliance requires a negotiation between stakeholders to enhance ownership across stakeholders to underpin a mutually beneficial outcome.

Additionally, financial compliance testing has become a feature of the relationship between government agencies and NPSOs. In the period 2013–2017, for example, Sport England is reviewing funding streams as part of the audit and assurance programme, not only funds acquired by NGBs, but also funds acquired through a grant where NGBs support clubs. In effect, the whole funding process in the non-profit sector is subject to review. In the case of NPSOs not complying with recommended changes to governance, a 'tailored' assurance review or a special investigation may be commissioned. This usually involves a more in-depth audit of specific aspects of governance. In some cases, arbitration may be necessary. In regard to arbitration in the sport sector, an independent body can mediate disputes between an NPSO and a government agency, for example.

CASE EXAMPLE: COMPLIANCE AND CHANGE IN NGBS

Over the 2009–2013 funding period, Sport England investment in NGBs was closely linked to sport-related outcomes and change in NPSO governance, finance and control frameworks. During the 2009–2013 funding period, NGBs were given time to develop their governance frameworks with support from Sport England within a self-assurance and on-site audit process and relationship management activities. Subsequently, for the 2013–2017 funding period, a number of key criteria for effective governance were identified and set. NGBs were required to devise and implement an action plan with targets aligned to timelines. Further, this governance arrangement was established by NGB boards and Sport England through negotiation. The idea for 2013–2017 is to build upon the minimum standards set in the previous four years. NGBs are required to disseminate new governance standards through their structures from county board or regional board level (depending on how the sport is organised) to local club level. The reform of sport governance (see Chapter 1) therefore consists of a significant re-organisation of the sector using a number of tools to encourage compliance from conditional funding arrangements to target-setting to monitoring and a re-negotiation of priorities.

Monitoring and evaluating compliance

In order to ensure sports organisations comply with codes of practice, decisions and actions can be monitored and evaluated. Data gathered through a monitoring process can be the foundation on which to establish governance change. Monitoring performs four major functions: accounting, auditing, explanation and compliance (Dunn, 2004: 355–356). In the case of compliance, monitoring helps to determine whether the processes, activities, resources and staff or volunteers are in compliance with standards and procedures featured in a code of practice, or in compliance with organisational objectives, for example.

Within an NPSO, board members can monitor legal compliance through a five-stage process:

1. Identify the offences to which the organisation and its members are exposed.
2. Determine how the organisation could breach the law and the likelihood of this occurring.
3. Design a programme to eliminate the risk of breaches.
4. Ensure that the programme guidelines are implemented.
5. Monitor compliance with a programme.

All of these strategies and tactics have formed a core element of the reform of the non-profit sport sector in recent years. Governance change in the UK has parallels with change in the international level too. The IOC, for example, has introduced recommendations for achieving compliance (see the case example to follow). In sum, ensuring that an NPSO meets compliance standards may require a comprehensive audit of policy, finances, internal controls, legal compliance and privacy. Also of note is that the 'comply or explain' principle that originated in the corporate sector (MacNeil and Li, 2006) is beginning to take effect in the sport sector as part of its reform or 'modernisation'.

CASE EXAMPLE: COMPLIANCE WITH ADMINISTRATIVE CHANGE – IOC RECOMMENDATIONS

The IOC (2008: 5) made precise recommendations in the area of governance. An overall recommendation for all its associated members states that 'Precise, clear and transparent regulations should be established and applied, and effective controlling systems and checks and balances should be put in place.' More specifically, this involves an internal control system (variable depending on the size of the organisation) regarding financial processes and operations, a compliance system, document retention system, information security system and the creation of audit committees for large sports organisations (IOC 2008: 8).

Compliance and risk management

Risks can be defined as uncertain future events that could impact on an organisation's ability or capacity to achieve its objectives. Hoye and Cuskelly (2007) note that sports boards must meet the challenge of implementing compliance measures in order to protect the organisation from not only breaching the law but in defending the reputation of the NPSO as one that seeks to implement a code of best practice. Compliance measures, if applied carefully, should not impact negatively on the work of volunteers, despite the additional bureaucracy that meeting a code can entail. The board is engaged in practice in an ongoing process of managing potential liabilities and risks that might impact on the loss of volunteers, staff, members, partner organisations or funding.

UK Sport (2004) note the importance of risk management for NPSOs as undertaking an analysis of risk can improve strategic thinking, effective decision-making and contingency planning. With the knowledge acquired through a risk analysis, resources can be allocated to complying with external demands. In summary, the potential benefits for NPSOs of managing risk include:

- more effective management of assets, events, programmes and other activities;
- a safer environment for participants, volunteers, spectators and officials;
- the development of longer-term strategic thinking and planning;
- enhanced image and reputation;
- higher morale and increased volunteer commitment;
- a better-managed organisation to support government objectives; and
- a clearer understanding of roles and responsibilities.

In turn, each of these potential and actual benefits can result in:

- improved compliance with laws, regulations and other formal requirements;
- improved compliance with best-practice guidelines and codes;
- the compliance of members with organisational objectives and practices;
- regular monitoring and assessment of compliance; and
- greater transparency and accountability.

Compliance in international sport: case examples

Given a relative lack of research into compliance by UK-based NPSOs, apart from Grix (2009) on athletics and Hindley (2004) on football, and in terms of the relationship between NGBs such as Sport England (Green, 2009; Green and Houlihan, 2006), for example, lessons learned from research into compliance at the international level of sport can be instructive for NGBs or county-, regional- or local-level NPSOs. A series of case examples follow.

CASE EXAMPLE: COMPLIANCE AND CODES OF PRACTICE – WADA

Although doping in the modern era has been an issue in sport and in some sports in particular since the 1960s, a series of scandals from the late 1980s onwards have received extensive media coverage, resulting in the founding of WADA in 1999. An extensive body of research now exists on this issue (see, for example, Houlihan, 2002, 2004, 2013, 2014). The issue of compliance with a code of practice by sports organisations, athletes and coaches has become key to tackling doping. A single code of practice (WADA, 2004) applies for all stakeholders underpinned by a harmonisation of policy and practice between sports organisations and public anti-doping authorities. Also, the *Olympic Charter* was amended in 2003 to state that 'The World Anti-Doping Code is mandatory for the whole Olympic Movement'. The Code, its most recent drafting in 2009, outlines the procedures for the legal implementation of a globally harmonised set of rules for future doping controls, testing procedures and penalties for athletes. Further, the 2009 Code established national anti-doping agencies harmonising anti-doping policies in all sport and all countries (see WADA, 2012).

Further, WADA implements code compliance monitoring that encourages sport sector and government acceptance of the Code. Apart from monitoring, WADA implements anti-doping education programmes in order for NPSOs to develop effective doping prevention strategies and in turn educate athletes and other stakeholders. If education measures fail, however, enforcement measures can include penalties and sanctions and, potentially, the removal of Olympic status for a sport. Nonetheless, there is some flexibility for how government agencies implement the WADA code given differing resources for sport and whether sport governance via regulation is an established norm and practice. The Court of Arbitration for Sport (CAS) can resolve disputes and all Olympic International Federations have recognised the jurisdiction of CAS for anti-doping rule violations (see Chapter 4). In sum, NPSOs and athletes must seek to be fully compliant with the WADA code in three stages: acceptance, implementation and enforcement. This can mean amending rules and policies in NPSOs to be in line with the articles and principles of the Code.

CASE EXAMPLE: ANTI-CORRUPTION COMPLIANCE – THE CASE OF FIFA

The International Federation of Association Football (FIFA) oversees international competition for affiliated national associations, including the World Cup, which it organises, promotes and, critically, assigns the host nation. Alleged corruption in mega-event procurement has attracted the attention of lawyers operating at a high level within European institutions and the United States, and more recently intelligence agencies, leading to the arrest of many senior FIFA officials. Critics for many years have suggested that the governing body should operate within a robust legislative and ethical framework, aligned to 'good governance' principles such as transparency and independent scrutiny in decision-making, accountability to stakeholders including the wider public and the implementation of financial controls to avoid 'loopholes' in monetary transactions (King, 2014).

In this context, there are pressures on FIFA to enact a 'world-class' compliance programme. This requires a clear code of conduct addressing both values and integrity issues. Based on the code of conduct, specific rules need to address the most important risks, notably clarification of FIFA's position towards gifts and hospitality, political and charitable contributions as well as the selection, contracting and supervision of third parties. The rules would then have to be communicated to FIFA officials and to member associations and other stakeholders (Transparency International, 2011).

FIFA has a *Code of Ethics* and the *Disciplinary Code*, but compliance with the codes is the issue. This raises the question of whether to employ direct or indirect controls and which approach will be more effective. Transparency International (2011) suggested that the existing *Code of Ethics* be overhauled and a full-scale *compliance programme* introduced and implemented. Subsequently, given the events of 2015 involving an FBI investigation, reform of the organisational structure is very likely. Pieth (2011) suggested that FIFA should elect a number of independent non-executive directors to change the extent of compliance with existing codes or revised codes. This may form one component of the final outcome for FIFA.

Summary

This chapter has explored the notion of compliance as a core component of sport sector governance, specifically for NPSOs. Achieving compliance implies meeting guidelines or standards set by external bodies, but also implies setting guidelines and standards for members and other stakeholders. Meeting standards within an NPSO requires commitment, responsibility, adequate resources, a clear policy statement and a culture of continuous improvement. It also requires personnel to operationalise the policy, which means that compliance issues need to be identified, with procedures put in place, and a level of enforcement, monitoring, record-keeping, reporting and supervision being necessary.

Finally, it can be argued that organisational improvement in performance and in meeting good governance criteria has to be driven by NPSOs, as regulation may deliver compliance but not necessarily improvements. Therefore, compliance with regulation, policy objectives or a code of practice may require education and training in upskilling board members and possibly other stakeholders in compliance issues and practices. The outcome of establishing coherent procedures and processes for compliance is intended to be extended accountability, improved communication and reputational benefits for NPSOs that in turn should assist in building the capacity and resilience of sports organisations. On the other hand, it can be argued that regulation is necessary to ensure a level of compliance that some NPSOs may be either unwilling or unable to achieve without intervention.

LEARNING ACTIVITIES

- Identify effective ways to achieve organisational compliance with codes of practice. Support your answer with examples from the sport sector.
- What role do external auditors play in sport governance? How does external audit differ from internal audit?
- Identify the legislation, codes, guidance and standards that sports organisations must take into account when designing a risk-management strategy.
- How does compliance relate to risk? Provide examples.
- Identify the key benefits of implementing and monitoring compliance standards.
- What lessons can be learned from international sport that are relevant for an NPSO board to understand compliance both nationally and locally?
- Make five specific recommendations aimed at ensuring compliance with a code of ethics, with reference to an NPSO of your choice.

Bibliography

Aguilera, R.V. and Cuervo-Cazurra, A. (2009). Codes of good governance. *Corporate Governance: An International Review*, 17, 3: 376–387.

Bonn, I. and Fisher, J. (2005). Corporate governance and business ethics: insights from the strategic planning experience. *Corporate Governance: An International Review*, 13: 730–738.

Chappelet, J.L. (2011) GRC [governance, risk and compliance] and you. Presentation at *IF Forum*, Lausanne, 14–16 November.

Chayes, A. and Chayes, A.H. (1995) *The New Sovereignty: Compliance with International Regulatory Agreements*. Cambridge, MA: Harvard University Press.

Chayes, A., Chayes, A.H. and Mitchell, R.B. (1998) Managing compliance: a comparative perspective. In: Brown-Weiss, E. and Jackson, H.K., eds, *Engaging Countries: Strengthening Compliance with International Environmental Accords*. Cambridge, MA: MIT Press, pp. 39–62.

Dunn, W. (2004) *Public Policy Analysis: An Introduction*. Upper Saddle River, NJ: Prentice Hall.

Garret, R. (2004) The response of voluntary sports clubs to Sport England's Lottery funding: cases of compliance, change and resistance. *Managing Leisure*, 9, 1: 13–29.

Green, M. (2009) Podium or participation? Analysing policy priorities under changing modes of sport governance in the United Kingdom. *International Journal of Sport Policy and Politics*, 1, 2: 121–144.

Green, M. and Houlihan, B. (2006) Governmentality, modernisation and the 'disciplining' of national sporting organisations: athletics in Australia and the United Kingdom. *Sociology of Sport Journal*, 23, 1: 47–71.

Grix, J. (2009) The impact of UK sport policy on the governance of athletics. *International Journal of Sport Policy and Politics*, 1, 1: 31–49.

Henry, I.P. (1999) *An Evaluation of Compliance with the European Sports Charter in the United Kingdom*. Loughborough: UK Sports Council.

Hindley, D. (2004) Stakeholding and trusts: a framework for good governance within the football industry. In: Papapanikos, G.T., ed., *4th International Conference on Sports*, Athens Institute of Education and Research, Athens, Greece, 31 May–2 June.

Houlihan, B. (2002) Managing compliance in international anti-doping policy: the World Anti-Doping Code. *European Sport Management Quarterly*, 2, 3, 188–208.

Houlihan, B. (2004) Civil rights, doping control and the world anti-doping code. *Sport in Society*, 7: 420–437.

Houlihan, B. (2013) Implementation and compliance of good governance in international sports organisations. In: Play the Game, *Action for Good Governance in International Sports Organisations*. Copenhagen: Play the Game, pp. 38–55.

Houlihan, B (2014) Achieving compliance in international anti-doping policy: an analysis of the 2009 World Anti-Doping Code. *Sport Management Review*, 17, 3: 265–276.

Hoye, R. and Cuskelly, G. (2007). *Sport Governance*. Oxford: Elsevier Butterworth-Heinemann.

International Olympic Committee (2008) *Basic Universal Principles of Good Governance of the Olympic and Sports Movement*. Lausanne: IOC. www.olympic.org/Documents/Conferences_Forums_and_Events/2008_seminar_autonomy/Basic_Universal_Principles_of_Good_Governance.pdf

King, N. (2014) Questionable ethics: good governance or terminal decline for FIFA. In *Governance and Compliance*. London: ICSA.

MacNeil, I. and Li, X. (2006). 'Comply or explain': market discipline and non-compliance with the combined code. *Corporate Governance: An International Review*, 14, 5: 486–496.

Oliver, C. (1991) Strategic responses to institutional processes. *Academy of Management Review*, 16: 145–179.

Pieth, M. (2010) *Harmonising Anti-Corruption Compliance: The OECD Good Practice Guidance*. Zürich: Dike Publishers.

Pieth, M. (2011) Governing FIFA. Concept paper and report, Universität Basel.

Sport and Recreation Alliance (UK) (2011) *Voluntary Code of Good Governance for the Sport and Recreation Sector*. London: SRA.

Tallberg, J. (2002) Paths to compliance: enforcement, management, and the European Union. *International Organization*, 56, 3: 609–643.

Transparency International (2011) *Safe Hands: Building Integrity and Transparency at FIFA*. Berlin: Transparency International.

UK Sport (2004) *Best Practice Principles of Good Governance in Sport*. London: UK Sport.

Wieland, J. (2005). Corporate governance, values management, and standards: a European perspective. *Business & Society*, 44, 1: 74–93.

World Anti-Doping Agency (WADA) (2004) *World Anti-Doping Code*. Lausanne: World Anti-Doping Agency. (For the most recent (2009) version, see www.wadaama.org/

Documents/World_Anti-Doping_Program/WADP-The-Code/WADA_Anti-Doping_CODE_2009_EN.pdf

World Anti-Doping Agency (WADA) (2012) *Compliance Reporting.* www.wada-ama.org/en/World-Anti-Doping-Program/Sports-and-Anti-Doping-Organizations/The-Code/Code-Compliance--Reporting

Wymeersch, E. (2006). Corporate governance codes and their implementation. Financial Law Institute, Gent University, Working Paper Series, 1–14.

9

GOVERNANCE CHALLENGES IN THE NEXT DECADE

LEARNING OBJECTIVES

At the completion of this chapter, students should be able to:

- identify and examine the key governance challenges NPSOs face today and in forthcoming years;
- locate governance challenges in a wider political and societal context;
- critically analyse and reflect on decisions and courses of action that can be taken in meeting governance challenges.

Introduction

This chapter identifies and assesses the key governance challenges facing NPSOs in the forthcoming years. These challenges can be more fully understood as inter-related rather than isolated components of a complex sport governance context. The challenges relate to the key themes of this study text, namely: sector reform, regulation, stakeholding, performance, good governance and compliance. The challenges facing NPSOs pertain to both the administrative and political understandings of governance, where issues of power and autonomy are central. How NPSOs respond to this context will be critical in forthcoming years. It is argued that although this text has mainly centred on the UK context, the governance themes cited here are largely applicable to the governance of sport in other nations and at international level, while recognising that distinct historical, organisational, administrative, economic, socio-cultural and political contexts shape specific challenges in different locations and at different levels of sport governance.

The chapter ends with a short conclusion to this study text. The Appendix provides learning resources for higher-level undergraduate study or postgraduate study, including research projects on key themes within sport governance.

Managing change and compliance

A key challenge facing NPSOs today and over the next decade is managing the ongoing programme of reform of the non-profit sector for sport (Chappelet and Bayle, 2005). This applies at the international level of sport governance and in countries where a 'modernisation' agenda is taking effect, such as the UK. The changing nature of sport governance is closely connected with change in central government sport policy and funding priorities (see Chapter 1). In brief, sports administrative structures are expected to become professionalised (Henry and Lee, 2004) in order to be able to implement government policy and, as stated, a corporate sector ethos has shaped organisational practice. In the UK non-profit sector, NGBs are at the core of performance-related plans, where objectives are aligned to conditional funding arrangements, operationalised via *Whole Sport Plans* (Sport England, 2005). To what extent NPSOs comply with government policy objectives and revisions to sport governance is a key issue (see Chapter 8).

Making generalisations regarding the relative success of the reform agenda will be problematic to ascertain as NPSOs are 'quasi-public' organisations in some countries with a resource dependency on government funding or in terms of legal status, while in other countries, and for different sports, there is a higher level of autonomy from government influence. Moreover, in another group of countries, it is in effect the state that governs sports organisations. The political context therefore shapes outcomes of reform processes.

Maintaining autonomy

As is central to this study text, defining, retaining, expanding or defending 'autonomy' has proven to be a key issue in the sport sector and poses a significant challenge in the context of 'modernisation'. The term is often assimilated with broader concepts such as 'independence' or narrower concepts such as 'self-determination' or 'self-regulation'. In sport governance, maintaining 'autonomy' can be understood as a political issue or a legal issue, or an issue with consequences for financial compliance. It can be claimed that in practice 'autonomy' is negotiated between stakeholders, although not always where an equitable balance of power exists. In the case of the 'modernisation' agenda, there is an element of supervised autonomy where discretion in decision-making is subject to national scrutiny and oversight. The notion of 'earned autonomy' (Green and Houlihan, 2006) also applies where sports funding is conditional upon meeting national objectives within a fixed timeframe.

The non-profit sport sector has a long history of 'autonomy' from state/government intervention, and where this is compromised or perceived to be compromised, non-profit sport organisations (NPSOs) face a challenge as to whether to modify their understanding of 'autonomy', comply with government agendas, resist change or revise current policy, provision or specific practices. Apart from Grix (2009), who investigated these issues in respect of athletics, research is scarce in regard to specific sports. What can be stated is that NPSOs, especially NGBs and international governing bodies, are engaged in a revision of practice as a result of the challenge of maintaining autonomy (however conceived). Specific challenges for specific NPSOs will vary across countries, as, for example, 'European sport is characterised by a multitude of complex and diverse structures which enjoy different types of legal status and levels of autonomy in Member States' (European Commission, 2007a: 18). However, following the corruption-related incidences across sports that have been highlighted in the media, the very understanding of 'autonomy' has been increasingly subject to scrutiny from a range of stakeholders, including government, athletes and the general public. In practice, maintaining a level of autonomy may necessitate that governing bodies operate within a framework of 'good governance'. Failing to do so is likely to result in further government intervention. Arguably, while freedom of association is worth defending robustly, the 'autonomy' of sport may in practice be an outdated concept that has been misused by unscrupulous individuals seeking to evade accountability for profiteering activities at the expense of sport and its stakeholders.

Tackling corruption in sport

Doping in athletics, match-fixing in football and cricket, and bribery in the award of major events to specific host cities are three of the serious issues in sport today. At the time of writing, there are numerous examples of weak governance highlighted by the media, which portrays sport governance as being in 'crisis', with some supporting evidence. For example:

- The Serious Fraud Office in the UK is investigating vote-rigging within FIFA in relation to a World Cup bid.
- The UK government is giving consideration to making doping a criminal offence.
- The Canadian soccer league is under investigation for claims of widespread match-fixing.
- The anti-doping agency in Russia is under investigation.
- Match-fixing in professional tennis is being investigated.
- FIFA officials have been suspended and others arrested for alleged financial fraud, with serious implications for the governance of football and a breakdown in relations between FIFA and its commercial sponsors.
- The Qatar World Cup 2022 bid is under investigation.
- IAAF officials have been suspended following an inquiry into financial 'mismanagement'.

- The South Korean government is monitoring corruption in sport and the Japanese government is considering adopting anti-doping legislation.
- Both the FBI and Interpol are investigating corruption in professional sport, which indicates the serious nature of the 'crisis'.

As a response, NPSOs are seeking to retain legitimacy for sport and those that govern it. For example:

- The ICC Anti-Corruption Unit has formed a partnership with the National Crime Agency to develop a memorandum of understanding regarding match-fixing in cricket.
- The IOC is intending to audit monetary contributions for developing sports in order to address claims of corruption and widespread doping.
- The German Olympic Sports Confederation has adopted a good governance policy.
- The IOC has suspended the Olympic body for Kuwait for political interference in sport.
- Concerns over gambling in sport have led to changes in governance, e.g. the introduction of a sports betting integrity action plan in horse racing.
- FIFA has established an Independent Governance Committee.
- WADA has produced a report into doping in athletics (see the case example in this chapter).

(SRA news releases, 2015–2016)

Given the perceived or actual scale of the 'crisis' in sport governance, involving corruption, nepotism, bureaucracy and mismanagement (Nanda, 2006), NPSOs either face a direct or indirect impact on how sport is governed (at least in professional, commercial sports organisations). How effective reform will be is the key issue here. Pro-active NPSOs have the option of bringing about reform themselves in order to minimise external intervention. For example, NPSOs can: replace board members, organise an internal investigation, audit or review; produce documentation to steer future action such as reports, codes of practice or changes to the organisation's constitution; establish an ethics committee or similar body; extend stakeholder engagement or co-production of NPSO policy or strategy; and if necessary, fine, suspend or ban members; or employ external agencies to manage a reform process.

However, sport governance structures are embedded in political and financial systems and therefore without exogenous change at this level, NPSOs will be constrained in the opportunities each has for embedding good governance as the 'new normal'. Instead, NPSOs have the option of minimising the impact of corrupt practices in their sport through establishing a robust framework for ethical governance. Such an outcome is clearly more feasible in a pluralistic society than within a society led by an authoritarian regime whose understanding of 'autonomy', 'stakeholding', 'good governance' and civil society–state relations differs considerably from states where sport governance is semi-autonomous from government intervention (Dorsey, 2016).

Maintaining the values of sport and volunteer involvement

Another significant challenge facing NPSOs today and over the next decade is the issue of maintaining the core values of sport and, in relation to this, the challenge of recruiting and retaining volunteers. Simply stated, without the volunteers to govern, manage and deliver services across clubs, the non-profit sport sector would not function. Volunteering may be affected, however, by a decline in the values that sport embodies, in the context of the rise of commercialisation and professionalisation in the sport sector. Most NPSOs do not have sufficient financial resources to introduce salaries for board members without increasing costs to participants, raising membership fees and forming relationships with commercial organisations to acquire sponsorship monies, for example. Not all sports attract commercial investment or are considered 'marketable' enough to gain access to broadcasting monies.

As a result, NPSOs are in many cases operating as small and medium-sized businesses, with limited company status, and employing governance practices that resemble corporate governance. With the emergence and gradual embedding of corporate governance practices in NPSOs, a shift in decision-making powers from volunteer boards to salaried professionals poses a challenge for sport governance. Maintaining the values normally associated with sport (e.g. fair play, civic engagement, voluntarism) requires NPSOs to both invest in developing volunteers (competencies) and to clearly set out the remit, roles and responsibilities of volunteers as distinct from those of professional staff with responsibilities for business development (e.g. procurement, marketing, corporate social responsibility).

Building legitimacy

Related to maintaining values and volunteers is the challenge of maintaining legitimacy as an organisation. NGBs, for example, face both opportunities and threats. Opportunities include: maximising revenue streams (from commercial sources) in order to invest in 'grass-roots' developmental activities and grow participation; investing in facility refurbishment or new buildings to attract and retain participants and to host events; investing in human resources to build a volunteer base; acquiring accreditation; and/or improving the governance and management of the NPSO. If, however, legitimacy is undermined, then NPSOs face threats, including the loss of financial support, members, volunteers and key partner organisations, for example. If authority is based on legitimacy, then where sports operate in a commercial environment characterised by corporate governance, NPSOs may no longer be the key authority. Sports that are commercial, professional and are organised by large international sports organisations, such as football, may undermine the legitimacy of the National Governing Body (NGB), leading to a decline in authority. However, most NGBs in the UK retain authority and legitimacy over a sport.

Nonetheless, looking ahead, sports boards will need to decide what their role is: whether regulatory, administrative or commercial, or a combination of roles. The purpose of the NPSO may be centred on recreational or competitive sport; extending or widening participation or performance-based activities; a sport or club for all or a few with a particular shared interest or ability; non-commercial or commercial; or could be split into distinct organisational structures. Where a sport has a layer of governance on the international stage, retaining specificity will be a challenge, especially for sports with a large commercial arm. Retaining self-organisation and self-regulation across the sport sector requires NPSOs to have a constructive relationship with government bodies so that legitimacy, authority and autonomy are maintained. Those sports operating on a smaller scale with no significant commercial arm may still experience pressures on legitimacy from national government sports agencies. NPSOs are therefore subject to both commercial and government (policy and legislation) pressures that can determine the level of self-determination. NPSOs must chart a course of action in a challenging financial and political environment through the next decade.

Implementing good governance: towards accountability

A key component of the ongoing reform process in the sport sector is the challenge of implementing practices that can be defined in terms of 'good' governance (see Chapter 7). The majority of NPSOs are already engaged in delivering components of best practice aligned to codes of good practice and meeting legal requirements. However, 'good governance' requires organisations to review all practices in terms of accountability, transparency and fairness, for example, and to operate within ethical guidelines. For NPSOs, implementation and assessment in this respect can be problematic. The *Voluntary Code of Good Governance for the Sport and Recreation Sector* (SRA, 2011) offers a gateway into assessing whether a sports club, for example, is accountable to its stakeholders, transparent in its financial operations and fair in its distribution of resources. Some organisations have established an ethics committee and a code of ethics or made adjustments to the constitution or other binding documentation that members must agree to.

As noted in Chapter 5, NPSOs are now operating within an environment of heightened expectations from stakeholders for increased transparency and accountability, coupled with the government-led emphasis on professional practice and other elements of 'modernisation'. Given the economic downturn in the UK since 2008, NPSOs are under greater scrutiny than at any other time, especially if the organisation depends or partly depends on public monies to function. Forward-thinking organisations have embraced the concept and practice of 'extended accountability' as opposed to making minor modifications to existing practices. This involves an extended role for multiple stakeholders in decision-making and challenges hierarchical forms of governance and centralised control.

The benefits of embedding 'good governance' in an NPSO and across the sport and recreation sector over the next decade need to be fully articulated and understood if organisations are to move beyond 'paying lip-service' to the ideas emerging from the good-governance debate. Specific governance practices are already identifiable and NPSOs can take action to: collate feedback from stakeholders and engage in open dialogue on the values of the organisation; adhere to disclosure requirements and establish reporting mechanisms to enhance transparency; take steps to monitor and evaluate good governance; and publish key information online, for example. It is clear to many NPSOs that implementing and embedding good governance practices builds legitimacy as a lead organisation and authority in a particular sport; develops a good reputation that attracts funding and new members; and acquires political support from government bodies. Employing good governance can therefore be viewed both as protecting the core values of sport and its organisations and as a strategy of empowerment, building capacity and resilience across a sector under increasing financial and political pressure.

Extending stakeholding: collaboration, interoperability and trust

Throughout the EU there are approximately 70,000 sports clubs and 70 million club members or 15 per cent of the EU population (Hoye and Cuskelly, 2007: 200). Although there appears to have been a reduction in UK sport clubs since the late 1980s (Taylor *et al.*, 2009), the UK still has a significant number of clubs and volunteers. At the national level are a raft of NGBs across over 120 recognised sports and many recreational activities. In between are regional and/or county bodies for many sports. The non-profit sport sector is therefore large and highly fragmented, making governance challenging. This is compounded by government departments and agencies, most notably local government and the UK sport councils. Given that the UK has semi-autonomous nations, governance is not uniform and the non-profit sport sector is organised and delivered differently across England, Northern Ireland, Scotland and Wales. Apart from the non-profit and public sectors, the private or commercial sector has formed partnerships with many NGBs and clubs. Many local clubs have partnerships with schools and community organisations and/or health agencies. Given this context, sports boards in clubs and the boards of NGBs face the major challenges of building collaboration, trust and interoperability across partners or stakeholders. Extending the notion of stakeholding to include not only members/participants, to funders, the local community and others, presents a challenge to the way in which clubs are traditionally governed. At the national level, NGBs have had to adjust in the last decade to having government agencies and commercial organisations as partners, with significant influence in many cases. The next decade will pose similar challenges for all NPSOs.

As noted in Chapter 5, managing multiple stakeholder relationships is at the heart of good governance and is a critical consideration for NPSOs when planning and implementing strategy. Effective governance in this regard can reduce disputes;

build trust between a range of actual and potential partners; and increase interoperability – how organisations work together effectively to their mutual benefit. Two main techniques that enable NPSOs to manage stakeholder relationships are: *stakeholder engagement*, which requires an organisation to consult with stakeholder groups that have relatively little influence on decision-making; and *stakeholder participation*, which involves building a more inclusive management strategy, allowing stakeholder groups to be actively involved in decision-making and integrating them within governance structures. Many NPSOs who have operated hierarchically within a 'command and control' model of governance will be challenged by new thinking around network governance (see Chapter 8) where the emphasis is on collaborative problem-solving, trust and negotiating priorities. Given a climate of scarce resources, affecting the majority of NPSOs, especially those at the margins of the reform agenda and performance-related sport, with few commercial sponsors, for example, clubs and some NGBs must pool resources and collaborate.

Embedding social responsibility

In corporate governance, an increasing number of companies have in recent years decided to voluntarily contribute to social and environmental goals. Corporate Social Responsibility (CSR) has emerged due to growing public, media and government criticism of corporate practice and as a response to a variety of social, environmental and economic pressures (European Commission, 2001). CSR was found to influence the success of a company, in terms of differentiation from competitors, building image and reputation, creating consumer goodwill and positive employee attitudes and behaviour. As is clear in this study text, changes in corporate governance tend to result in changes in governance in the non-profit sector. Therefore, NPSOs are facing a higher demand to meet 'good governance' goals (see Chapter 7) connected to ethical, social and environmental concerns and government agenda (Babiak, 2010). As with corporations that prioritise shareholders ahead of the public benefit, some sports organisations have prioritised specific stakeholders ahead of the wider community interest. However, an emphasis on social responsibility is now typical among many NPSOs, where an extended understanding of stakeholding (see Chapter 5) has emerged inclusive of the public interest (and especially if legally bound if an NPSO has charitable status).

It is argued that because sport embodies socio-cultural values, there is the potential for NPSOs to have a positive impact on the wider society (European Commission, 2007a, 2007b). Moreover, if sports organisations acquire public funding or in any way depend on public-sector support (see Euro-strategies *et al.*, 2011), then it can be plausibly argued that NPSOs should contribute to outcomes that benefit the wider community, beyond its membership. Public money pays for the building of facilities, including training centres, parks and green spaces, and can take the form of grants and National Lottery funding that NPSOs can access. Elite professional sports organisations rely on government funding for major events, for example, and, more broadly, transport infrastructure, security and so on (Bruyninckx, 2012). In summary, NPSOs are expected to introduce social responsibility into their codes of practice and governance documentation. This can mean operationalising a strategy to extend access to its services to the wider community beyond its members.

Mediating liability and risk

A complex and ever-changing legal context at the national and EU level poses challenges for sports organisations. As noted in Chapter 3, the sport sector is a diverse and disparate sector characterised by legal uncertainty and raised stakeholder expectations. Within an increasingly litigious society, the NPSO must steer a course through what can resemble a 'regulatory minefield' where legal liabilities for managers/organisers have increased in the areas of spectator safety, public rights, risk in schools, safeguarding, disability discrimination, health and safety and athlete doping, among others. The challenge for sports board members is acquiring the relevant information that applies to the particular organisation and the sport or recreation, and then taking the necessary steps to safeguard the NPSO against the many potential legal hazards.

To meet what can be a daunting challenge, NPSO directors clearly need to assess liability, including vicarious liability, and risk. NPSOs must understand 'duty of care', take steps to fulfil the duty and avoid negligence. Developing an expertise in these issues will serve to pre-empt potential litigation and legal costs that may impact negatively on the resources and reputation of the NPSO and the sport.

Measuring performance, impact and legacy

Increasingly, NPSOs are challenged by funders, members and the wider public to demonstrate the impact of services provided, and over the longer term the legacy of provision in terms of stakeholder benefit. Good practice in this respect can include:

- proceeds of sport being re-invested back into sport (development);
- revenues distributed fairly/equitably and efficiently;
- the clear and transparent allocation of resources;
- policies and procedures in place to measure the quality of provision, dedicated staff to undertake any assessment, evaluation or audit and funding set aside for measuring impact;
- reducing administrative costs in order to maximise development funding (building capacity); and
- seeking advice on how to assess impact/legacy.

Fundamentally, for NPSOs to measure performance, impact and legacy is to enhance the learning capacity, flexibility and adaptability of the organisation in a challenging decade ahead.

Developing knowledge

Hoye and Cuskelly (2007) observe that in order to strengthen the non-profit sport sector, the functioning of boards will be the most promising point of leverage. The authors state that dysfunctional board–staff relations are a major issue for specific NPSOs and across the sport and recreation sector. This is one area where developing knowledge will benefit understanding and inform practice in the next decade. Other areas where an extended knowledge base is needed for the effective functioning of sport governance include understanding:

- the distinction between the principles and practices of corporate governance from non-profit and sport-specific governance;
- the management of risk in an increasingly litigious culture;
- the application of the transparency agenda without compromising confidentiality of data and anonymity of personnel where applicable;
- the expertise needed for self-governance and local autonomy;
- service modification to fulfil good-governance criteria and codes of practice;
- how to acquire and allocate funding that builds organisational capacity;
- modes of compliance that do not compromise the commitment of volunteers; and
- methods of assessing best practice, impact and legacy.

Clearly, there are many other key areas of sport governance to research, learn lessons from, and apply in practice, in order to build a resilient sport and recreation sector over the next decade and beyond.

Leadership in governance: towards transformation

NPSOs require effective leadership from volunteers and professionals if the non-profit sport sector is to thrive. It has been argued that leaders create and change cultures, while managers and administrators live within them. In this sense, effective administration is 'doing things right', whereas leadership is 'doing the right things'. Board chairs, directors or CEOs require a vision for a sport and the organisation being governed and this needs to be translated and communicated across many stakeholders in an organisation. In this sense, governance can be transformational and not simply a matter of conducting transactions to meet targets; procure funding; manage budgets; monitor compliance and so on. Visionary leadership motivates staff and volunteers to lead themselves and seeks to empower, not control.

Adapting to changing relationships between government and non-profit organisations

Since 2010, the coalition government has introduced an agenda (under the banner of the *Big Society*: see report at www.culture.gov.uk) to reduce citizen dependency on state services and shift the focus of service delivery to the non–profit sector. Alongside this shift has been the increased emphasis on the private sector delivering public services. The relationship between the three sectors has therefore changed to an extent (by 2015): in the case of sport and recreation, service providers have in some cases changed, with sports clubs, for example, taking on an increasing workload. This in turn can affect sport governance.

Research by King/APSE (2012) found that an extended role for both non–profit and private–sector sport organisations and trusts has emerged with the demise of local authority sport-related services, alongside community ownership and/or delivery of sport services, parks management and play services in some areas of the UK. Further, the rise of academy schools (centrally financed but with devolved powers to the local level) has led to schools bringing in private or voluntary/ community providers. Moreover, with local authorities modifying in-house services and outsourcing services that were formerly directly managed, it can be anticipated that there will be further pressures on NPSOs operating at the local level to take on more responsibilities. In turn, this may impact on the governance and operations of clubs where new expertise may be required to manage stakeholder relationships; procure funding; form mergers; and mobilise influence.

Selecting an appropriate legal form and 'business model'

Finally in this list of inter–related challenges facing NPSOs over the next decade is perhaps the most fundamental of challenges, namely to undertake a review of governance within the NPSO and decide on the legal form and 'business model' best suited to the sport and organisation. For many NPSOs who do not or cannot qualify for charitable status and the advantages this offers, the social enterprise model is gaining in popularity, assuming there is a clearly defined social purpose for the organisation to fulfil. The 'business case' moving forward may be strengthened too through a merger of smaller organisations assuming a level of autonomy can be retained, so that the administrative and political components of sport governance are addressed to the satisfaction of the board. Independent board members may also be considered to bring in new expertise in a challenging financial climate. A closer working relationship with both government sports bodies and the Sport and Recreation Alliance (SRA) as the umbrella body for the voluntary/non–profit sector would also benefit both sports organisations and the sector.

Managing media influence and commercialisation

In many sports, NPSOs have been subject to rapid commercialisation and one aspect of this has been the rise of mass media influence on sport governance. Several 'global' sports acquire monies from broadcasting rights and through sponsorship (Boyle and Haynes, 2000) and the Olympic movement itself has been commercialised (Magdalinski and Nauright, 2004). In this context, NPSOs are required to manage sponsors and the media as organisations become corporate entities subject to scrutiny and compliance with business practices. In other sports, commercialisation has had relatively little impact and media interest is limited. However, this can change in a short time, as has been the case in the growth of women's football (soccer) and for Paralympic sports to some extent since the Games were televised. With government funding decreasing in some sports, NPSOs are increasingly operating within a competitive environment that mirrors the corporate sector.

The issues and challenges cited in this chapter can act as a starting point and possibly a catalyst in NPSOs for a fundamental review of governance. As organisations seek 'best practice' and 'good governance' on a firm financial footing into the next decade, it is clear that competent and informed administrators and practitioners will be needed to manage this complex and changeable context.

Summary

This chapter has sought to identify the key challenges facing NPSOs in the next decade based on current trends in policy, funding, the non-profit sport sector and the wider economic and political environment. Accountability is a core theme in this respect. Other themes clearly relate to performance, effectiveness, impact and liability. NPSOs are in effect at the hub of pressures for reform of the sport sector and must develop strategies and tactics to not only survive but also to thrive through capacity building. A high quality of sport governance in the UK will ensure the sector is resilient for the foreseeable future despite the many challenges NPSOs face.

LEARNING ACTIVITIES

- Identify the key drivers of governance change for sport in the UK. Draw a diagram to make your insights explicit.
- For a specific sport, assess the challenges facing those who govern the sport. Illustrate your answer with a SWOT analysis.
- How can the NPSO board leadership manage governance change? Provide examples.
- Given the many challenges NPSOs face, how can sports organisations become more resilient?
- Enacting the role of a consultant, create a series of recommendations for an NPSO facing some of the challenges identified.

Conclusion to the study text

This study text has highlighted and analysed sport governance in the UK (within the EU context for legislation), with a particular focus on NPSOs. The board sits at the hub of NPSOs and it is the decisions made by the board that can make a difference to the health of the sector. Therefore, much of the text is written with the board members in mind, while acknowledging the importance of a wider set of stakeholders. This text has identified the key themes in sport governance, including: administrative components; legal and regulatory aspects; leadership and performance; stakeholding; compliance; and good governance and ethics. The context of reform or 'modernisation' is considered important too in assessing the future prospects for NPSOs and the challenges ahead. The text also sought to explain sport governance via the inclusion of theoretical perspectives for readers to utilise in considering how best to improve performance, extend accountability and meet good practice codes and standards, despite a relative absence of published research on sport governance in the UK, especially as it pertains to the local level.

Finally, it is noted that not all of the content of this text applies to all sports or recreational activities across all levels of organisation in all the geographical areas of the UK, especially as the sector is so diverse and includes small clubs with few resources dependent on volunteers, to larger resource-rich organisations driven by salaried professionals operating with a business model akin to a corporate-sector body. However, generalisations can be made that apply to all organisations, aligned to the core themes identified in this text. Those working in sport governance, or planning to, will need to become familiar with the governance of specific sports in an environment subject to changes in the law, political priorities, social and cultural trends, financial instability and administrative reform.

Bibliography

Babiak, K. (2010). The role and relevance of corporate social responsibility in sport: a view from the top. *Journal of Management & Organization*, 16, 4: 528–549.

Boyle, R. and Haynes, R. (2000) *Power Play: Sport, Media and Popular Culture*. Harlow: Longman.

Bruyninckx, H. (2012). Sports governance: between the obsession with rules and regulation and the aversion to being ruled and regulated. In: Segaert, B., Theeboom, M., Timmerman, C. and Vanreusel, B., eds, *Sports Governance, Development and Corporate Responsibility*. Oxford: Routledge, pp. 107–121.

Chappelet, J.L. and Bayle, E. (2005) *Strategic and Performance Management of Olympic Sport Organizations*. Champaign, IL: Human Kinetics.

Dorsey, J.M. (2016) *The Turbulent World of Middle East Soccer*. London: Hurst.

European Commission (2001) *Promoting a European framework for Corporate Social Responsibility*. Green Paper COM (2001) 366 final.

European Commission (2007a) *EU White Paper on Sport*: http://ec.europa.eu/sport/documents/wp_on_sport_en.pdf

European Commission (2007b). *The EU and Sport: Background and Context, Accompanying Document to the White Paper on Sport*. SEC(2007) 935 final.

Euro-strategies, Amnyos, CDES, and Deutsche Sporthochschule Köln (2011). *Study on the Funding of Grassroots Sports in the EU with a Focus on the Internal Market Aspects Concerning Legislative Frameworks and Systems of Financing*. Final report No. 1. http://ec.europa.eu/internal_market/top_layer/docs/Executive-summary_en.pdf

Green, M. and Houlihan, B. (2006) Governmentality, modernisation and the 'disciplining' of national sporting organisations: athletics in Australia and the United Kingdom. *Sociology of Sport Journal*, 23, 1: 47–71.

Grix, J. (2009) The impact of UK sport policy on the governance of athletics. *International Journal of Sport Policy and Politics*, 1, 1: 31–49.

Harris, S., Mori, K. and Collins, M. (2009) Great expectations: voluntary sports clubs and their role in delivering national policy for English Sport. *Voluntas*, 20, 4: 405–423.

Henry, I.P. and Lee, P.C. (2004) Governance and ethics in sport. In: Chadwick, S. and Beech, J., eds, *The Business of Sport Management*. Harlow: Pearson Education.

Hoye, R. and Cuskelly, G. (2007) *Sport Governance*. Oxford: Elsevier Butterworth-Heinemann.

King, N./APSE (2012) *Local Authority Sport and Recreation Services in England: Where Next?* Manchester: APSE.

Magdalinski, T. and Nauright, J. (2004) Commercialisation of the modern Olympics. In: Slack, T., ed., *The Commercialisation of Sport*. New York: Routledge, pp. 185–204.

Nanda, V.P. (2006) The 'Good Governance' concept revisited. *Annals of the American Academy of Political and Social Science*, 603, 1: 269–283.

Nichols, G. (2013) Voluntary sport clubs and sports development. In: Hylton, K., ed., *Sports Development: Policy, Process and Practice*, 3rd edition. London: Routledge.

Nichols, G., Padmore, J., Taylor, P. and Barrett, D. (2012) The relationship between types of sports clubs and English government policy to grow participation. *International Journal of Sport Policy and Politics*, 4, 2: 187–200.

Play the Game (2016) Corruption 'embedded' in the IAAF: second WADA report. www.playthegame.org/news/news-articles/2016/0140_corruption-embedded-in-the-iaaf-second-wada-report

Sport England (2005) *Whole Sport Plans: Key Performance Indicator Manual*. London: Sport England.

Sport England/DCMS (2012) Creating a sporting habit for life: a new youth sport strategy. www.sportengland.org/about_us/what_we_do.aspx

SRA (Sport and Recreation Alliance (UK)) (2011) *Voluntary Code of Good Governance for the Sport and Recreation Sector*. London: SRA.

Taylor, P., Nichols, G., Holmes, K., James, M., Gratton, C., Garrett, R., Kokolakakis, T., Mulder, C. and King, L. (2003) *Sports Volunteering in England*. London: Sport England.

Taylor, P., Barrett, D. and Nichols, G. (2009) *Survey of Sports Clubs 2009*. London: CCPR.

UK Sport (2003) *'Investing in Change': High Level Review of the Modernisation Programme for Governing Bodies of Sport*, London: Deloitte and Touche.

Walters, G., Trenberth, L. and Tacon, R. (2010) *Good Governance in Sport: A Survey of UK National Governing Bodies of Sport*. London: Birbeck University.

APPENDIX: LEARNING RESOURCES

UK government documentation

Carter, P. (2005) *Review of National Sport Effort and Resources*. London: Sport England/ DCMS.

Department for Culture, Media and Sport (DCMS) (2000) *A Sporting Future for All*. London: DCMS.

Department for Culture, Media and Sport (DCMS) (2005) *Five Year Plan: Living Life to the Full*. London: DCMS.

Department for Culture, Media and Sport (DCMS) (2008) *Before, During and After: Making the Most of the 2012 Olympic Games*. London: DCMS.

Department for Culture, Media and Sport (DCMS) (2008) *Playing to Win: A New Era for Sport*. London: DCMS.

Department for Culture, Media and Sport (DCMS)/Strategy Unit (2002) *Game Plan: A Strategy for Delivering Government's Sport and Physical Activity Objectives*. London: DCMS/ SU.

Department of Health/Department for Children, Schools and Families (2008) *Healthy Weight, Healthy Lives: A Cross-Government Strategy for England*. London: DoH/DCSF.

Department of National Heritage (1995) *Sport: Raising the Game*. London: DNH.

House of Commons Committee of Public Accounts (2006) *UK Sport: Supporting Elite Athletes* (54th Report of Session 2005–2006, HC 898). London: HMSO.

National Audit Office (NAO) (2005) *UK Sport: Supporting Elite Athletes* (HC 182, SE/2005/9 Session 2004–2005). London: HMSO.

National Audit Office (NAO) (2008) *Preparing for Success at the London 2012 Olympic and Paralympic Games and Beyond* (HC 434 Session 2007–2008 SG/2008/22). London: HMSO.

Sport England (1999) *Investing for Our Sporting Future*. London: Sport England.

Sport England (2004) *Driving up Participation: The Challenge for Sport*. London: Sport England.

Sport England (2005) *Whole Sport Plans: Key Performance Indicator Manual*. London: Sport England.

Sport England (2008) *Sport England Strategy 2008–2011*. London: Sport England.

Sport England (2008) *Sport England's Partnership with National Governing Bodies of Sport.* www.sportengland.org/sport_englands_partnership_with_national_governing_bodies_of_sport.htm

Sport England (2011) Speeches and presentations of the Promoting Grassroots Sport Forum. www.sportengland.org/support__advice/promoting_grassroots_sport.aspx

Sport England (2011) *Good Governance Guidance.* London: Sport England.

Sport England (2013) *2013–17 Whole Sports Plan Investments.* www.sportengland.org/our-work/national-work/national-governing-bodies/sports-we-invest-in/2013–17-whole-sport-plan-investments

Sport England/DCMS (2012) Creating a sporting habit for life: a new youth sport strategy. www.sportengland.org/about_us/what_we_do.aspx

Sports Council (1996) *Valuing Volunteers in UK Sport.* London: Sports Council.

UK Parliament (2015) Governance of Sport Bill. www.publications.parliament.uk/pa/bills/lbill/2014–2015/0020/15020.pdf

UK Sport (2003) '*Investing in Change': High Level Review of the Modernisation Programme for Governing Bodies of Sport.* London: Deloitte and Touche

UK Sport (2004) *Best Practice Principles of Good Governance in Sport.* London: UK Sport.

UK Sport (2004) *Good Governance: A Guide for National Governing Bodies of Sport.* London: Institute of Chartered Secretaries and Administrators.

UK Sport (2005) New responsibilities vital to 2012 success. Press release. www.uksport.gov.uk/news/2152

UK Sport (2008) World class governance. www.uksport.gov.uk/pages/world_class_governance

UK Sport (2008) No compromise funding strategy. www.uksport.gov.uk/pages/no_compromise

European Union documentation

Copenhagen Declaration on Anti-Doping in Sport, (2003) www.wadaama.org/Documents/World_Antidoping_Program/Governments/WADA_Copenhagen_Declaration_EN.pdf)

Council of Europe (1989) Anti-Doping Convention, Strasbourg: Council of Europe. http://conventions.coe.int/Treaty/en/Treaties/Html/135.htm

Council of Europe (1992) *European Sport Charter.* Strasbourg: Council of Europe.

Council of Europe (2004) *Resolution I on the Principles of Good Governance in Sport.* Strasbourg: Council of Europe.

Council of Europe (2005) *Recommendation Rec (2005)8 of the Committee of Ministers to Member States on the Principles of Good Governance in sport.* https://wcd.coe.int/ViewDoc.jsp?id=850189&Site=CM

Council of Europe (2012) *Good Governance and Ethics in Sport.* Parliamentary Assembly Committee on Culture, Science Education and Media. Strasbourg: Council of Europe.

European Commission (1991) *The European Community and Sport.* Communication from the Commission to the Council and the European Parliament. SEC (91) 1438 final.

European Commission (1999) *The Helsinki Report on Sport: Report from the European Commission to the European Council with a View to Safeguarding Current Sports Structures and Maintaining the Social Function of Sport within the Community Framework,* COM 644 final, 10 December.

European Commission (2000) *Nice Declaration on the Specific Characteristics of Sport and its Social Function in Europe.* http://ec.europa.eu/sport/documents/doc244_en.pdf

European Commission (2001) *European Governance: A White Paper.* COM (2001) 428 final.

European Commission (2001) *Promoting a European Framework for Corporate Social Responsibility*. Green Paper COM (2001) 366 final.

European Commission (2003) *Commission Communication on Governance and Development*. http://eur-ex.europa.eu/smartapi/cgi/sga_doc?smartapi!celexplus!prod!DocNumber&lg=en&type_doc=COMfinal&an_doc=2003&nu_doc=615

European Commission (2007) *EU White Paper on Sport*. http://ec.europa.eu/sport/documents/wp_on_sport_en.pdf

European Commission (2007) *The EU and Sport: Background and Context, Accompanying Document to the White Paper on Sport*. SEC(2007) 935 final.

European Commission (2011) *Developing the European Dimension in Sport*. COM (2011) 12 final, January. http://eurlex.europa.eu/LexUriServ/LexUriServ.do?uri=COM:2011:0012:FIN:en:PDF

European Commission (2011) Expert Group 'Good Governance', report from the 1st meeting (6 December). http://ec.europa.eu/sport/library/documents/b24/xg-gg-20111206-final-rpt.pdf

European Commission (2012) Expert Group 'Good Governance', Report from the 2nd meeting (13 March): http://ec.europa.eu/sport/library/documents/b24/xg-gg-201203-final-rpt.pdf

European Commission (2012) Expert Group 'Good Governance', Report from the 3rd meeting (5–6 June): http://ec.europa.eu/sport/library/documents/b24/xg-gg-201206-final-rpt.pdf

European Council (1997) *Declaration No. 29, on Sport, Attached to the Treaty of Amsterdam Amending the Treaty on European Union, the Treaties Establishing the European Communities and Certain Related Acts*. Nice: EC.

European Council (2000). *Declaration on the Specific Characteristics of Sport and Its Social Function in Europe, of which Account Should be Taken in Implementing Common Policies*, Presidency Conclusions. Nice: EC.

European Parliament (1989) *Resolution of the European Parliament on Sport in the European Community and a People's Europe*, Rapporteur: Jessica Larive. OJ C 69/1989, 20 March, p. 234.

International governing bodies of sport documentation

FIFA (2009) *FIFA Code of Ethics*. Zurich: FIFA. www.fifa.com

FIFA/Independent Governance Committee (2014) *FIFA Governance Reform Project. Final Report by the Independent Governance Committee to the Executive Committee of FIFA*. Basel.

International Olympic Committee (2001) Athletes' Commission terms of reference. http://multimedia.olympic.org/pdf/en_report_712.pdf

International Olympic Committee (2007) *The White Paper on Sport, Joint Statement with International Sports Federations*. IOC 10268/2007/mgy, 3 April.

International Olympic Committee (2008) *Basic Universal Principles of Good Governance of the Olympic and Sports Movement*. Lausanne: IOC. www.olympic.org/Documents/Conferences_Forums_and_Events/2008_seminar_autonomy/Basic_Universal_Principles_of_Good_Governance.pdf

International Olympic Committee (2009) *Codes of Ethics and Other Texts*. Lausanne: IOC.

International Olympic Committee (2011) *Olympic Charter*. IOC: Lausanne, Rule 1(2). www.olympic.org/Documents/olympic_charter_en.pdf

International Olympic Committee and FIFA (2007) *IOC–FIFA Joint Declaration: EU White Paper on Sport: Much Work Remains to be Done*. www.olympic.org/news?articleid=54916

International Non Governmental Organisations Accountability Charter (2005) www. ingoaccountabilitycharter.org/wpcms/wp-content/uploads/INGOAccountability-Cha rter.pdf

Codes of practice

ICSA (2010) *Good Governance: A Code for the Voluntary and Community Sector.* www. governancecode.org/wp-content/uploads/2012/06/Code-of-Governance-Full1.pdf

National Council for Voluntary Organisations (NVCO) (2005) *Good Governance: A Code for the Voluntary and Community Sector.* London: NVCO.

Sport and Recreation Alliance (UK) (2011) *Voluntary Code of Good Governance for the Sport and Recreation Sector.* www.sportandrecreation.org.uk/sites/sportandrecreation.org.uk/ files/web/GovernanceCodeFINAL.PDF_.easyprint%20Version.pdf

Sport and Recreative New Zealand (2005) *Nine Steps to Effective Governance: Building High Performance Organizations,* 2nd edition. www.sportnz.org.nz/Documents/Sector Capability/Web_PDF_11.10.06.pdf

Good practice guides

Canadian Institute of Chartered Accountants (CICA) (2010) *20 Questions Directors of Not-for-Profit Organizations Should Ask about Governance.* CICA: Toronto.

Canadian Institute of Chartered Accountants (CICA) (2010) *20 Questions Directors of Not-for-Profit Organizations Should Ask about Strategy.* CICA: Toronto.

Canadian Institute of Chartered Accountants (CICA) (2010) *20 Questions Directors Should Ask About Building a Board.* CICA: Toronto.

Canadian Institute of Chartered Accountants (CICA) (2010) *20 Questions Directors Should Ask about Codes of Conduct.* CICA: Toronto.

Canadian Institute of Chartered Accountants (CICA) (2010) *20 Questions Directors Should Ask about Governance Assessments.* CICA: Toronto.

Canadian Institute of Chartered Accountants (CICA) (2010) *20 Questions Directors Should Ask about Internal Audit.* CICA: Toronto.

Canadian Institute of Chartered Accountants (CICA) (2010) *20 Questions Directors Should Ask about Risk.* CICA: Toronto.

Canadian Institute of Chartered Accountants (CICA) (2010) *20 Questions Directors Should Ask about Strategy.* CICA: Toronto.

Vicsport (2010) *Good Governance Tool Kit.* www.vicsport.asn.au/Assets/Files/FINAL_ Good_Governance_ToolKit_Update.pdf

Wales Sports Council (2006) *Sound Governance and Good Management Characteristics.* Cardiff: WSC.

Miscellaneous documentation: governance and sport

Carter, P. (2005) *Review of National Sport Effort and Resources.* London: Sport England/ DCMS.

Cunningham, J. (2001) *Elite Sports Funding Review.* Report to the Prime Minister and the Secretary of State for Culture, Media and Sport, August.

David, P. (2008). *A Guide to the World Anti-Doping Code: A Fight for the Spirit of Sport.* Cambridge: Cambridge University Press.

Euro-strategies, Amnyos, CDES and Deutsche Sporthochschule Köln (2011). *Study on the Funding of Grassroots Sports in the EU with a Focus on the Internal Market Aspects Concerning Legislative Frameworks and Systems of Financing.* http://ec.europa.eu/internal_market/top_layer/docs/Executive-summary_en.pdf

Financial Reporting Council (2010) *The UK Corporate Governance Code.* London: Financial Reporting Council.

Global Reporting Initiative (2011) *Sustainability Reporting Guidelines.* Amsterdam: GRI.

Hindley, D. (2007) *Resource Guide in Governance and Sport.* www.heacademy.ac.uk/assets/hlst/documents/resource_guides/governance_and_sport.pdf

Organisation for Economic Co-operation and Development (OECD) (2004) *Principles of Corporate Governance.* Paris: OECD

Pieth, M. (2011) Governing FIFA. Concept paper and report, Universität Basel.

Play the Game (2011). Cologne consensus: towards a global code for governance in sport. End statement of the conference. *Play the Game Conference*, Cologne, 6 October.

Pound, R. (2011) Responses to corruption in sport. *Play the Game Conference*, 3 October.

Transparency International (2009) *Business Principles for Countering Bribery: A Multi-Stakeholder Initiative led by Transparency International.* Berlin: Transparency International.

Transparency International (2009) *Corruption and Sport: Building Integrity and Preventing Abuses.* Berlin: Transparency International.

Transparency International (2011) *Safe Hands: Building Integrity and Transparency at FIFA.* Berlin: Transparency International.

Turnbull Committee (1999) *Internal Control: Guidance for Directors on the Combined Code.* London: Institute of Chartered Accountants in England and Wales

UNESCO (2012) *International Convention against Doping in Sport.* www.unesco.org/eri/la/convention.asp?KO=31037&language=E&order=alpha

World Anti-Doping Agenda (2004) *World Anti-Doping Code.* Lausanne: WADA. (For the most recent (2009) version, see www.wadaama.org/Documents/World_Anti-Doping_Program/WADP-The-Code/WADA_Anti-Doping_CODE_2009_EN.pdf

World Anti-Doping Agenda (2012) *Compliance Reporting.* www.wada-ama.org/en/World-Anti-Doping-Program/Sports-and-Anti-Doping-Organizations/The-Code/Code-Compliance--Reporting

World Bank (2003) *Toolkit: Developing Corporate Governance Codes of Best Practice.* Washington, DC: World Bank.

Website resources

British Olympic Association: www.teamgb.com

British Paralympic Association: http://paralympics.org.uk

Charities Commission: www.gov.uk/government/organisations/charity-commission

Chartered Institute for the Management of Sport and Physical Activity: www.cimspa.co.uk/

Companies House: www.gov.uk/government/organisations/companies-house

English Federation of Disability Sport: www.efds.co.uk

Football Governance Research Centre: www.football-research.org

Governance in Sport: www.governance-in-sport.com

Play the Game: www.playthegame.org

Runningsports: www.clubmark.org.uk/news

Skills Active: www.skillsactive.com

Sport and Recreation Alliance (SRA): www.sportandrecreation.org.uk

Sport England: www.sportengland.org
Sport Northern Ireland: www.sportni.net
Sport Scotland: www.sportscotland.org.uk
Sport Wales: www.welshsports.org.uk
Sports Coach UK: www.sportscoachuk.org
UK Sport: www.uksport.gov.uk

Additional reading

Andreff, W. (2000) Financing modern sport in the face of a sporting ethic. *European Journal for Sport Management*, 7: 5–30.

Cornforth, C. (2003) Introduction: the changing context of governance – emerging issues and paradoxes. In: Cornforth, C., ed., *The Governance of Public and Non-Profit Organisations: What Do Boards Do?* London: Routledge, pp.1–19.

Foster, J. (2006) Global sports organisations and their governance. *Corporate Governance*, 6, 1: 72–83.

Forster, J. and Pope, N. (2004). *The Political Economy of Global Sporting Organisations*. London: Routledge.

Heald, D. (2006) Varieties of transparency. In: Hood, C. and Heald, D., eds, *Transparency: The Key to Better Governance?* Oxford: Oxford University Press.

Henry, I.P. and Ko, L.M., eds (2013) *Handbook of Sport Policy*. London: Routledge.

Hodgkin, C. (1993) Policy and paper clips: rejecting the lure of the corporate model. *Nonprofit Management and Leadership*, 3: 415–428.

Jennings, A. (2006) *Foul! The Secret World of FIFA: Bribes, Vote Rigging and Ticket Scandals*. London: HarperSport.

Jennings, A. and Sambrook, C. (2000) *The Great Olympic Swindle: When the World Wanted its Games Back*. London: Simon & Schuster.

Kikulis, L.M., Slack, T. and Hinings, B. (1995) A structural taxonomy of amateur sport organisations. *Journal of Sport Management*, 3, pp. 129–150.

Michie, J. (2000) The governance and regulation of professional football. *The Political Quarterly*, 71, 2: 184–191.

Monks, R. and Minow, N. (2011) *Corporate Governance*. Chichester: Wiley & Sons.

Montel, J. and Waelbroeck-Rocha, E. (2010) *The Different Funding Models for Grass-root Sports in the EU*. http://ec.europa.eu/internal_market/services/docs/sport/conference 20100216/2-the_different_grassroots_sports_funding_models_in_the_eu_en.pdf

Oliver, R.W. (2004) *What is Transparency?* New York: McGraw-Hill.

Pierre, J. (2000) *Debating Governance: Authority, Steering and Democracy*. Oxford: Oxford University Press.

Rhodes, R.A.W. (1997) *Understanding Governance: Policy Networks, Governance, Reflexivity and Accountability*. Milton Keynes: Open University Press.

Rhodes, R.A.W. (2007) Understanding governance: ten years on. *Organization Studies*, 28, 8: 1243–1264.

Segaert, B., Theeboom, M., Timmerman, C. and Vanreusel, B., eds (2014) *Sports Governance, Development and Corporate Responsibility*. London: Routledge.

Stone, M.M. and Ostrower, F. (2007) Acting in the public interest? Another look at research on nonprofit governance. *Nonprofit and Voluntary Sector Quarterly*, 36, 3: 416–438.

Sugden, J. (2002) Network football. In: Sugden, J. and Tomlinson, A., eds, *Power Games*. London: Routledge, pp. 61–80.

Sugden, J. and Tomlinson, A. (1998) *FIFA and the Contest for World Football: Who Rules the Peoples' Game?* Cambridge: Polity Press.

Tricker, B. (1984) *Corporate Governance: Principles, Policies and Practices.* Oxford: Oxford University Press.

Vanreusel, B., ed. (2010) *Sports Governance, Development and Corporate Responsibility.* Oxford: Routledge.

Weiss, T. (2000) Governance, good governance and global governance: conceptual and actual challenges. *Third World Quarterly,* 21, 5: 795–814.

Zakus, D.H. and Skinner, J. (2008): Modelling organizational change in the international olympic committee. *European Sport Management Quarterly* 8, 4 421–442.

Zwart, F. de and Gilligan, G. (2009) Sustainable governance in sporting organisations. In: Rodriguez, P., *et al.,* eds, *Social Responsibility and Sustainability in Sports.* Oviedo: Universidad de Oviedo, pp. 165–227.

INDEX

Page numbers in *italic* denotes a table